# Memories of War

# Memories of War

Visiting Battlegrounds and Bonefields
in the Early American Republic

THOMAS A. CHAMBERS

Cornell University Press
Ithaca and London

First published 2012 by Cornell University Press
Printed in the United States of America

Library of Congress Cataloging-in-Publication Data

Chambers, Thomas A.
    Memories of war : visiting battlegrounds and bonefields in the early American republic / Thomas A. Chambers.
        p. cm.
    Includes bibliographical references and index.
    ISBN 978-0-8014-4867-6 (cloth : alk. paper)
    1. United States—History, Military—18th century.   2. United States—History, Military—19th century.   3. Battlefields—United States—History—18th century.   4. Battlefields—United States—History—19th century.   5. Cemeteries—United States—History—19th century.   6. Heritage tourism—United States—History—19th century.   7. Memorialization—United States—History—19th century.   8. Collective memory—United States—History—19th century.   I. Title.
    E181.C49 2012
    355.00973—dc23          2012013902

Cloth printing          10  9  8  7  6  5  4  3  2  1

# Contents

# *Illustrations*

**Maps**

**Tables**

*Preface*

Americans love their battlefields. In 2010 alone, over 8.5 million people visited the twenty-two battlefields administered by the National Park Service, and millions more likely visited the many other sites run by state, local, or private organizations. At these battlefields Americans do more than learn about their past—they enact their patriotism by commemorating, preserving, and remembering the places where patriot blood won our nation's independence. Gettysburg attracts over one million yearly visitors because American history was forged there, and people seek out a personal connection with an evocative place to understand their nation's past.[1] Many tourists claim to feel something special at Gettysburg, a "sense" that transformative events occurred there, and frequently comment on the chill that runs down their spine while on the battlefield. Twenty-first-century Americans assume that all battlefields have always elicited this kind of emotional response, that the National Park Service has been offering guided tours for hundreds of years, that monuments have dotted the terrain since Washington chopped down the cherry tree, and that we have always been able to engage our nation's past by visiting battlefields.

We expect to discover history at historic sites, and that the conveniently placed markers and interpretive signs will allow us to better understand our nation's past. Yet this kind of reverence for place did not begin immediately after 1776, and was not a standard part of American life until fairly recently. It took more than fifty years, as veterans of the Revolutionary War dwindled in number and few founding fathers remained alive, for Americans to even begin commemorating battlefields, much less make touring them a required part of an American family's summer vacation. In writing this book I wanted to investigate why it took so long for Americans to remember their battlefields, and what kind of memories they constructed once they began viewing such sites as "sacred places" worth visiting.[2] The cultural work required to construct memory at battlefields, and to deem them worthy of preservation and commemoration, took decades to accomplish, and during the period addressed in this book some of the crucial foundation was laid for the type of battlefield tourism that is so pervasive today.

My interest in battlefield commemoration comes in large part from one of the earliest and most vivid memories of my childhood. During the nation's bicentennial, my family observed what so many other Americans witnessed during that celebration—a battle reenactment. It took place in the familiar setting of Ballston Center, New York, a few miles west of my grandparents' house and barn, and just a short distance east of "dee farm" where my Scots-Irish ancestors faltered as agriculturists and where my paternal great-uncle and great-aunt still resided. The family's ties to the area were real but also attenuated. No one from my parents' generation lived in the area, and my family had driven twenty miles from our suburban subdivision to attend the event.

Ballston Center is the principal crossroads of a farming community settled in the late eighteenth century. Where the east–west Charlton Road meets the north–south Middle Line Road, amid rolling hills and mediocre soil, stand a few houses, a cemetery, a Grange hall, and a white clapboard Presbyterian church. This is all that marks what was once the hub of an agricultural community. My family and hundreds of others descended on the intersection one late-summer day as the town held its bicentennial event. I can still see the heat rising from the asphalt as the shrill sound of fifes and drums drifted across the fields, heralding the approach of British soldiers from the direction of my great-uncle's farm. Defending the crossroads was a motley crew of "minutemen" dressed in fringed hunter's garb of James Fenimore Cooper's Leatherstocking.

After what seemed to a child to be hours of waiting, the redcoats crested a rise in the road a hundred yards from the church. Rough battle lines were formed—the minutemen being a bit more unpolished than the supposed British regulars—and each side opened fire. The clatter of musket fire rose and fell in waves, and the acrid smoke of gunpowder wafted over soldier and civilian alike. The minutemen gave way after a few rounds of musketry, and the British made a show of "burning" the church before turning left up Middle Line Road and marching off toward what as a ten-year-old I assumed was the famous battle of Saratoga.

I interpreted the Revolution as a contest between well-dressed British regulars dead set on disturbing a pleasant community of humble farmers. It didn't matter that the Saratoga battlefield was almost twenty miles to the east, or that this reenactment converted what the historical record demonstrates was a Loyalist guerrilla raid into a fictionalized, organized march along paved roads. This was how I remembered the Revolution. Shortly after the staged battle, and once the smoke cleared, the townsfolk, militiamen, and British soldiers joined together under the trees of the churchyard for a barbecue. This community celebration featured familiar people, food, smells, and buildings. The pretense of historical reenactment was over.

The events of the day and the landscape on which they took place remain etched in my memory.[3] On the infrequent occasions when I visit my grandfather's grave near Ballston Center, I am reminded of the bicentennial reenactment; the churchyard and "battlefield" are just down the road from the cemetery, and my mind goes back to that childhood visit. During one recent stop the historian in me contemplated how place, whether it be a specific site with a personal connection or a battlefield with broader historical significance, serves as a prompt for constructing memory. In my visits to Ballston's historic sites during the bicentennial era and afterward, I engaged in activities that many Americans have done millions of times, and continue to do today. Perhaps my responses to this particular historic site belonged to the larger American impulse to remember our past.

In writing this book I sought evidence of the kind of highly personal, vivid responses to battlefields that I possessed—memory influenced by specific places with historical and social context—in the primary sources. This book's research depends upon some sources that historians have already employed, such as newspaper articles, formal commemorative ceremonies, broadsides, and published histories from the post-Revolutionary period. More important, it also exploits the many travel guidebooks and travelogues printed during the early republic and antebellum periods, as well as the personal letters and diaries of people who visited the Revolutionary War's decaying battlefields.

I attempted to understand the interaction between place and memory by visiting archives at many of the battlefields under study, where manuscript and printed sources told the stories of the people who fought and later visited each battlefield. During the 1970s, the National Park Service began writing administrative histories and historical resource surveys of its sites, and these rich documents helped me to understand each battlefield's neglect and eventual commemoration; they also revealed additional primary sources. Far from the battlefields themselves, I conducted research at nineteen different libraries and archives up and down the eastern United States and into Ontario. The most important locations, in terms of the amount and quality of material I discovered, are listed in the acknowledgements below. Important archives that did not require travel include the Niagara Falls (NY) Public Library, the Buffalo and Erie County Historical Society, the Old Fort Niagara archives, and the Niagara Falls (Ont.) History Museum at Lundy's Lane.

To supplement the manuscript and print sources located in these wonderful libraries, I also drew on electronic databases of historical documents that were not available just a few years ago. In collaboration with the American Antiquarian Society, EbscoHost has produced several invaluable collections of historical newspapers and printed material, including the Historical Periodicals Collection and American Broadsides and Ephemera. Combined with Readex's America's Historical Newspapers, HarpWeek (a compilation of Civil War–era *Harper's Weekly Magazine* issues), and ProQuest's Historical Newspapers: *New York Times,* researching and reading nineteenth-century periodicals has become far easier than when I started graduate school in the early 1990s. Being able to keyword search full-text editions of thousands of newspapers and periodicals, and then view the actual pages and articles in a scalable PDF document, makes the researcher's task far easier than it was in the days of microfilm rolls that arrived via InterLibrary Loan. Of course this also means that there is more material to read and an ever-expanding realm of possible sources. But compared to dusting off my university's one remaining microfilm reader and hoping that it worked, as I did for research in several smaller local newspapers, I'll take the electronic databases any day. The main challenge to accessing these source collections is cost, which is prohibitive for smaller institutions that lack research libraries or generous endowments. In my case, I accessed many of these databases while visiting other university libraries on fellowships. The Library of Congress's American Memory Project helps to address the privatization of historical material by making important collections like the "Journals of the Continental Congress" and the "American Notes: Travel in America, 1750–1920" series electronically available to researchers free of charge. Google Books, archive.org, Project Gutenberg, American Journeys, and the Making of America websites provided additional electronic resources vital to the research for this book.

The incredibly rich sources that I found revealed many aspects of personal interactions with battlefields that formal speeches and ceremonies omit, and filled the gap between the response to place and history prescribed by published guidebooks and how people actually felt when they retraced soldiers' steps. I have walked almost every battlefield, climbed every monument, and viewed practically each marker that I discuss in this book. If anyone has an appreciation of the interaction between place and history, I now do. The resulting book reveals the importance of people interacting with specific battlefields, not just listening to or reading speeches and ceremonies, in constructing American memories of war. Preserving battlefields and remembering soldiers' sacrifices requires reverence for place, something that during the early republic took Americans many decades to learn. Until they visited battlefields, little sacred ground existed.

*Memories of War* ranges across three conflicts and dozens of battlefields over a century of American history. My chronological focus is the years between the conclusion of the Seven Years' War and the onset of the Civil War, with individual chapters emphasizing specific, if sometimes overlapping, time periods. Throughout this era the formalized ceremonies and monument dedications common during the nation's centennial rarely occurred. The limited Revolutionary War–era commemoration of the 1750s battles at Braddock's Field and Ticonderoga contrasts with the early nineteenth-century cultivation of battlefield tourism and place-centered memory along the Hudson River Valley and nearby lakes (the locus of America's first tourist route). The rise of tourism and battlefield memory occurred simultaneously during the early republic, although Southern battlefields lagged far behind in this cultural development, even after the Marquis de Lafayette visited sites such as Yorktown, Virginia, and Camden, South Carolina, in 1824–25. The lack of sufficient tourist infrastructure left many Southern battlefields unremembered and often in ruins. A much different story emerged along the Niagara River, where visitors to America's first great tourist destination, Niagara Falls, used the area's well-developed transportation networks and hotels to visit the battlefields where the War of 1812 had raged. There they constructed memories that emphasized sentiment and scenery, unlike the sectional memories that Americans advanced at Revolutionary War battlefields during the antebellum period. By the 1850s Cowpens or Saratoga served the purposes of Southern or Northern nationalists intent on dividing or preserving the Union, according to their occasionally complementary sectional and partisan interests.

I deliberately avoided extensive discussion of well-studied locations such as Bunker Hill or Lexington and Concord in favor of lesser known and, in some cases, more militarily significant battlefields in rural areas and especially in the South. At such locales the romance of picturesque landscapes merged with veneration of the past in ways that troubled very few Americans.

Generous support from Niagara University's Research Council and the Albion College Small Grant program enabled me to travel to archives at Fort Ticonderoga, the Massachusetts Historical Society, the American Antiquarian Society, the Saratoga Springs Public Library, the William L. Clements Library at the University of Michigan, the Southern Historical Collection, the Duke University Special Collections, the Guilford Courthouse National Military Park, the Kings Mountain National Military Park, the Cowpens National Battlefield, the South Caroliniana Library, and the South Carolina Historical Society. Two separate fellowships from the Gilder-Lehrman Institute funded research at the New-York Historical Society and an invaluable monthlong residential fellowship at the Colonial Williamsburg Foundation. The latter allowed me time to visit the College of William and Mary Special Collections Research Center, the University of Virginia's Small Special Collections Library, the Yorktown Victory Center, and the Colonial National Historical Park archives at Yorktown. A Mellon Fellowship provided valuable research time at the Virginia Historical Society. The ability to access manuscript sources at these wonderful libraries and historic sites proved an invaluable part of my research and composes the foundation of this book.

I have accumulated more debts in writing this book than mere words can acknowledge. The History Department at Niagara University has as fine a collection of scholars as can be found at any liberal arts college, and I am grateful for the supportive, intellectually curious atmosphere that my colleagues there have created. The College of Arts and Sciences punches well above its weight in terms of scholarship, and I appreciate the supportive environment fostered by my fellow faculty and our Dean, Nancy E. McGlen. I never lacked for funds to travel for research or conference presentations, and for this I thank Niagara University. Colleagues and friends who read parts of the manuscript include Jerry Carpenter, Suzanne Cooper-Guasco, Doug DeCroix, Doug Kohler, Bob Kane, Scott Krugman, and Nick Westbrook. I appreciate their insights, and especially the always trenchant and thorough comments of Bob Gross, whose graceful writing and precise analysis continue to be my model. Commentators and audience members offered suggestions on my conference papers at meetings of the Society for Historians of the Early American Republic, Omohundro Institute of Early American History and Culture, Conference on New York State History, and British Group of Early American History—suggestions that greatly improved this book. The anonymous reviewers of a very early version of chapter 2 reshaped that argument, as did the expert critiques provided by the referees for Cornell University Press. Cornell asked me to submit a book proposal as early as 2004, and only the persistence and good humor of Michael J. McGandy convinced me to do so. Because of his sharp eye for detail and keen ability to distill abstract arguments into concise interpretations, this book is far better than it would have been with my efforts alone. I deeply appreciate his interest and commitment to the project. Every author should be so lucky as to have him as an editor! The expert and friendly help of the superb people at Sage House, including Susan Specter, Sarah Grossman, and Susan Barnett, and the copy editor, Glenn Novak, helped to make the final product clean and attractive. In a world where too many books are slapped together with little editorial oversight, it is a relief to know that some presses still do things the right way. Of course, these colleagues deserve all of the credit and none of the blame for what follows. Any errors, misinterpretations, or infelicitous phrases are mine alone.

Countless archivists answered my arcane queries and requests for many more documents than appear in this book. In particular, Frances Pollard and Katherine Wilkins at the Virginia Historical Society; David F. Riggs at the Colonial National Historical Park; Neal Polhemus at the South Carolina Historical Society; Ginny Fowler and Layton Carr at Cowpens National Battlefield; Chris Revels and Leah Boshell at Kings Mountain National Military Park; Rachel Ingram and Hannah Craddock at the Duke University Rare Book, Manuscript, and Special Collections Library; Graham Duncan at the South Caroliniana Library; Del Moore and George Yetter of the John D. Rockefeller Jr. Library at Colonial Williamsburg; Brian Leigh Dunnigan at the William L. Clements Library; Chris Fox at Fort Ticonderoga; Jere Brubaker at Old Fort Niagara; Kevin Windsor at the Lundy's Lane Historical Museum; and Cynthia Van Ness at the Buffalo and Erie County Historical Society provided friendly and expert assistance. Tracy Snyder was a helpful graduate assistant who tracked down the book's illustrations and secured permissions. Bill Nelson drew wonderful maps and graciously accepted my suggested revisions. Samantha Gust is quite simply the greatest Interlibrary Loan librarian I have ever known and found every single obscure microfilm I requested. And for the second time in my career, the inimitable Margaret Cook located several important sources in the Earl Gregg Swem Library Special Collections Research Center that I never would have found without her help.

There are three people, however, who deserve special thanks for helping make this book possible. Teddy and Henry Chambers were always willing to trudge along to an old battlefield and listen to their father "make a big speech about blah, blah, blah." Their enthusiasm for all things historical, especially those involving guns or cannons, inspired me. And they provided a welcome respite from research and writing to read books, play soccer, have a catch, construct elaborate Lego scenes, battle at Wii, or ride bikes. Anne Ward has been my partner-in-crime since our graduate school days and has both tolerated and supported my obsession with battlefields and frequent trips to distant archives and conferences. This book would not have been as enjoyable, nor as worth writing, if not for her companionship, support, and love. Together, we make a pretty good team. Writing this on our wedding anniversary makes my dedicating this book to her especially important.

*Introduction*

## The Changing Nature of Battlefield Tourism and Commemoration

The Yorktown monument cornerstone-laying ceremony on October 18, 1881, the battle's centennial, had been a long time coming. Two years before the commemoration of that final battle, the *New York Times* asked, "What permanent memorial can be founded at Yorktown to record for future ages the historic glories of the spot?"[1] For nearly a century, Americans had not been able to provide an answer to this question, at least in the form of a significant monument on the Yorktown battlefield. Throughout the late-eighteenth and nineteenth centuries, Yorktown remained a sleepy, undistinguished port on the York River. Its Revolutionary War history was inscribed in textbooks but was not legible on the landscape.

During the Revolutionary War's centennial, the *New York Times* noted, "trivial engagements and even melancholy Indian massacres have furnished forth agreeable and successful celebrations," but the American victory at Yorktown, a far more significant event that heralded the war's conclusion, "has thus far been left without any fit memorial." Congress's century-old promise to erect a suitable marker remained unfulfilled. But with France, the thirteen colonies' ally during the Revolution, ready to celebrate that old alliance by donating a "colossal figure" in New York Harbor, "surely national gratitude should be eager to put on record afresh" American appreciation of French assistance at Yorktown, "the brightest example of the effects of this alliance."[2] Congress answered the call of newspaper editors and the American public, capping a half dozen years of centennial monument building across the nation with a bill to erect a fitting tribute to the Franco-American alliance at Yorktown. With the 1881 cornerstone laying and official completion in 1884, the United States had at long last commemorated one of its most significant battlefields.[3]

The Yorktown Centennial Association, formed by local citizens in 1879, made every effort to ensure a grand celebration of the monument's erection and the battle's anniversary. The association held preliminary events in 1879 and 1880, and the governor of Virginia led his fellow governors of the thirteen founding states in persuading Congress to sanction and fund a centennial event and monument. Congress passed a bill, which President James A. Garfield signed on June 7, 1880, appropriating $100,000 for a monument and $20,000 "for the purpose of defraying the expenses incurred in said Centennial celebration."[4] This was no small feat, as Congress had been reluctant to fund monuments in the past. During the nation's centennial, though, Congress suddenly expressed interest in funding "monuments on all sorts of battle-fields where a hundred years have elapsed" without any formal commemoration. Congress preferred to "go no further than State or local patriotism would go"; Yorktown's successful local organization provided "an exception" where Congress supported a monument.[5]

The president and Senate soon appointed a committee of thirteen men to plan the event and select a monument design. With just over a year remaining before the centennial, they scrambled to make ready for the commemoration. The committee quickly selected a four-sided column honoring the victory and the Franco-American alliance. A much larger group representing Congress and "each of the Colonial States" planned the actual centennial event. They invited representatives from every state in the Union, militia groups and U.S. military units, naval vessels, descendants of the European officers who had fought with the Americans at Yorktown (including the Marquis de Lafayette, the Comte de Rochambeau and Baron von Steuben), Masons and Knights Templar, state and national politicians, and the general public to a nine-day festival honoring the great victory. It seemed that everyone would be there.[6]

The festivities began on October 13, 1881, with gala balls, speeches, fireworks, a regatta, and religious services for members of civic associations and militia units in attendance. The national ceremonies commenced on October 18, with President Chester A. Arthur—just in office a few weeks, after Garfield's death—attending the cornerstone-laying ceremony. Arthur's steamboat approached the wharf below Yorktown village and received a military salute. A marching band escorted his party to the reviewing stand, where the crowd greeted him with cheers. The Reverend Robert Nelson, "grandson of Governor Nelson, who commanded the Virginia militia at Yorktown," delivered the opening prayer. Virginia governor Frederick W. M. Holliday followed Nelson and lauded "the fulfillment of the Republic's promise" to build a monument on "the spot where we are now gathered." He concluded his discourse on Yorktown's history by declaring, "So may the principles this Monument is intended to represent not fall from the memory of men!" The Masons in attendance performed the cornerstone ceremony, and a host of dignitaries expounded on the event's significance. "The scene," wrote a Richmond newspaper, "was an inspiring one."[7]

The United States, one hundred years after the British surrender at Yorktown, had properly commemorated that momentous event. Hitherto, Yorktown had not been completely without attention; parades and speeches had occurred before, including Lafayette's 1824 visit to the battlefield. Yet it took more than a half century after Lafayette's visit until a major monument stood at Yorktown. Even in 1881, accomplishing the feat required significant effort and revealed many shortcomings in battlefield tourism and commemoration and the changing nature of that endeavor over the course of the late eighteenth and nineteenth centuries.

In confronting history at battlefields like Yorktown where the Revolution was fought, Americans performed memory in a manner that was less about the distinctly nationalistic concerns emphasized by politicians such as those gathered at Yorktown in 1881 than it was about the transatlantic trend of picturesque scenery and sentiment that pervaded early nineteenth-century Anglo-American culture. Battlefield tourism did not fully develop until fifty years after the Declaration of Independence. In its formative years attention to battlefields grew alongside the "Northern Tour" and an American fascination with landscape. Early tourists to battlefields formed their *own* emotional, patriotic memories based on Romantic ideals of the picturesque, melancholy, and nostalgia, as well as a generic Revolutionary War history. Their battlefield visits and responses to those sites occurred within a larger context of shared cultural assumptions. Americans maintained an ambivalent relationship with the past; most possessed only partial knowledge of their nation's history, and sought to keep it that way. They had been performing nationalism at July Fourth parades and political rallies throughout the early republic and antebellum periods, but tourism to distant battlefields was far different from listening to Daniel Webster speak at Bunker Hill or hearing Edward Everett drone on for several hours recounting the militia movements of April 19, 1775, on Lexington Green.[8] These and other speeches made near urban centers to dedicate what few monuments existed struck on political and military themes and lacked the melancholy responses tourists experienced at barren battlefield sites often situated in magnificent landscapes. By the time the larger American public focused on battlefield commemoration, in the 1850s, this Romantic impulse had faded and memories of war were subsumed by sectional politics. Before that moment, however, people did visit battlefields, and in growing numbers. Their visits slowly made these battlefields into "sacred places," but this early sacralization was barely interested in politics and was ill-fitted with the patriotic purposes to which these sites would eventually be put.[9]

## Getting to Battlefields

The nation's inefficient transportation system and insufficient accommodations hindered visits to battlefields. Even as late as the Yorktown centennial, for instance, just reaching the battlefield proved difficult. The Yorktown Centennial Association promised "hourly ferry service" between nearby cities and Yorktown aboard "some of the handsomest excursion steamers" imported from New York.[10] The Chesapeake and Ohio Railroad planned to extend its line from Richmond all the way to Yorktown, with four trains running each day. But the railroad "failed to make its connection" by the commemoration's first day, and as a result the crowds proved much smaller than promoters had expected.[11]

Those who did attend the centennial balked at the "absence of suitable accommodations."[12] Since Yorktown lacked lodging for more than a few dozen people, the committee laid out tent cantonments on the plain adjacent to town. Military academy cadets and regular army units managed to establish their camps, but the militia, "working men, clerks and merchants," lacked the skills and discipline to pitch tents and situate latrines.[13] More prestigious visitors, like the French delegation and American politicians, were to be housed in a hastily constructed hotel or in two historic buildings dating to the Revolution that required renovation "from cellar to garret."[14] Organizers failed to make these accommodations ready, and instead "barns and old buildings" had been "arranged with bunks." Barges moored in Yorktown's harbor served as floating hotels, "with the upper deck crowded with cots."[15]

The Yorktown Centennial Committee blamed Congress for the crude accommodations, since its $20,000 appropriation was "wholly inadequate to meet the requirements of a celebration which will be commensurate with the historical significance of the event and the present grandeur of our country."[16] Yet even the nation's parsimony could not dampen the celebration's patriotic enthusiasm. America's "patriotic ancestors...only asked or secured the earth for a couch and the heavens for a covering." If Washington had spent much of the war sleeping not in a house but in a tent, at the centennial patriotic and appreciative Americans could sleep for a few uncomfortable nights under canvas.[17] This temporary fervor made events such as Yorktown's centennial and monument dedication a success, but could not and did not sustain battlefield tourism and commemoration over the long run. Americans had to be able to get to battlefields before they could memorialize them.

Little had changed in Yorktown and on the Virginia Peninsula more generally between 1781 and 1881. During the decades after the Revolutionary War, the slow rise of tourism in the United States hindered attempts to commemorate Revolutionary War battlefields. Across the nation, travel proved hard, and lodging was difficult to find. Few Americans caught the traveling bug during the eighteenth century, in large part because of the colonies' and young nation's limited transportation infrastructure. The era's best-known traveler, Dr. Alexander Hamilton (no relation to the Federalist politician), encountered a mere seven bridges but crossed fifty-five ferries on his four-month journey in 1744 from Virginia to Maine.[18] Without advanced roadways, bridges, guidebooks, or maps, eighteenth-century travelers generally stuck to major cities along the eastern seaboard. At their most adventurous, they might venture roughly 150 miles up the Hudson River, a tidal estuary navigable by oceangoing ships as far north as Albany. The hills and mountains of the Appalachian west remained inaccessible to all but the most intrepid, and the lands there were largely unvisited except by yeoman farmers pushing west and claiming the land.

No matter the state of the roads, most travel served business purposes or sought to connect friends and family separated by distance. The idea of traveling merely to see something new or be somewhere different was not current in early America. The letter of introduction, not today's Fodor's or Lonely Planet guidebooks, helped travelers find their way, and those letters tended to lead them to familiar cities and towns, where they could lodge with people they, or a friend, knew. During the early republic era only an elite few, mostly those wealthy enough to enjoy leisure time and morally flexible enough to view touring as something other than sinful sloth, ventured more than a few dozen miles from their homes. These nascent tourists concerned themselves with scenery, health, or commingling with their social equals at seaside resorts such as Newport, regional mineral springs such as Ballston Spa, or cosmopolitan cities including Charleston, Philadelphia, and New York. The political and military history of the republic was not their concern. No matter their interests, the number of tourists remained small, and tourism constituted a minor part of American life and culture during the late eighteenth century.[19] Before battlefield tourism could become a significant part of American tourism or culture, an impetus to visit such places needed to develop. That pull factor came from the landscapes around battlefields.

## The Grand Tour and the Romantic Landscape

During the 1790s relative peace and prosperity established conditions that made travel more possible than it had been previously. Gradually, infrastructure such as roads, bridges, regular ferry and steamboat service, better-built carriages that softened the often bone-jarring ride—all these developments led to faster, more convenient travel, although getting around was by no means easy or luxurious. The commercial impetus to transmit information and goods as quickly and cheaply as possible moved such internal improvements along.[20]

Hotels and resorts began to appear along these routes, and almost every crossroads town that boasted a bubbling rock hoped to become a mineral springs resort attracting regional tourists. By the 1820s prominent resorts such as Saratoga Springs, New York, and White Sulphur Springs, Virginia, emerged as destinations of choice for the national tourist class. Visiting a mineral spring resort offered Americans a justification to travel—they did so for health, not amusement. Southern planters claimed they needed to escape to the Blue Ridge Mountains in order to avoid the summer fevers that ravaged the tidewater region, and Northern urbanites insisted that the heat was unbearable inside their town houses but was much less taxing on the Hudson River. Even if health was merely an excuse to dine, flirt, and dance, the search for physical well-being provided a necessary foundation for travel in a nation anxious about leisure.[21] During the early nineteenth century, tourism developed to the point where the purpose of traveling was "to see and be seen, to chat, laugh and dance, and to throw each his pebble on the giant heap of the general enjoyment."[22] As Washington Irving declared, people traveled "to exhibit their equipages and wardrobes, and to excite the admiration, or what is much more satisfactory, the *envy* of their fashionable competitors."[23]

The further development of canals, turnpikes, and railroads as reliable transportation during the 1820s and 1830s, at least in the Northern states, connected American farms, towns, factories, and ports in increasingly regional networks of trade and travel. Tourists took full advantage of these new networks, and the "travel system" grew so quickly that guidebooks appeared, catering specifically to the tourist trade. Any traveler could now identify the quickest routes, best lodgings, and most fashionable destinations for the price of a pocket-size volume. Travel expanded to the point that by 1828 "all ages and sexes are to be found on the wing, in perpetual motion from place to place."[24]

By the 1820s the standard tour route allowed tourists to sail up the Hudson River from New York City, gaze at the Catskill Mountains just at a remove from the river's west shore, visit Saratoga Springs and Lake George, and then head west along the newly opened Erie Canal, to gawk in wonder at Niagara Falls. After reaching this westernmost point, travelers followed Lake Ontario and the St. Lawrence River to historic Montreal and Quebec. They returned home either via the St. Lawrence to Lake Champlain (reached by a brief overland trip

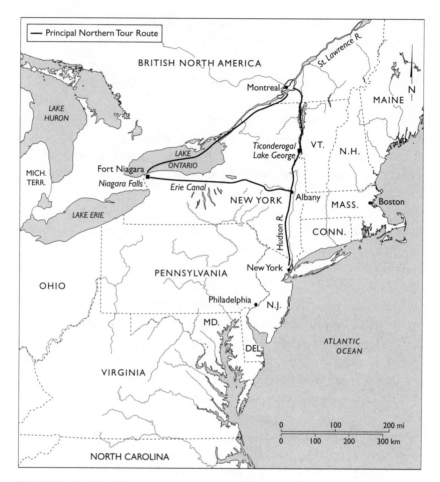

**Map 1.** The Northern Tour.

from Montreal to the Richelieu River) and then descended the Hudson River to New York City, or traveled overland to the Connecticut River Valley, New Hampshire's White Mountains, and finally to Boston. They frequently commented on bad hotels and atrocious food, cramped canal boats or lake sloops, boomtowns and rustic locals, and the general challenges of travel in an age of poor roads and improvised accommodations. But travelers had defined routes to follow and reliable (if not always pleasant) accommodations and food along the way.

In and through their travels, Americans sought to imitate the European Grand Tour, a rite of passage for young British aristocrats who visited ancient ruins, painters' studios, and homes of their fellow nobles before returning home to assume responsible roles in society. As part of their gaining worldly experience, these travelers sought emotional responses to landscape and history. A model for this activity was Edward Gibbon, who, while in Rome in 1764, felt that he could "neither forget nor express the strong emotions which agitated my mind as I first approached and entered the *eternal City*."[25] Such reactions to landscapes and historic places evolved into the tradition of English landscape painting and picturesque tourism during the late eighteenth century, as articulated by William Gilpin's influential 1792 "Essay on Picturesque Travel." Gilpin moved beyond the dichotomy between the sublime and the beautiful that Edmund Burke had articulated earlier in the century, wherein raw nature produced terror in those who viewed it, and reverence for God's power. In contrast, beauty, Burke stated, was characterized by smoothness and less threatening landscapes, such as a sloping garden, which produced joy and pleasure. Gilpin amended Burke and described an intermediate landscape that possessed both the roughness of nature and the calmness of man-made scenery. Viewing and sketching such scenery became commonplace in late-Georgian Britain, as people pursued "the love of novelty" in finding new landscapes. They also looked to landscapes for evidence of the unchanging essence of Great Britain in a time of profound technological and social upheaval. Scenes untouched by the modern—be it roads and bridges or smokestacks and factories—prompted emotional responses to what the country had lost, mixed with pride in what it had gained. In defining landscape in this way, Great Britain's cultural elite redeemed nature from social change, imagining a past of untrammeled and unchanged scenery. The reality that very few such landscapes existed made the yearning for them all the stronger. A key motivation in viewing the picturesque, then, was to expand one's capacity to express longings for the vanished past and to signify one's membership in a broader, exclusive cultural group. Gilpin asked his readers, "Is there a greater ornamental landscape, than the ruins of a castle?" and they responded enthusiastically by searching for such scenes.[26]

Experiencing picturesque scenery became an American cultural trend a bit later, by the 1820s. The few Americans who had crossed the Atlantic before that decade to complete the Grand Tour returned with an appreciation for European cultural standards, and they considered

British ways superior to all others. Just as the British had been and were using picturesque tourism to articulate their nation's vanished golden age and national character, Americans just returned from Europe began cultivating an American Grand Tour as a symbol of their nation's cultural maturity.[27] But American scenery was quite different from English gardens or meadows, much less the cathedrals and ancient ruins that drew British travelers to Italy or Paris. The United States' wild and undiscovered—at least by tourists—landscapes offered the opportunity to sketch new scenes and to construct new narratives.[28] Because it lacked Europe's ancient ruins and cultivated scenery, the nation's relative youth became an asset. Its unspoiled landscapes could actually hold *more* meaning than Europe's ancient places. The English-born painter Thomas Cole seized upon this "distinctive" aspect of American scenery as its main attraction. "Nature has shed over *this* land beauty and magnificence, and although the character of its scenery may differ from the old world's, yet inferiority must not therefore be inferred," Cole wrote in his influential 1835 "Essay on American Scenery." America's wild and unsettled scenery provoked more than reflections upon a specific castle's legend or an associated poem. Surrounded by untrammeled mountains and ancient forests, "the consequent associations are of God, the Creator; they are his undefiled works, and the mind is cast into the contemplation of eternal things." Cole added that America's sights "are not destitute of historical and legendary associations; the great struggle for freedom has sanctified many a spot." American scenery struck the perfect balance between historical associations and unspoiled wilderness; it provided a source of national pride while simultaneously conforming to British ideals of the picturesque.[29]

Cole's earliest work sparked the rise of the Hudson River School of landscape painting and scenic tours of the Hudson River Valley and nearby Catskill Mountains during the same years that writers such as Washington Irving and James Fenimore Cooper searched for national meaning in the vanishing wilderness and the history of the United States. In subsequent decades Ralph Waldo Emerson and Nathaniel Hawthorne expanded this ideology to emphasize individual experiences and nostalgia for a simpler past.[30] Like earlier British conceptions of the relationship between nature and industrialization, American painters and authors looked to the imagined past for useful national myths. The Transcendentalist and Romantic movements lauded the beauty and power of America's wild scenery as evidence of the nation's unspoiled origins, while simultaneously asserting the republic's ability to conquer and improve nature. Americans hastened to view their nation's wild and historic places. When they arrived at the Catskill Mountains, Niagara Falls, or an abandoned fort or battlefield, they responding emotionally. The Romantic impulse toward nostalgic reflections on landscape and history allowed tourists to express their membership in a cultural elite conversant in the vocabulary of the picturesque but also interested in their nation's origins and unique character. The new American Grand Tour was, by virtue of being closer to home, more affordable and achievable for more Americans and appealed to Americans casting about for ways to appreciate the wonders of the continent. Visiting America's natural wonders and historic sites served nationalistic as well as cultural purposes; the nation's scenery revealed America's "errand into the wilderness" far better than did the scenery and castles of Europe.[31]

At historic sites such as Fort Ticonderoga, a ruined eighteenth-century lakeside fort and battlefield in northern New York State, visitors reveled in the chance to walk historic ground and to touch the fort's stone walls, viewing the ruins' "scenes of desolation" as positive attributes.[32] Vines tangled around earthen embankments, stone doorways leading into roofless rooms, and walls toppling to the ground piece by piece evoked "a very romantic appearance."[33] As Benjamin Silliman noted in 1819, "This scene is very fine, and the whole outline of the spot—the mountains near, and the mountains at a distance—the shores—the bay—and the ruins, all unite to make a very grand landscape." He felt "that I was beholding a striking emblem of the mutability of power, and of the fluctuations of empire."[34] Visiting old battlefields along the Northern Tour enabled tourists to express their cultural sophistication, national identity, and emotional nuance, in order to engage larger questions about the nation's creation and its meaning. Battlefields like Ticonderoga perfectly suited the imperatives of the emerging American culture, because, as *The Picturesque Tourist* guidebook said, such sites were "varied in scenery, and deeply interesting in historical incidents."[35]

Tourism to picturesque historic sites proved so popular that the leading guidebook, Theodore Dwight's *The Northern Traveller*, went through six editions between 1825 and 1841. From one edition to the next, Dwight gradually added more information on visiting battlefields located along the route.[36] The steady development of transportation routes, hastened by the expansion of railroads in the 1840s and 1850s across the northeastern United States, eased travel to the point that by 1858 a traveler "on my way home from the coal regions of central Pennsylvania" could hop off the train at "the Wyoming depot to view the ground" of the 1778 battle and its monument, before catching the next scheduled train and reaching his destination on time. While the traveler was reading inscriptions on the obelisk, "the shrill sound of the whistle" announced "that the train was approaching; so I left in haste, arrived at the depot in time to get comfortably seated, and was swiftly borne from the beautiful valley of Wyoming."[37] The commercialization of leisure occurred almost simultaneously with the evolution of memory at many but not all battlefields, with history provided as a whistle-stop attraction for American travelers.[38]

## Memory and Place

Once Americans arrived at battlefields, they sought meaning in these "sacred places." Politicians and cultural arbiters attempted to shape how Americans remembered battlefields by organizing formal ceremonies and making serious speeches, but with limited success. In the era of picturesque tourism and emotional responses to landscape, encountering place mattered more than the words uttered by a famous orator. That changed during the antebellum era, when attempts to memorialize the Revolutionary War to advance sectional political identity coincided with increased tourist visits to abandoned battlefields. During this brief period "official" memory merged with battlefield tourism.[39] Once Americans realized the result of such politicized memory—a bloody Civil War—they retreated from embracing formal commemorations for a time.

Twenty years after Confederate troops fortified Yorktown, Americans gathered to dedicate a monument to the 1781 battle. "Dead earnest" Masons presided with their usual pomp and circumstance, but their "patriotic and chaste sentiments" enervated the Yorktown centennial. As an aged Mason presided over the ceremony, "alluding to one after the other of [his] Biblical friends," the crowd grew impatient. "The seats were half deserted, but the President and his Cabinet could not sneak away and wipe their fevered brows in the shade and murmur sarcasm on the orator's knowledge of antiquity." The printed version of the grand master's speech plodded along for almost nineteen single-spaced pages. An afternoon of "long sitting in the broiling sun, while Masons of various degrees held forth," was less attractive than the fireworks and general revelry that evening. In an earlier era, the monument's bluff-top site, "one of the finest here, overlooking York-town, the field of battle as well as the sea," might have overcome the torpid ceremony. But in 1881, rather than admire scenery or listen to "the brunt of heavy speeches that everybody knows must be listened to, and that nobody wants to hear," Americans preferred "a national jollification and festival."[40] The ages of genteel picturesque tourism and sectional memory had passed.

The kind of historical memory that many Americans desired strayed far from the dull speeches of elected leaders, whether in 1881 or 1825. Americans preferred less instructive, more personal commemorations and a good show, either in the form of evocative landscapes or exploding fireworks. Their interaction with battlefields and historic ruins was about something other than erecting monuments or hosting formal ceremonies. Pilgrimages to hillocks and meadows where armies had engaged were more personal than political in character. Even while those Americans visiting battlefields hailed from the wealthy and culturally sophisticated segments of society that might be most inclined to support the "official" memory expressed in speeches, ceremonies, and published works, they rejected "the eloquent utterances of the distinguished speaker." Instead, such tourists preferred to walk over Lexington Green and muse on its melancholy past when Edward Everett was not pontificating on its significance.[41]

Battlefield tourism reveals the multiplicity of memory constructed by Americans after the Revolutionary War. "Official" memory found expression in the formal commemorative events that frequently took place in American towns and occasionally on the nation's battlefields. These scripted events constituted a small fraction of Americans' interaction with battlefields. During less structured encounters with battlefields from the Seven Years' War (often called the French and Indian War in North America), the Revolutionary War, or the War of 1812, Americans constructed highly personal and emotional memories of war that were closely tied to place.[42] By the middle of the nineteenth century, Americans wanted to encounter the past rather than listen to someone tell them about it.

Almost every speaker at the 1881 Yorktown centennial made reference to the events that took place "on this soil 100 years ago." The fact that the commemoration occurred "on the spot where we are now gathered" lent it greater legitimacy and emotive power.[43] These orators spoke to the broader relationship between memory and location. Our senses of sight, sound, smell, taste, and touch combine with symbols and landscape cues, such as monuments, cemeteries, or battlefield ruins, to create place as "a center of meaning constructed by experience."[44] Our memories are strongly connected to place and landscape, because topographical features remain relatively unchanged over time. A distinctive hillside boulder might conjure up long-forgotten recollections of a particular event near that rock that are far more vivid than those elicited by reading a book or listening to a story about the same occurrence. The durable nature of place, at least over the course of a few decades, renders it a potent stimulus to remembering a past event that occurred there. Encountering place fosters corporeal rather than abstract ideas, forming a type of memory that is powerful and emotional.[45]

These largely individual memories, for all their force, still lack the power to construct collective memory. Only community-based interaction with place involving common rituals and commemorations results in durable memory that can be reenacted and reconfirmed in future years.[46] "Past events make no impact in the present unless they are memorialized in history books, monuments, pageants, and solemn and jovial festivities that are recognized as part of an ongoing tradition."[47] The visibility of the past gives it meaning, and tourists were often—and still are—the earliest and most frequent visitors to remote yet significant historic sites.[48] Their trips to battlefields often followed a set itinerary listed in published guidebooks—perhaps even eliciting similar responses to landscape in different parts of the United States—in the process constructing fundamental memories and identities through interaction and relationship with historic sites. "Place attachment" enables people to render historical landscapes meaningful and constitutes a core value of the touristic impulse. People go to a place so that they can better understand it through personal experience.[49] Locations such as battlefields become *lieux de memoire,* sacred contexts where remembrance is preserved and encountered once the events and actors recede in time. Battlefields provide a particularly rich cultural context for such constructions of memory. They serve as loci where societies and nations invent and legitimize their histories, traditions, and myths. Tourists constituted a core population in that endeavor.[50]

## Touring History

Well into the nineteenth century, the ways in which Americans interacted with historic sites reflected greater interest in landscape aesthetics than preoccupation with historical knowledge. At decaying forts and overgrown battlefields, Americans reached a consensus where landscape and scenery merged with responses to history. Tourists searched for sites that evoked melancholy along well-traveled tourist routes better known for picturesque scenery than famous battlefields. Not until the late 1840s and 1850s did Americans explicitly interpret battlefields from the nation's earlier wars as patriotic sites crucial to the nation's creation. Instead, American tourists preferred picturesque landscapes tinged with veneration for the past.

Tourists' responses to battlefields and scenic landscapes produced memories far different from those evoked by more-formal commemorations of past events in part because "as tourists, people reveal about themselves more than they might have wished." Tourists' responses to place—either as individuals or as part of a small group of friends or family, the normal mode of early travel—provide a view into "individual motivations and intimate values" rarely expressed beyond an inner dialogue or within a close personal circle. These individualized memories contrast with the inability of cultures to physically represent the painful memories experienced at sites of destruction such as battlefields. The United States' paltry early monument-building efforts make the distinction between official and vernacular memory less important to understanding how early republic and antebellum Americans remembered war. The participatory nature of walking blood-soaked battlefields enacted a type of memory far more personal and place-dependent than did attending drier speeches and ceremonies intended to convince listeners of a particular view of the past.[51] This type of memory prevailed from the Revolutionary era until the sectional crisis.

Only the Civil War's onset combined these various memories into a more formal, public memory focused on great men, their deeds, and the persistent values of an ordered Revolution, albeit with distinctly Northern and Southern perspectives. Such nascent collective memories later formed the basis of a nationalism rooted in the Revolution's martial sacrifice. Not until the Revolution's centennial would governmental commemorative efforts begin in earnest, tied in large part to efforts to heal the Civil War's wounds by binding the nation together in what was depicted as a nonsectional past. This "reconciliationist vision" of the past romanticized the Civil War by emphasizing the valor and struggle of soldiers at the expense of the emancipationist ideology of the war's conclusion and the conflicts of the Reconstruction years. It sought common points of cultural unity, such as battlefields where soldiers from both North and South suffered and demonstrated valor in a cause that, according to this vision, had little to do with race or slavery.[52] For post-Reconstruction Americans, the Revolutionary War, fought during an idealized golden age of national unity against a common foe, provided an ideal subject for unifying commemoration, even if that idealized past had never existed. To further the point of national unity, "no representatives of the British nation or descendants of the British benefactors of America were invited" to the Yorktown centennial.[53] The omission seems glaring, considering that militias from Northern and Southern states camped next to each other on Yorktown's plains in 1881, a spot where not even two decades earlier North and South shed each other's blood. Instead of remembering that recent fighting, Americans imagined a past rooted in martial sacrifice, which provided the basis for a shared nationalism. New Jersey troops fraternizing with Virginia militia at Yorktown in 1881 declared "it to be disingenuous and unmanly to indulge in recriminations as to responsibility for the [Civil] war when the struggle was the outgrowth of generations." Amid a sumptuous banquet and extensive speechifying, "not one word was uttered on either side that would mar the occasion."[54]

Before they could use battlefields to unite a nation divided by the Civil War, Americans first had to believe that visiting, understanding, and commemorating their battlefields was a worthwhile endeavor for more than a cultural elite. In order to understand that process, it is necessary to look closely at how, across the late eighteenth and early nineteenth centuries, American travelers and tourists encountered the battlefields of not just the Revolutionary War but also the Seven Years' War and the War of 1812.

CHAPTER ONE

*Accidental Tourists*

The Bonefields of Braddock's
Defeat and Ticonderoga

During the summer of 1776, when the Revolution's outcome seemed far from certain, George Washington claimed, "I did not let the Anniversary of the 3d or 9th of [July] pass of[f] without a grateful remembrance of the escape we had at the Meadows and on Banks of the Monongahela."[1] He referred to his military experience at Fort Necessity in 1754 and Braddock's Field in 1755, two early battles during the Seven Years' War that helped shape the future of western Pennsylvania, as well as the legacy of Washington himself. In each case he experienced defeat and witnessed death at close range, yet escaped with his person and reputation intact. The site where he earned his greatest early fame, Braddock's Field, remained largely undisturbed for many years, "the bones of men who were killed at the battle laying very thick" on the ground.[2] In subsequent years soldiers stationed at nearby Fort Pitt, as well as the many travelers who passed by the bonefields, remarked on the decaying human remains. The memories they constructed of Braddock's Field, as well as of a Seven Years' War site in northern New York State, Ticonderoga, relied on interaction with place. Relatively few people visited these battlefields as tourists during the Revolutionary War and for the rest of the eighteenth century, but the response to history and place by those who did set the pattern for constructing memory in the decades to come. The differing memories of accidental tourists visiting Braddock's Field or Ticonderoga depended on connecting the bones and landscapes they viewed with the events that shaped the Revolution.

## Braddock's Defeat

Jasper Yeates traveled from his home in Lancaster, Pennsylvania, to the relatively wild western portion of his state in 1776 on official business. Congress had appointed him a commissioner to negotiate peace treaties with the Indians living near the Forks of the Ohio River in the hopes of keeping them neutral in the Revolutionary War against Great Britain. The negotiations took place where the Allegheny and Monongahela rivers joined to flow westward, the strategic location that Britain, France, and native peoples had fought to control just two decades earlier during the Seven Years' War.[3] The massive Fort Pitt, built next to French Fort Duquesne after its destruction in 1758, had been abandoned by the British in 1772 but continued to provide a reminder of imperial might. A small garrison manned Fort Pitt, but just a few hundred feet away at Duquesne "a little irregular ground, a few graves and the fosse of the Fort are only visible." Just these earthworks remained from a place "celebrated...in my youth." Yeates considered the fighting for "this little spot...a waste of blood and treasure." At least "the prospects around here are most charming...and the walks pleasant beyond description." As an actual military site, Fort Pitt and the remains of Fort Duquesne failed to impress the well-educated lawyer with an eye for scenery.[4]

But other remnants of the Seven Years' War lay nearby, and Yeates "made a party to visit Braddock's Field" on August 20, 1776, perhaps the first pleasure trip to the site. He and his fourteen companions traveled in style, with their "large canoe of six oars" fitted out with sleeping platforms at the bow and stern, and blankets stretched across poles above the boat "to keep off sun or rain." In four hours' time they paddled several miles up the Monongahela River as one passenger "played delightfully on a German flute." Stopping near the battleground at "a fine spring," the party enjoyed "a hearty dinner." As Yeates noted, "it was wise in eating before we visited the field, for I would have had but little appetite, if we had pursued a different course." From the moment Yeates, also a volunteer in the Pennsylvania militia, and his companions "commenced our ramble, our Hearts sickened; the skulls and bones of our unburied countrymen met our eyes, and we contemplated in imagination as an event but recently happened." Marks from cannon and musket balls "are still to be seen on the trees" twenty feet above the ground, and "any person of common humanity would have experienced pain from the reflection that between five and six hundred brave men fell victims to the merciless savages." Yeates benefited from the narration provided by fellow traveler Dr. Walker, "an eye witness" who pointed out the ford where British troops had crossed the river in 1755, far different from how "they cross the river now,—without arms, order or music, the hellish yells of the Indians and the groans and shrieks of the dying and the wounded falling upon their ears." More jarring than the contrast between the locale's current peaceful repose and the bloody warfare of twenty-one years earlier were the human remains still visible. After the battle "the dead bodies of our troops were suffered to remain a prey to wolves and crows." Hundreds of skulls and bones had been interred since the battle, but "many remain as monuments of our shame." Shocked by the sight of bleached bones, Yeates "returned home late in the evening; the music of the flute was delightful and solemnly impressive."[5]

The Seven Years' War site that Yeates and his companions encountered represented perhaps the most humiliating defeat suffered by the British Empire in North America, and certainly the greatest feat of Native American arms during the 1750s. Braddock's Field stood near a key crossing of the Monongahela and a few miles above the crucial Forks of the Ohio, a gateway to the continent's interior. The wayside witnessed one of the earliest and bloodiest engagements of the Seven Years' War when a British army marched north from Winchester, Virginia, during the summer of 1755. On July 9, a French, Canadian, and Native American force of nearly 900 men collided with Major General Edward Braddock's 2,200 British, provincial, and Native American troops shortly after they crossed to the east bank of the Monongahela River and before the British reached the outnumbered French garrison at Fort Duquesne, which could hold only 200 of the total 1,600 French forces inside its earth-filled log walls. Marching in formation down a narrow forested path, Braddock's men spotted the enemy first

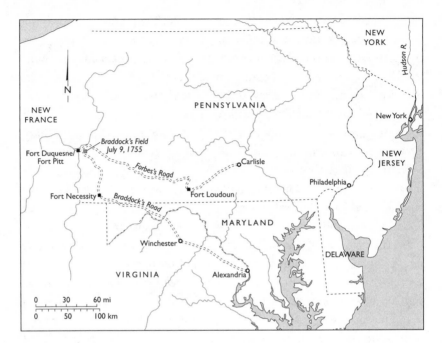

**Map 2.** Braddock's Field and Forbes's Road.

and opened fire but were quickly surrounded on both sides by irregular tactics.[6] As twenty-three-year-old George Washington remembered, the British "soon f[e]ll into irretrievable disorder...a general
panic took place among the Troops from which no exertions of the
Officers could recover them." Having suffered two-thirds casualties—
including Braddock and his senior officers—the British retreated and
were psychologically unable to regroup. Serving as an aide to Braddock
because of a dispute over rank, the ambitious Virginian whose actions
at Jumonville Glen the previous year may have started the great war for
empire noted: "The shocking Scenes which presented themselves in
this Nights March are not to be described—The dead—the dying—the
groans—lamentation—and crys along the Road of the wounded for
help...were enough to pierce the heart of [the] adamant. the gloom &
horror of which was not a little increased by the impervious darkness
occasioned by the close shade of thick woods."[7]

Such horrific slaughter remained fresh in Anglo-American minds
long after the battle. When in 1758 the British next attempted to capture

Fort Duquesne, they moved deliberately. George Washington, once again involved in the advance on the French position at the Forks of the Ohio, recalled the "hapless spot" and "the cruel butcheries exercised on our friends, in the unfortunate day of General Braddock's defeat."[8] His musings came from the army's base at Fort Loudoun seven months before the British approached Fort Duquesne, suggesting some trepidation in marching to the spot of the previous slaughter. Likewise, when British scouts approached the Forks of Ohio in August 1758, they "came up across the place of Braddock's engagement, and stayed there until sunset." The soldiers remembered the defeat as they "marched down the road and saw the bones of men who were killed at the battle laying very thick."[9] Not wanting to repeat this destruction, General John Forbes had made sure to win the allegiance of Native Americans. This time the Delaware and other regional native peoples sided with the British, and western Indians had returned home after the 1755 battle, having proven their valor by taking trophies and prisoners in the earlier conflict. Left in a vulnerable defensive position, on November 23, 1758, the French commander set fire to Fort Duquesne and detonated fifty barrels of gunpowder under its walls, reducing the fort to smoldering ruins.[10]

The British took possession of the site the next day. Wasting little time, Forbes built a log stockade near the ruins of Fort Duquesne and on November 28 ordered "thirty men" to parade at 8 a.m. "with a proportion of Tools in order to march & bury the bones upon the Field where General Braddock had his engagement." Owing to the chaotic nature of that battle and the wounded stragglers who might have died on the retreat or in the woods, Forbes ordered that "any bones that they find upon the Road are likewise to be interred."[11] The troops buried at least 450 human skulls on the field.[12] Even the body of Sir Peter Halket, the veteran colonel of the Forty-fourth Regiment of Foot and Braddock's deputy commander, had been left unburied in 1755, along with that of his younger son, a lieutenant in his father's regiment. Halket's other, elder son formed part of the 1758 detachment sent to rebury the dead on Braddock's Field, the standard practice for British forces after an engagement, even if several years had passed. With the aid of Pennsylvania militia captain Samuel West, the brother of the painter Benjamin West, and an "Indian warrior" who had fought in the battle, Major Halket located "the remarkable tree" under which his father and brother had died. The Indian claimed to have seen a British officer fall near the tree, and then witnessed a junior officer run to the first man. The younger officer was "shot dead on reaching the spot, and fell across the other's body." This detail convinced Major Halket that the men were his father and brother. When they reached the tree, the officers with Major Halket formed a circle around the spot and had the Indians remove "the leaves, which thickly covered the ground." They quickly found the two men's skeletons "lying across each other." Unable to determine the remains' identity, Major Halket mentioned that his father possessed the identifying trait of "an artificial tooth." He ordered the Indians to "remove the skeleton of the youth, and bring to view that of the old officer." Halket needed only moments before he exclaimed, "'It is my father!' and fell back into the arms of his companions." The accompanying soldiers "then dug a grave, and the bones being laid in it together, ... they were interred with the customary honors."[13]

Improper burial or disturbing the dead profoundly upset eighteenth-century Anglo-Americans, especially when the remains belonged to an officer or relation. Common soldiers might be wrapped in cloth and covered with a thin layer of soil, but officers were expected to receive a formal burial and perhaps even a coffin. The "customary honors" that the Halkets posthumously received included "a highland plaid" spread over their remains, in honor of their Scots heritage and in recognition of their noble lineage. That when he died several days after the battle General Braddock's body was interred under the road his army soon marched over—in an attempt to conceal and preserve his bones—while his men's corpses decayed on the battlefield, subject to the ravages of weather and scavengers, reflects the varying concepts of death and burial across class lines. Apparently proper burial extended only to some of the dead men, especially the officers.[14] In leaving the bodies behind, and allowing scavengers and nature to reduce the corpses to bones, Braddock's army produced a stark reminder of defeat and death. Yet even the Forbes expedition's effort to bury the remains of Braddock's Field proved incomplete.

While the work of burying soldiers' bones remained, provincial and British troops completed Fort Pitt in 1759, intending to impress local Indians with the empire's powerful reach. Perhaps unintentionally, the wide roads protected by the British guardhouses and small forts that stretched across western Pennsylvania provided a perfect avenue for settlers to follow the soldiers into the Ohio Country. And because

**Figure 1.** John Rogers, *Burial of General Braddock* (1858). By the early nineteenth century, Braddock's death and burial became a central part of American mythology, proving the intransigence of Great Britain and the general's refusal to listen to George Washington. This engraving's depiction of a placid, mournful burial, based on a painting by John McNevin, contrasts with the fate of Braddock's fallen soldiers, whose corpses and bones remained unburied on the battlefield. Courtesy of the Library of Congress.

Braddock's Field lay near the confluence of the two main westward routes—Forbes's Road and Braddock's Road—many people interacted with the battlefield without intentionally setting out to encounter the past. The influx of settlers and soldiers quickly populated the area around Fort Pitt, a movement that the British army could do little to stop. Even though the region lay west of the Proclamation Line of 1763, which was designed to halt the westward migration of American settlers, by the late 1760s several hundred Europeans populated the land near Braddock's Field. Thousands more would pass by the battlefield in ensuing years, encountering the past in the process.[15] These migrants were men like the Philadelphia shipwright Jehu Eyre, at Fort Pitt to construct bateaux for the British forces plying western Pennsylvania's many rivers. Eyre broke the monotonous "cutting of knees for the bateaux" by pretending to enter the wood for that chore. Instead, he and another man "set off through the woods to go to Braddock's field." At the point where Braddock's men had crossed the Monongahela, Eyre "saw a great many men's bones along the shore. We kept along the road about 1½ miles, where the first engagement began." Five years after the battle, he still could find "men's bones lying about as thick as the leaves do on the ground; for they are so thick that one lies on top of another for about a half a mile in length, and about one hundred yards in breadth." Eyre's detailed description of the scattered remains sticks out in a terse diary otherwise filled with the daily entry, "We were at work on the bateaux."[16] The bones impressed a man seeking diversion from his daily toil. For the Moravian missionary John Heckewelder, they proved more sobering. The "dismal music" of his horse's hooves "continually striking against…skulls and bones of the unfortunate men slain" on "this memorable battle ground" hastened his departure from Braddock's Field. On his way to the mission towns of Christianized Indians in the Ohio Valley in 1762, he felt "relieved from an insupportable weight" when he arrived at Fort Pitt and was once again "in the company of the living."[17] Few travelers found the bonefields alluring, merely noting that they had "pass'd thro' the Field of Battle (the Bones yet in Sight)."[18]

Those who did pause to contemplate the scene were deeply moved. One missionary, the Reverend David McClure, made an explicit attempt to visit the battlefield, riding there the day after preaching to settlers near Fort Pitt in August 1772. "It was a melancholy spectacle to see the bones of men strewed over the ground, left to this day, without the solemn rite of sepulture." His catalog of death included still intact horses' harness, "bones gnawed by wolves, the vestiges of their teeth appearing on them," and several hundred skulls lying on the ground. McClure examined the specimens and "found the mark of the scalping knife on all." He scooped handfuls of grapeshot into his satchel, along with one skull "and a jaw bone," which he later donated to a museum. His preservationist instincts noted with thanks that the farmer "whose corn field takes in a part of" the bonefield "had humanely collected a great number of the bones and laid them in small heaps." The minister failed to realize that the farmer might merely have wanted to clear his field for planting and harvesting. McClure's more religious mind pondered "serious and solemn reflections on the vanity of life, and the deep depravity of our fallen nature, the dreadful source of fighting and war, and all the miseries that man delights to inflict on man." Disgusted with the sight of such slaughter, he cried, "'Oh! Why will men forget that they are brethren!'" His Christian faith informed his condemnation of the battlefield as an insult to God's creation but provided him little reason to comment on General Braddock's leadership or the merit of the British cause, as later observers would do. He merely noted that neglecting to inter the soldiers' remains was "a disgrace to the british commanders at Fort Pitt."[19] In the two decades after the battle, those few people who passed Braddock's Field primarily noted the physical remains of battle and paid little attention to cause or consequences. They merely observed the misfortunes and horrors of war.

The British abandoned Fort Pitt in 1772, and five years later American forces converted its remains into the headquarters of the western army, using it until the Revolutionary War's end. Still, the bonefields remained. Migrants traveling Braddock's Road mentioned "great quantities of broken Bombshells, cannon, bullets, and other military stores scattered in the woods." They barely noticed "the vestiges of Fort Necessity" or the more substantial "place where Colonel Dunbar was encamped when he received the news of General Braddock's defeat in 1755."[20] Military detritus constituted such an omnipresent part of the western Pennsylvania landscape that residents often ignored shell fragments and rusted armaments, overlooking them as part of their natural surroundings. It was not until 1781 that local inhabitants near Braddock's Field, not the American army or government, "gathered and carted several loads of human bones and deposited them in a hole dug for the purpose."[21] For twenty-six years the remains of Braddock's men rotted in the earth or bleached in the sun. Not until a century later, during the Civil War, with its massive scale of death, did Americans begin to identify and inter every single soldier in a separate grave, regardless of rank. Eighteenth-century battlefields left behind ample, visible reminders of human suffering.[22]

## Blundering Braddock / Heroic Washington

The meaning of Braddock's Field changed with the American rebellion against British colonial rule in 1775. What had been the main goal of the western theater during the Seven Years' War saw no major combat during the Revolutionary War, serving instead as the diplomatic mission to prevent native peoples in the Ohio Country from attacking the rebellious colonies. But in the context of the rebellion against British tyranny, Braddock's Field, even if it lay fallow, resounded with comparisons to the current cause. Jasper Yeates went beyond previous sentimental responses to the bones he witnessed in 1776. "My indignation was greatly excited against the commander of the British army, in suffering so many brave men to perish from an obstinate adherence to European rules of war." He imagined a dramatic scene before the slaughter: "A finer sight could not have been beheld" than the ordered ranks of well-dressed soldiers carrying their shining muskets, with the military music echoing off the mountains. "How brilliant the morning,—how melancholy the evening!" he enthused. But this romantic recollection belied the fact that "Braddock appeared almost to have courted defeat." As the Indian and French force adopted irregular tactics in the dense woods, the stubborn General Braddock insisted on maintaining formation in ranks, and "fired in platoons against no object. How very dispiriting to a gallant soldier." In Yeates's remembered version of the battle, the enemy, "observing the *infatuation,* of the General, felt assured of victory" and pressed the attack, sending the British troops into chaotic retreat. Because of "the blunder of Braddock…the dead bodies of our troops were suffered to remain a prey to wolves and crows."[23] Blame lay only at Braddock's feet, as his American officers had warned against traditional tactics.

As one Revolutionary War soldier declared in evaluating the previous war, "The destruction of General Braddock is a melancholy instance: by his haughty demeanour, and strict adherence to his own plan, in direct opposition to the counsel of experienced chiefs, he lost their friendship, and died unlamented."[24] Years after the battle George Washington emphasized "the folly & consequence of opposing compact bodies to the sparse manner of Indian fighting, in woods, which had in a manner been predicted, was now so clearly verified that from hence forward another mode obtained in all future operations." Although attempting to solidify his reputation as a great military leader and to absolve himself of blame for this disastrous campaign, in his 1787 recollection Washington articulated an essential point of the Revolutionary War mythology: Americans won because they fought like Indians.[25] This battle pointed out the foolishness of British tactics; as in battle, so in politics. Braddock's Field provided an object lesson in why Americans' interests and instincts diverged from those of Great Britain.[26] Washington gained a reputation for having saved the British army from total destruction at Braddock's Field in 1755, and his personal deliverance mirrored the new nation's precarious existence.[27] From Washington and Braddock's Field Americans not only learned a hard lesson, but also gained an admirable hero.

## Carillon / Ticonderoga

Washington's judgment was not always so keen. Hundreds of miles to the northeast, along what is now the New York–Vermont border, another Seven Years' War battlefield reminded Revolutionary War–era Americans of their difference from the British. In 1758 a massive British and provincial army moved against the French Fort Carillon, later called Ticonderoga, in hopes of expelling their imperial rivals from Quebec. Outnumbering the French garrison by four to one, British general James Abercromby chose a frontal assault on outlying French entrenchments before advancing his artillery. During the battle "we got behind trees, logs and stumps, and covered ourselves as we could from the enemy's fire," wrote seventeen-year-old Massachusetts provincial soldier David Perry. He "could hear the men screaming, and see them dying all around me." The French musket balls came "by the handful" and struck any man who so much as raised his head. The battle ended shamefully at sunset as "the men crept off, leaving all the dead, and most of the wounded."[28] Abercromby's haste resulted in nearly two thousand casualties, including over three hundred provincials. It was, recalled another Massachusetts soldier, a "sorefull Si[gh]t to behold. The Ded men and wounded Lay on the ground having Som of them thir legs their arms and other Lims broken, others shot threw the body and very mortly wounded." Even though General Jeffery Amherst took the fort the next year, Ticonderoga possessed specific associations and vivid, unpleasant memories for New Englanders: "their cries and...their bodies lay in blood...a mournful [h]our as ever I saw."[29]

The British rebuilt Carillon—whose powder magazine the French had detonated as they evacuated the fort in 1759—and renamed it Fort Ticonderoga. They also built a much larger fort at Crown Point, a dozen miles closer to Canada, and Ticonderoga lost some of it strategic importance. British military officers, however, sought out the "famous lines, which we attacked Unsuccessfully in 1758."[30] The "French Lines," as Fort Carillon's outer defenses were usually called after the Seven Years' War, "still remain entire, and are very strong," wrote a Scottish traveler in 1767. Eight feet thick at the bottom, as tall as a man, and extending two miles across the peninsula, the French lines impressed, as "nothing could be stronger of the sort." Fort Ticonderoga itself, however, was "reckoned too small" for effective defense soon after the war.[31] British military minds declared that Ticonderoga's "works are ruinous…all of Wood and some bad Casemates."[32] Ticonderoga's inadequate defenses, old French fortifications, and scattered outer works suffered from neglect during the brief peacetime.

British commanders strengthened Ticonderoga's defenses in 1774–75 as tensions within the colonies increased. Captain William De La Place commanded twenty men at Ticonderoga, a force grossly inadequate to defend the fortification, much less its outer defenses.[33] In the spring of 1775, in one of the Revolutionary War's first actions, Ethan Allen and Benedict Arnold seized "the fortress Ticonderoga" in an early morning surprise attack, declaring "the sun seemed to rise that morning with a superior lustre" after an event that Allen considered "of signal importance to the American cause."[34] During the next winter, of 1775–76, American soldiers hauled over two hundred cannon captured at Ticonderoga across the frozen lakes, rivers, and roadways of eastern New York and Massachusetts to Boston. Their commanding presence on Dorchester Heights helped American forces end the British occupation of Boston on March 17, 1776.[35] Yet the artillery itself may have been of less significance than Ticonderoga's legend. The fort's symbolic value as a major battlefield during the Seven Years' War outweighed its actual strategic utility. Ethan Allen didn't just steal some cannon, he captured one of North America's most famous fortresses.

That mythic importance prompted both sides to overemphasize Ticonderoga in future campaigns. Congress ordered "that the fortress at Ticonderoga be repaired and made defensible" during the winter of 1776.[36] George Washington, now commander of the Continental army, assumed that "Ticonderoga properly Garrisoned and Supplied, is almost impregnable."[37] But Washington based his opinion on Ticonderoga's reputation, not actual observation of the battlefield itself.

During his April–June 1776 diplomatic mission to Canada, Maryland congressman Charles Carroll reported that felled tree trunks at Ticonderoga "remain piled up" along the 1758 French lines, but "they are fast going to decay." He considered the fort to be "in a ruinous condition" and its location not "judicially chosen for construction of a fort." Yet remembering the slaughter on the French lines as he walked that ground changed his opinion. "The event of the day is too well known to be mentioned," wrote Carroll, and he categorized the 1758 British attack as "morally impossible to succeed," its failure due to Abercromby's being "so infatuated as to attack with musquetry only." Had he only deployed his artillery, Abercromby would have taken Fort Carillon.[38] "The Misconduct of General Abercrombie [sic] who it is said was not equal to the Command" explained his army's slaughter and defeat.[39] Carroll's memory combined the arrogance of British commanders with the strength of Fort Ticonderoga, which he exaggerated when it suited his purposes, to absolve provincial forces from any fault in the failed assault. They faced a staunch foe defending a formidable position while commanded by an incompetent British general. The attack was doomed from the start, and this history shaped what Carroll saw at the decrepit fortification. So long as Ticonderoga stood, he wrote, it would prevent the British "from ever having it in their power to invade these colonies."[40] After all, Americans had failed to take it, or more accurately the "French lines" of Fort Carillon, previously.

The British tested Carroll's confidence in 1776 and 1777. As Richard Montgomery and Benedict Arnold's invasion of Canada collapsed during the spring of 1776, American forces beat a hasty retreat southward up Lake Champlain to Ticonderoga, considered their best hope to make a stand against the British counterinvasion. Thousands of American troops strengthened the French lines and erected new entrenchments at Mount Independence on the Vermont shore, relegating the actual Fort Ticonderoga to minor tactical importance. The naval battle at Valcour Bay on October 11, 1776, delayed the British expedition enough that "the Rigour of the Season" compelled them to withdraw to Canada for the winter; Ticonderoga remained in American hands for another year.[41] But the winter of 1776–77 was not without peril. As early as Christmas Eve, 1776, Congress fretted over the "critical state of the Fortress" and the "extreme danger" of British forces capturing it by crossing Lake Champlain's ice-covered waters.[42] Washington requested "a proper Reinforcement to secure the important pass of Ticonderoga," lest the British "make themselves Masters of that valuable fortress."[43] He overestimated the mostly earthen entrenchments that could hardly be called a "fortress" by anyone who had actually seen them.

Only Pennsylvania Colonel Anthony Wayne and roughly one thousand soldiers secured the spot. And they suffered. Joseph Wood endured "a Lame leg, in a D—d Smoakey house, metamorphic'd from a Stable, with ten thousand Crevices, that lets in rain hail & snow."[44] Wayne sympathized with "the hardships and Miseries these poor fellows have endured (on this Infectious Spot) the bare Recital of which wou'd shock Humanity."[45] Few men seemed willing to reenlist, apprehensive of "being Immediately sent back again to a place which they Imagine to be very unhealthy." The soldiers' complaints may have owed to the cold weather or the cramped conditions in hastily built log huts, but Ticonderoga spooked many soldiers as well.[46] Some of the troops "went round to see what our old soldiers did in the last war" and didn't like what they saw.[47] With their enlistments about to expire, the soldiers told their commanders to "march us off this Ground and then we will Cheerfully Re-engage."[48] Wayne agreed with his men, terming the old fort an "ancient Golgotha or place of skulls—they are so plenty here that our people for want of other vessels drink out of them whilst the soldiers make tent pins out of the shin and thigh bones of Abercrumbies men."[49] The remains of six hundred Anglo-American dead had been reduced to banal utensils in a place Wayne referred to as "the last part of God's work, something that must have been finished in the dark."[50]

The arrival of summer relieved their troubles. British general John Burgoyne invaded south from Canada and approached Fort Ticonderoga in early July 1777. Once Burgoyne's engineers hauled cannon up Mount Defiance, a hill overlooking both Ticonderoga and Mount Independence from Lake Champlain's western shore, American commander Arthur St. Clair rapidly evacuated his garrison and fled headlong to the south. Incredulous at news of Ticonderoga's July 6 loss, George Washington insisted, "If those posts were carried it must have been by assault." The interval between the British arrival outside Ticonderoga and its fall—two days—"was too short for it to be done by Blockade."[51] If Washington had been looking up from inside the fort's walls to the nearby heights, he might have felt differently. Almost all Americans, like Washington, remembered the Ticonderoga, or

Carillon, of 1758: a small defending force bloodily defeating what was then the largest army ever assembled in North America. Without having seen the fort or its widely scattered defenses, Washington and others failed to imagine how the American army could have abandoned Ticonderoga without a fight. "Our *Evacuating* Ticonderoga," wrote one American officer, created "a circumstance that has drawn us all into an unexpected dilemma."[52] Courts-martial and political infighting among American officers seeking to cast and escape blame for Ticonderoga's loss indicate the site's importance in the American mind.[53]

British prime minister George Germain went so far as to posit that capturing Ticonderoga "may make that impression upon the rebels as will incline them to submission."[54] Perhaps this was wishful thinking from across the Atlantic, but it reflected Ticonderoga's significance to the British establishment. Burgoyne sent word back to London of his victory at Ticonderoga. He must have done so the moment he entered the fort's stone walls in early July, as his dispatch reached England in mid-September. Lord Germain gushed at the news. "His Majesty's wisdom in appointing you to the command, was immediately seen and universally applauded." Ticonderoga's capture was worthy of reporting to King George III, as Germain wished "to express the high opinion that His Majesty entertains of the services which you have rendered Him." Hoping for further good news, Germain detained Burgoyne's aide until a July 30 dispatch arrived announcing Burgoyne's arrival at the Hudson River. Germain's October 1 letter termed it "an event of such great moment, that the news thereof could not fail of being extremely acceptable."[55] Unbeknownst to Germain, Burgoyne had already lost one major battle at Freeman's Farm and was six days from meeting defeat at Bemis Heights and his subsequent surrender at Saratoga. Ticonderoga, the battlefield that had claimed so many British lives in 1758, held such mythic importance that its capture lowered a rose-colored lens over Germain's thinking. To his mind, its fall predicted the success of the king's arms despite any other obstacles.

The Americans attacked but never retook Fort Ticonderoga during the 1777 campaign, and the British abandoned it that winter as their overall strategy shifted to the South. Congress continued to insist on controlling Ticonderoga, although not for use as a garrison. In March 1778 they ordered the "fortifications and works...demolished."[56] Fort Ticonderoga fell into disrepair, as military planners finally realized that its value was more symbolic than strategic. Most soldiers who observed Ticonderoga realized its limited military utility. But its legendary 1758 battle convinced sober men such as Washington and Germain, neither of whom had ever walked the crumbling French lines, that Ticonderoga held the key to the continent. Memory could distort the reality of place.

## Post-Revolution Memory

The continued presence of the bonefields at Ticonderoga and Braddock's Field made forgetting these 1750s battles physically impossible for those who interacted with place—the bleached remains or ruined fortifications stuck out of the ground. Yet, as few soldiers or travelers visited the battlefields, memory diminished. During the immediate postwar period, Ticonderoga faded into obscurity. George Washington, who spent many of the Revolution's early years worrying about Ticonderoga, left no comments from his July 1783 visit, one designed "to wear away some time" as the war wound down.[57] Only a European traveling with Washington's party noted that they "went ashore to see Ticonderoga where there are remnants of the English defenses of the War of 1754."[58] The passage is brief, suggesting that Washington's entourage chose not to reflect too long on the spot. As blundering as Abercromby's attack was, no post–Revolutionary War American visitors critiqued his tactics or commented on the lessons it provided for American warfare and the Revolutionary cause. Instead, the 1785 words of an English officer, Joseph Hadfield, emphasized Ticonderoga's sentimental past. During his visit he "saw with regret the place where the gallant Lord Howe was killed."[59] He did not need to recount the confused skirmish at a French outpost along the portage from Lake George where a French musket ball felled Howe, a thirty-three-year-old, charismatic officer beloved by both regular and provincial troops. Howe's unmarked grave avoided the more complicated story of the Fort Carillon debacle.

But Hadfield's is one of only a handful of travel accounts before 1800, and perhaps the only one that does more than mention the existence of the overgrown French lines or "buildings in ruins."[60] When Thomas Jefferson and James Madison visited the "northern lakes" in

1791, neither offered extended commentary on the "scenes of blood" they passed along the way. The two men "were more pleased however with the botanical objects which continually presented themselves."[61] The lack of historical reflection is at least partly due to the short passage of time between the Seven Years' War and the Revolution, which may have prevented a new generation of Americans from interpreting Ticonderoga on their own terms. In addition, Ticonderoga's multiple losses implied failed masculinity, and were more easily forgotten.[62] More important, however, with soldiers no longer stationed there, few people visited Ticonderoga shortly after the Revolution. One man who did, the Scottish minister George Hamilton, waited days to hire a boat to carry him north along Lake Champlain in 1783. The lack of taverns forced him to lodge in local farms. Delayed by thunderstorms and trees fallen across the road, he took refuge "in one of the most wretched Cabbins" he had ever seen. Near Ticonderoga he stayed in a hovel without glass panes and found his "breeches as dirty as my boots." After "walking around the French Lines," up Mount Defiance and overland to Lake George, Hamilton "felt as much pleasure at the sight of the rising sun from the top of Mount Independence, and to behold the blue mists sailing along the side of the distant hills, as ever I felt at the same scenes in gayer mansions or more elegant walks."[63] Hamilton, a "Pilgrim," sought out historic battlefields where his fellow Scotsmen had fought. His sentimental response to scenery, rather than historic ruins, made him perhaps the first of many tourists who privileged landscape over history in his response to place. But Ticonderoga remained too remote in the late eighteenth century to attract visitors. Without interaction with place, they lacked the materials from which to construct memory.

Braddock's Field remained a locale that people noticed. Nearby Pittsburgh grew into a busy trade center, and travelers passed the battlefield on their way westward. The old roads carved by British generals Braddock and Forbes became the main migration routes across Pennsylvania to the booming Ohio River Valley. Simple proximity to byways and people made Braddock's Field a place where memory *had* to be constructed. One traveler noted "many memorials to the battle are still to be seen, but none so characteristic as the bones which lay bleaching by the way side." These sacred relics became souvenirs, as "one of our company, being an anatomist, carried one away as a curiosity."[64] As late as 1825 "the plough could not trace a furrow without turning up bones whitened by time, and fragments of arms corroded by rust."[65] A few years earlier workers building the National Road near Fort Necessity had unearthed the grave of what appeared to be a British officer, most likely the ill-fated General Braddock.[66] His gravesite lay forty miles from the actual battlefield, though, diverting attention from the place where Braddock earned his infamy.

As the years passed, Braddock's defeat was beginning to be seen in a new light. In this early engagement, wrote one French visitor in 1802, "the youthful Washington, gathered some of his earliest laurels."[67] By 1820, travelogues declared that Washington "saved the English troops from total destruction" and proved his valor by having "two horses shot under him, and received two balls through his clothes."[68] Here Washington "signalised himself by bringing off the wretched remains of the army."[69] Later accounts, as had Revolutionary War–era sources, faulted Braddock for "rejecting the advice of Washington."[70] Indeed, some early nineteenth-century authors added the claim that Braddock "with his dying breath . . . acknowledged to Colonel Washington the error he had committed in not following his advice."[71] It was only "owing to [Washington's] courage and coolness that the wreck of the conquered army was saved."[72] By the 1820s Washington, not Braddock, became the commemorative focus of the battlefield, and allowed Americans to refashion the defeat into an object lesson in nationalism.

Braddock's Field provided the perfect confluence of history and hagiography, the legend of Washington corresponding nicely with the mythology of the Revolution. It provided a "clean" story and a single narrative thread, with blame easily placed at the feet of General Braddock for his refusal to listen to George Washington's advice. Braddock's Field offered both an example of American distinctiveness and the spot where the nation's first hero—the father of the country—made his mark and came of age. During the Marquis de Lafayette's triumphant tour of the United States in 1824–25, he made special efforts to visit "the field of Braddock's defeat, where the military talents and heroism of Washington were first elicited."[73] So great was Washington's legacy that antebellum patriots proposed a fifty-foot-high iron monument "be built to Washington at Fort Necessity, Pa., his first battle ground," regardless of the fact that he lost that engagement, as well as participated in Braddock's debacle the following year.[74]

The differing significance of Braddock's Field and Ticonderoga in late eighteenth-century American memory would reverse in the decades to follow. Braddock's Field faded into the background as local residents buried the few remaining bones, converted the battlefield to agriculture, and transformed the landscape into a non-martial space. By 1840 one traveler passed by the field and instead stopped nearby, where "a tavern keeper preserves a fence by way of speculation ... there is a hitching post in front of his inn to allure travelers to stop [at] 'Braddocks grave.'"[75] Apart from this fledgling wayside a few miles from the battlefield, Braddock's Field itself attracted few visitors. At Ticonderoga, however, the rise of tourism, and specifically battlefield visits, created a new form of memory dependent on interaction with place, romantic scenery, and sentiment. When steamship lines ran up and down Lake Champlain to Montreal after the 1820s, Ticonderoga's ruins became a favorite stop on the emerging Northern Tour. Visits to battlefields appealed to historical enthusiasts such as Nathaniel Hawthorne, who in his 1835 essay "Old News" described leafing through yellowed newspapers containing "tales of military enterprize [sic], and often a huzza for victory; as, for instance, the taking of Ticonderoga, long a place of awe to the provincials, and one of the bloodiest spots in" what he called "the Old French War." But Hawthorne lamented that newspapers could not fully bring the past back to life or "paint a more vivid picture of their times."[76] For that kind of experience, Americans, including Hawthorne, would have to visit the old battlefields.

# CHAPTER TWO

# *Forsaken Graves*

## The Emergence of Memory
## on the Northern Tour

One of the most introspective early records of a tourist's visit to Ticonderoga came from the pen of Abigail May, a young Massachusetts woman spending the summer of 1800 at Ballston Spa, New York, in an attempt to improve her faltering health. To relieve the tedium of spa life she and a dozen others embarked on a multiday trip to Lake George. They found delightful scenery, wretched accommodations, and several historic sites along the eighty-plus-mile journey. May's most extensive musing focused on Ticonderoga, where her party viewed the crumbling fort walls, dined, and paused only briefly before retracing their steps to Ballston Spa.

> I wanted to know all, every particular, of a spot that interested my feelings so much, but could obtain very imperfect information—that a vast sight of blood has been spilt on this spot, all agree—for several miles round, every object confirms it—the heaps of stones on which the soldiers used to cook, the ditches, now grass grown, and forsaken graves!! All, every thing makes this spot teem with melancholy reflections. I knew not how to leave it, and ascended the wagon with regret.[1]

May's journey occurred in the early stages of two significant cultural developments in the early republic—the rise of tourism and changing memories of the Revolutionary past. That neither was fully developed in 1800 reflects the fledgling state of American culture, but also the ways in which tourism and memory grew hand in hand. Where May found romantic ruins and "melancholy reflections," a half century later pictorial history innovator Benson Lossing identified other reasons why Ticonderoga constituted "one of the most interesting relics of the Revolution." He agreed that "broken arches and ruined ramparts are always eloquent and suggestive of valiant deeds...but manifold greater are the impressions which they make when the patriotism we adore has hallowed them."[2] Yet few visitors agreed with Lossing. The divergent interests of these two visitors over the span of the early republic highlight the inability of ideologues such as Lossing to transform private Revolutionary War memories from exercises in personal sentiment to explicit searches for nationalistic historical fact and a patriotic past, much less to develop Ticonderoga into a major tourist attraction. In traveling, Americans encountered and began to understand their past, but in highly personal ways that differed from histories constructed by cultural arbiters. History served to complement landscape and emotion, never occupying the sole focus of the touristic gaze.

## Sacred Places

The key sites of the Revolutionary War's 1777 northern campaign—the lower Hudson River forts, Saratoga, and Ticonderoga—lay along the increasingly popular Northern Tour but were at best an addendum to the main project—viewing scenery and displaying class status. Guidebook author Theodore Dwight termed the route's final leg, along the upper Hudson River and the Lake George / Lake Champlain corridor "the high road of war" and a region offering "scenes of the most important military operations which have ever been carried on in the United States." The area was replete with "spots of high interest for their historical associations...that [have] been sprinkled with blood."[3] As the nineteenth century progressed, more and more people visited the sites along this route and responded to the historic places they encountered. Yet tourists paid little heed to their forefathers' struggles to forge liberty on this sacred ground, preferring to contemplate landscapes and melancholy along the route of the Northern Tour. As Elizabeth Ruffin remarked in 1827, "What pleasure is there in looking at the ruins of forts, none earthly to me, so I contrive to shift the matter off quite phil-osophically."[4] The evolution of tourism and the tourist class depended, ironically, on the underdevelopment of historic sites; tourists sought overgrown ruins and scenic landscapes. Tourism in the early nine-teenth-century Anglo-American world depended on visual cues that allowed visitors to interpret the landscape and then to construct mean-ing from its features. Gazing at scenery allowed them to express senti-ment and class in a process that consumed landscape and paid relatively little attention to history.[5] Ruined fortifications and storied battlefields added variety and interest to the scenery, meaning that something other than history constituted the main goal of battlefield tourism.

Over time, unvarnished experiences such as Abigail May's disap-peared, to be replaced by a scripted experience at a well-maintained site influenced by guidebooks, artists, and cultural arbiters. Such pre-scribed responses to place belong to a much larger American trend of using memory "as a bulwark for social and political stability—a means of valorizing resistance to change."[6] But at sites along the Northern Tour this struggle to control meaning proved to be far more diffuse and democratic than respectable authorities would have liked. Old forts and battlefields continued to attract tourists enthralled by crumbling ruins and tree-covered lakeside slopes. These sites continued to dete-riorate, which only added to their charm. Authors such as Lossing and the cultural conservatives who sought to formally commemorate and preserve historic sites exerted their influence to sanction official histo-ries of specific forts and battlefields, and of the Revolution in general, in order to unite the nation both politically and socially.[7] Battles and heroism served their purposes far more effectively than did scenery and sentiment, yet tourists focused on landscape aesthetics far into the mid-nineteenth century, performing a nationalism shaped by personal interactions with place more than by reading the learned tomes of his-torians.[8] The early republic's collective memory of the Revolution-ary past developed in two distinct, complementary strands—personal memory based upon interaction with place, and a scripted memory advanced by guidebook authors and historical writers—that prevented battlefield tourism from evolving into an overtly patriotic pilgrim-age. The performative nationalism that developed at battlefields along the Northern Tour lacked the conflict between official and vernacu-lar memory that characterized the later nineteenth century.[9] Instead, personal and emotional responses to place provided complementary, yet alternative, memories to the monuments and formal commemorations that dominated official memory. On the unrestored grounds of battlefields and at ruined forts, Americans performed their own memories of the Revolution.

## Lower Hudson River Valley Forts

The Hudson River Valley constituted perhaps the first American tourist region, due to the juxtaposition of affluent New York City and scenic landscapes, connected by an easily traveled river. Tourists began their journey by passing a series of American and British forts used in the 1776 battles and siege of New York City. Most were crumbling or overgrown, like the stockade at Paulus Hook on the Jersey shore, which in 1794 "serve[d] the better purpose of inclosing the farm yard." Of artillery batteries, soldiers' huts, and even gravesites, "so lately the scene of destructive warfare...few traces now remain."[10] To the north the Hudson Highlands were "celebrated for the natural strength of [their] situation and for having contained a strong garrison during the war." For tourists moving up the river, "the ruins of the several forts, Barracks, and the Arsenal are still to be seen." With its steep mountains and narrow passage of the river, "nature has rendered this spot almost impregnable."[11] Washington's headquarters at Newburgh, the ruins of Fort Putnam, and especially West Point also attracted people's attention. West Point "was *historic* ground—had been trodden by Washington, was his favorite post, and his own selection!" But British traveler John Maude spent more time commenting on the "most sublime and magnificent" scenery there.[12] Others found West Point's fortifications insufficient "to induce us to remain on deck" as their ships glided up the Hudson. They might glance at Fort Montgomery's "nearly obliterated traces" on the heights above the river, but only with difficulty.[13] Poet and Philadelphia clergyman Charles West Thomson displayed far more enthusiasm for the Erie Canal, Cohoes Falls, and the Catskill Mountain House. Tourists like the Episcopalian minister Thomson viewed fortifications as something else besides historic ruins. As he approached Manhattan by boat, Thomson noted "the castellated forts that frowned in gloomy grandeur amid the smiles of evening—and the dawning of that beautiful scenery which makes the noble Hudson a very nice region of romance—all combined to render the view at once striking and interesting."[14] As lovely as the Palisades west of Manhattan were, the steeply wooded hillsides farther upriver among the Hudson Highlands convinced Thomson of that region's "superior grandeur and Sublimity."[15] Tourists expected to be moved by landscape, with the Hudson River's Revolutionary War fortifications framing the scene.

The rise of reliable and efficient steamship travel on the Hudson between New York City and Albany in the late 1810s stimulated heritage tourism. Chugging up the river with time to kill, many travelers gazed at the "beautiful scenery of North River" from their boat's deck.[16] But even if the river's scenery "bears nature's grandest imprint, . . . the impressions which crowd into the spectator's mind in this region are not all derived from river, mountain, or valley,—tradition and history lend a melancholy glory to this revolutionary ground." The Hudson River from New York to the highlands contained numerous "spots, where the life-blood of the free has been poured out like water, and where the traces of the revolutionary ditch and mound still remain, are altars sacred to the recollections of freedom." Tourists visited, or at least passed by, this "classic ground . . . to pay their tribute of affection and honor."[17] That they could do so amid "those happy groupings of mountains and water scenery" eased the task. The region "combines historical interest with picturesque beauty." Unlike a mere landscape, the Revolutionary War's events "give an interest to the scenery of this picture, beyond that which attaches to situations where the track of war has never been."[18]

The lower Hudson River Valley's sites benefited from well-known stories and visual depictions of their history. This added interest became an essential part of the reason to visit a site. Almost every tourist, especially those who took the carriage road up the eastern shore of the river, paused to view "a giant Tulip tree . . . which goes by the name of Arnold's tree, and which as long as it stands will be regarded and preserved as a memorial" of Benedict Arnold's attempted surrender of West Point. It was not Arnold, but "the unfortunate major [John] Andre," the British spy who brokered Arnold's treason, who in 1780 hanged at this "commanding situation" overlooking the Hudson, wrote an 1810 tourist.[19] This spot captured the writer Washington Irving's attention, and he placed "the great tree where Major André was taken" at the center of the "haunted region" depicted in "The Legend of Sleepy Hollow." Most prominent among the town's spirits was the Headless Horseman, "the ghost of a Hessian trooper, whose head had been carried away by a cannon ball, in some nameless battle during the revolutionary war." Sleepy Hollow sat amid history: "the British and American line had run near it during the war." The tale's protagonist, Ichabod Crane, heard of the "galloping Hessian of the Hollow" as he exchanged ghost stories with the town's "old Dutch wives." After one evening of unsuccessfully courting local beauty Katrina Van Tassel, Crane approached André's tree on his ride home. "His teeth chattered, and his knees smote against the saddle," provoked by "the tales of strange sights, and doleful lamentations, told concerning" the tree. Farther down the dark forest road, Crane came to a more frightful spot, the bridge where "the unfortunate André was captured." Irving chose landmarks steeped in local legend and recognizable by the many travelers who passed by the sites on their way up and down the Hudson as the places where his gangly schoolteacher would be most frightened. The "common people" of Sleepy Hollow regarded the "haunted stream" and "gnarled and fantastic" tree "with a mixture of respect and superstition" because of these sites' historical associations. More than the sound of "the rubbing of one huge bough upon another," the legend of events occurring in these places caused Crane's fear. He responded to encountered history as readers might expect him to, just as visitors to battlefields responded to their encounters with place in predictable ways. When a headless rider emerged from the woods to ride beside him, Crane spurred his own horse, Gunpowder, in an attempt to escape what he assumed to be the Hessian ghoul. Terrified at the encounter, he fled Sleepy Hollow. "The old country wives...maintain to this day, that Ichabod was spirited away by supernatural means." Irving published his story in 1820, several years after tourists began remarking on André's tree and its historical legend. Like the fireside chroniclers of Sleepy Hollow, "just sufficient time had elapsed to enable each story teller to dress up his tale with a little becoming fiction."[20]

The André tree became one of the few sites along the Hudson River where Americans openly contested memory. When one of the three militiamen who captured André, John Paulding, filed for an increased pension in 1817, Americans quarreled over the proper place of these men in the pantheon of the nation's heroes. Supporters lauded the three militiamen who seized the spy, casting them as patriotic soldiers doing their duty. Critics countered that the three acted out of mercenary motives and succeeded only because of André's carelessness. The competing visions clashed in 1821 when Great Britain reclaimed Major André's bones. As Anglophilic conservatives saw it, the "gallant active officer" deserved repatriation and praise as an example of the kind of gentleman-soldier who should lead the republic, even if he had fought for Great Britain, while the militiamen represented the baser motives of men on the make during the early republic. Elites in both the United States and Great Britain used the André incident in an attempt to regain the lost civility of a previous era, if it had ever existed.[21] As one observer lamented, André's capture had amounted to "the British exchanging one of their best soldiers for the worst man in the American Army."[22] André's remains healed old wounds, creating sympathy among refined citizens on both sides of the Atlantic.

The story was also retold in James Fenimore Cooper's 1821 novel *The Spy: A Tale of the Neutral Ground.* Cooper's "partisan" novel engages memory directly by putting aside André, "that darling of nostalgic Anglophiles," in order "to resuscitate the Revolution as the beginning of American political experience rather than the end of the colonial system." André's hanging takes place offstage, as Cooper chooses to emphasize the struggles among fictionalized participants in the surrounding events rather than repeat the historic narrative. The book's alleged spy, the "ill-educated peddler" Harvey Birch, "suggested future possibilities as well as historical truths." Birch was perhaps "the first great commoner in American literature" and represented a new model of democratic possibility in a "rough but noble" America. Both *The Spy* and Irving's "The Legend of Sleepy Hollow" sentimentalized history and converted it into a usable past that emphasized the "emergent class-bound interpretations" of the Revolution.[23]

The path up the Hudson and Lakes George and Champlain offered a perfect venue for contemplating the type of scenery and history that James Fenimore Cooper wrote about. Appealing to the newly emergent tourist class who were following the Northern Tour, Cooper "linked his historic settings with their present-day counterparts so as to give readers a perceptual fix on the 'old' scenes the plot was exploring." He had visited Saratoga and the northern lakes region in 1824, a trip that informed *The Last of the Mohicans* at a moment when Cooper was "primed to explore [the region's] historical associations." The novels acted as prompts that allowed tourists to "*imagine* the past as much as Cooper did in writing the books," in effect compensating for the lack of visible historic ruins.[24]

## American Scenery

Cooper and Irving both based their fiction on historic sites that many Americans knew and that some of their readers would have seen. Based on his own interactions with historic sites along the Northern Tour, Cooper developed an increasingly complex "relationship between place and action" in his novels.[25] These authors worked within a broader movement to construct a distinctly American culture that included identifying the unique features of the American landscape, a source of national meaning. Even more important than these authors to the process of connecting memory and landscape, though, was the painter Thomas Cole, who had immigrated to the United States at age seventeen. His initial career depended on the scenic tourism and the emerging cultural preference for landscape and historical allegory. Many of Cole's early paintings depicted the Hudson River Valley, the hearth of cultural tourism conveniently located near fashionable tourists and wealthy art patrons in New York City. The third painting that he sold, to the engraver Asher B. Durand in October 1825, depicted Revolutionary War–era Fort Putnam in the lower Hudson River Valley, and historic images paid Cole's bills. His aristocratic patrons readily bought historically themed landscapes—including two different 1827 paintings of a scene from Cooper's popular 1826 novel *The Last of the Mohicans*—around the same time that he executed two allegorical paintings, *The Garden of Eden* and *Expulsion from the Garden of Eden* (1827–28), without a commission.[26]

Travelers could have it both ways, then. Yale College president Timothy Dwight asserted that his 1802 journey to northern New York "had two principal objects in view. One was to examine the scenery of Lake George; the beauty of which had always been mentioned to me in strong terms of admiration: the other, to explore the grounds, on which the military events of former times had taken place, at its two extremities."[27] Unspoiled scenery and historic legend lay inscribed on the landscape; the picturesque could be patriotic. American ruins were

**Figure 2.** Thomas Cole, *A View of Fort Putnam* (1824–25). The site of the ruins of Fort Putnam, part of American defenses along the lower Hudson River, was a popular vista for travelers from New York City. It helped to launch Cole's career as a painter of historical landscapes. Philadelphia Museum of Art: Promised gift of Charlene Sussel.

newer, but they also reminded visitors of the significant struggle that had created the United States while preserving the nation's forward-looking optimism. But for culturally sophisticated Americans, scenery's dual role relegated historic sites to a secondary rank in cultural importance. Fort Washington, located on a bluff above the Hudson in upper Manhattan, saw fighting in 1776, but more important, it was "one of the most beautiful and picturesque localities on the banks of the Hudson, and affords a view of the scenery for thirty miles up and down the river." Scenery, it seems, reigned supreme over history. As the *New York Herald* reported in 1858, Germany's vaunted Rhine River, over which "poets and travelers may rhapsodize and work themselves into ecstacies [*sic*] over [its] natural and artificial beauties, and the old ruins that are strewed along its banks," remained "inferior to the Hudson in point of grandeur and magnificence, and even in quiet landscape scenery. And who is there that would exchange the glorious memories of the Revolution for all the old ruins and remains of feudal or kingly rule?"[28] That opinion required many years to develop.

## Old Saratoga

The Hudson River's northern reaches lacked the detailed historical context or stunning scenery of the Hudson Highlands, which led to different reactions to place. Once the steamboats had ascended the river to Albany or Troy, passengers transferred to horse-drawn carriages or railroad cars for the next leg of the Northern Tour. Saratoga Springs, the fashionable spa resort located thirty miles north of the navigable limit of the Hudson, had nothing to do with the 1777 battles of Saratoga—the "turning point of the Revolution"—which had been fought ten miles southeast of the spa. Two epic battles in September and October of 1777 saw nearly 12,000 American regulars and militia under Generals Horatio Gates and Benedict Arnold defeat General John Burgoyne's 6,800 British and Hessian troops. Burgoyne's surrender marked perhaps the first time that a British army had capitulated in the field. More important, it ended the British strategy of splitting the rebellious colonies along the Hudson River / Lake Champlain corridor and defeating each region in turn. Shortly after news of Burgoyne's surrender reached Europe, France recognized the Continental Congress and began overtly aiding the rebellion.[29] Visitors to Saratoga Springs combined edification with recreation when they assembled their fashionable carriages in front of the hotel piazzas along Broadway, which were "crowded with guests" awaiting the daily afternoon jaunt to the "Old Saratoga" battlefield. The ride itself might prove boring, "but then it is a distinction here to ride out in one's own carriage when so many stand to gaze and admire, and envy the fortunate ones who ride, while they must go on foot." The scantily concealed social competition "bore more the appearance of a race course, than any thing I can compare it to." Display, not patriotic edification, was the object.[30]

Excursionists needed reminding of the battlefield's significance. Yale scientist Benjamin Silliman insisted that "he who venerates the virtues and the valour, and commiserates the sufferings of our fathers, and he who views, with gratitude and reverence, the deliverances which heaven has wrought for this land, will tread with awe on every foot of

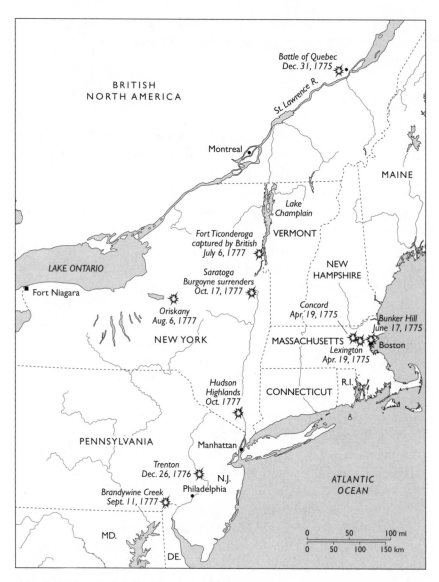

**Map 3.** Northern battlefields.

ground" around Saratoga.[31] Dutiful tourists recorded in their diaries that the battlefield was "rendered celebrated by the surrender of the British army."[32] By 1821 the Saratoga battlefields were "daily becoming more interesting to travelers, and many resort here for the gratification of a laudable curiosity."[33] One visitor found "an Inn under the heights, where with the remembrance of the deeds, which transpired on those grounds, I contented myself to repose." Ketchum's Tavern stood three miles south of "the house which the British army made their hospital." Still standing and "in good repair" in 1824, it was termed by locals "*The house where Frazer [sic] died.* It is now Smith's Tavern" or the "Sword House."[34] Yet with only two taverns to receive the traveling public, the battlefields near Bemis Heights lacked the accommodations necessary to become a major tourist attraction. Most visitors stayed a half day's ride to the west at the bustling resort of Saratoga Springs. In the many editions of his *Fashionable Tour* guidebooks, Saratoga Springs publisher and developer Gideon Minor Davison included descriptions of the Saratoga battleground and its history as addendums to his listing of spa lodging, amusements, and travel distances. Historic sites such as Old Saratoga played a secondary role in the rise of American tourism.

Part of Saratoga's attraction depended on its undeveloped state. It was more than a "truly *memorable* place, which may be considered the spot where independence was sealed." The surrender field also "remains exactly as it then was, excepting the sole circumstance that the bushes, which were cut down in front of the two armies, are since grown up again." In 1799 visitors could still report that "not the least alteration has taken place since that time. The entrenchments still exist; nay, the footpath is still seen."[35] Near one redoubt that experienced heavy fighting, "the fir trees which are torn by musket and cannon-shot, will long be a testimony" to the battle's brisk action.[36] In 1822 the "entrenchments of the two camps can to this day be traced," but not for long. One line running from the top of Bemis Heights to the Hudson River had become "overgrown with bushes." The earthen and log fortifications, thrown up of necessity on a bluff overlooking a bend in the Hudson River, were "almost razed in some place, and in others over-grown with bushes and tall forest trees." Some redoubts "are very perceptible," but the main British camp "is visible, daily washing away, and exposing rotten logs which in part composed the breastwork." One extant "wide redoubt, is turned into a buckwheat field, with its venerable moats and parapets forming the enclosures." Perhaps the only structures on the battlefield dating to September 1777, the farmhouse and barns used as an American hospital after the battle of Freeman's Farm, were "untenanted and ready to fall."[37] Three years later "the foundation only remains to mark the spot" where wounded patriots suffered.[38]

By the 1820s "few vestiges" of Saratoga's military past remained. No longer a battlefield, the lands around Freeman's Farm and Bemis Heights "now present, in some parts, fields under cultivation. The plough has strove with invidious zeal, to destroy even these few remaining evidences of revolutionary heroism. Each succeeding year, the agriculturist turns afresh the sod of the weather-beaten breastworks." Breymann's Redoubt and other "temporary works…are now nearly obliterated." At the Balcarres Redoubt, "little remains to be seen." The area's farmers "level alike mounds and ditches."[39] Only the "stump" of a tree planted to mark General Simon Fraser's grave remained in 1824, and even the "railing" of "rough stakes" installed to mark the spot had disappeared.[40] One 1821 resident claimed that "our plows are constantly striking against cannon balls or dead men's bones, or turning up grape shot or bullets." That day he had unearthed "only a skeleton." The farmer offered his interrogator several bullets to take home to Virginia, as well as a skull. William Wirt took the musket balls but declined the cranium, demurring that "it will not be convenient to carry it."[41]

When local residents discovered such remains, they often used them to piece together the battle's history. Mr. Walker operated a farm and blacksmith shop behind the old British lines. He had recently "discovered and disinterred the skeleton of a man killed in the action by a ball which perforated the back of the skull." A nearby circular skull fragment "was found, exactly fitting the perforation." Analyzing the skeleton's large size and proximity to "the position of the British grenadiers in the first action, we concluded [he] must have been one of that corps."[42] Yet the supply of such relics proved finite. "Some foolish mortals have dug holes" in the various redoubts, "hoping to get treasure which they hope was buried" there. This "common practice" drew treasure-hunters from as far away as Canada, and continued until at least 1843. That year the discovery of "several valuable coins…in a ploughed field on the old battleground" proved sufficiently rare to merit mention in a Rhode Island newspaper, perhaps because the coins were found near "a thigh bone, from which it was inferred that the money was deposited in the breeches pocket of the unfortunate owner."[43]

For most visitors to Saratoga, however, the "sensation of awe" came not from inspecting coins, bones, or bullets, but from encountering "the spot, where our forefathers fought and conquered."[44] As Yale's Timothy Dwight opined in 1799, "It was impossible not to remember that on this very spot a controversy was decided upon which hung the liberty and happiness of a nation." Dwight had predicted "future travelers will resort to this spot with the same emotions which we experienced, and recall with enthusiasm the glorious events of which it is the perpetual memorial."[45] Such visitors sought to duplicate Benjamin Silliman's experience on the "memorable ground" where "much precious blood was shed." During his 1819 visit to Saratoga Silliman slept in Sword's House, once occupied by British officers but now a humble tavern. As American forces pounded the trapped British army, "bleeding and dying men" filled the house in October of 1777. Their blood was "visible here, on the floor, till a very recent period." Silliman slept in the room where General Fraser, shot by an American marksman, "breathed his last." Unable to sleep through the "very dark and rainy night" surrounded by the "sublime and tender images of the past," Silliman recorded his thoughts while he glanced at a bullet gleaned from the battlefield. Such "painful specimens...were battered and mis-shaped, evincing that they had come into collision with opposing obstacles."[46] By 1825, visitors to Saratoga's "sanguinary fields" contemplated "the value of our dear bought liberties."[47] With fewer physical reminders of the battlefields' past, memory became less personal and more representational, a collection of predictable responses to scenery and place, with history providing context.

## The Ruins at Ticonderoga

At Fort Ticonderoga in 1805, the noted agriculturalist, traveler, and writer Elkanah Watson declared, "In examining the ruins of this celebrated fortress, it appears as if I was in Europe examining the works of antiquity, for really there is nothing in America that carries the appearance of an antiquated Castle so strikingly." Ticonderoga was one of the few historic sites that retained extensive physical reminders of its Revolutionary past, and these ruins made it into perhaps the most contemplated and depicted battlefield in the early nineteenth century.[48] Its ruins required much greater effort to reach than sites along the lower Hudson River, and possessed far fewer amenities. Travel by carriage and boat took at least two days from Saratoga Springs. Halfway along the journey the "mounds and trenchments" of Fort William Henry and Fort George, two Seven Years' War British outposts, remained visible "with tolerable distinctness" at the base of Lake George. Town booster James Caldwell accommodated history-seeking travelers at a hotel "on the ground of the French encampment" of 1757.[49] His Lake House overlooked the water, and in 1817 Caldwell launched a steamboat that carried passengers along the lake's steep, wooded shores. Passengers remarked on the places that had seen action during previous wars, including Sabbath Day Point, "so named as having been the scene of a battle between the French and English upon that day." Yet Caldwell's was better known for its fishing and scenery than its historic associations, even after the 1826 publication of Cooper's *The Last of the Mohicans,* written after the author had toured the ruins of Fort William Henry and scavenged for relics.[50] By 1834 the "ruins still exist as a monument of deeds long past; but those ruins are rapidly mouldering to decay, and soon traditions and History alone will be able to point to the spot, where they once stood."[51]

Once tourists had sailed or rowed the thirty-two miles north down Lake George and portaged the three miles around the rapids that flowed into Lake Champlain, they reached the dilapidated ruins of Fort Ticonderoga. The fort's original walls consisted of a stone base topped with logs backfilled with earth and rubble. The most famous feature, the French lines, had been hastily carved from the woods and erected virtually overnight from logs and earth in 1758. Nothing but overgrown earthen mounds and the crumbling walls of the stone barracks remained. As late as 1818 the fort's stonework supplied "the house below on the shore, which is being inhabited by a farmer, with building materials."[52] Bricks and stones from the structures traveled as far away as Missisquoi Bay on the northern end of Lake Champlain, used "to build an earthen-ware factory" in 1784.[53] A quick carriage ride past the ruins in 1804 revealed only "Two Old bastions and a pile of stone chimneys presented to our view." One early English observer labeled the fort in "a state of decay."[54] Decades past serving as a military installation, Ticonderoga allowed visitors to wander about the ruins, poking their heads into rooms and forcing open locked doors. One 1800 visitor scrambled over "the sally ports, the Guard room, the bakers room, and descended into some subterraneous cells supposed to be places of confinement, a powder room &cc." She even found "some human bones in one of the cells."[55] In this ruined state Ticonderoga was "no longer an object either of hope or fear." The fort's "mossy ruins, and the beautiful green declivities, sloping on all sides

**Figure 3.** R. W. Sherman, *Ruins of Fort Ticonderoga* (1852). Travelers reached Ticonderoga via waterways, whether on a steamboat or sailboat. To the right of the fort's ruins, along the shore, is the "Pavilion" hotel run by William Ferris Pell. Collection of the Fort Ticonderoga Museum.

to the water, were still and motionless as death." The once "venerable Ticonderoga" served now only as "a pasture for cattle," Benjamin Silliman reported matter-of-factly in 1819.[56]

Attempts to develop the ruins into a tourist destination fell short of success. Only "an old one Story, long stone house" provided rustic accommodations at the turn of the nineteenth century. The proprietress, the widow Hays, offered "fine dinner" and a "charming" view of Lake Champlain. Her pretensions to gentility—she claimed to be the sister of a British naval officer who had once shone in Montreal society—fared poorly.[57] When Elkanah Watson asked Hays what part of England she hailed from, his hostess whirled about suddenly and "all the apparatus, corking pins, and all which held her *small cloths* in suspense, gave way at once, and down they drop't." The dinner guests covered their eyes as Hays "jump[ed] out of the prostrait *coil;* and cut, and run for the door."[58] The accommodations improved slightly when wealthy New York merchant William Ferris Pell purchased 546 acres that included the fort's ruins from Union and Columbia Colleges in 1820. Meaning to construct a rural estate accented with historic ruins, he built a sizable Greek Revival house, planted ornamental gardens, and sought to improve Ticonderoga as a historic and tourist site. Visitors stayed at his Pavilion hotel, and Pell leased the land to his son on the condition that "the Lessee is not allowed to cut any timber or injure the fort in any way."[59] By 1826, guidebooks praised William Ferris Pell's "fine inn" at Ticonderoga, but tourists didn't linger in the luxurious accommodations, which held no more than a few dozen guests at any one time.[60]

Ticonderoga's remote location and imperfect transportation links limited the number of tourists who visited its ruins during the short summer tourist season. The same guidebook that lauded Pell's hotel advised steamboat travelers "to inquire the hour when [the steamboat] passes, and regulate their time accordingly," lest they miss the irregularly scheduled boats.[61] Steamboats plied Lake Champlain on their way to Montreal but stopped only on the Vermont shore opposite Ticonderoga. The inn's proprietors waited until 1840 to "erect a good & efficient Wharf" on the New York shore.[62] In the meantime, intrepid tourists hired ferry boats to cross the narrow lake "and followed such directions as we could get from the boatman across the fields to Ticonderoga."[63] Several other tourists commented on Ticonderoga from the vantage point of a steamboat deck as they cruised by the ruins, never bothering to disembark. The aspiring novelist Catharine Maria Sedgwick "regretted extremely" her boat's nighttime passage, but did not join her brother in viewing the fort "by the imperfect light of the waning moon."[64] Many travelers saw Ticonderoga as a mere transfer point between Lake Champlain and Lake George steamers. They paused for dinner at "the Fort House...on the old Fort grounds" before riding a stagecoach to the steamboat landing on Lake George.[65] The lack of regular steamboat service and scant tourist facilities relegated Ticonderoga to a lesser role on the Northern Tour.

## Romantic Ticonderoga

William Ferris Pell was only a summer resident, but the care he invested in the site paid off. By the early 1830s authors considered Ticonderoga "fine in its natural beauty and grandeur," but what made it worthy of consideration was that it was "finer still in its historical associations."[66] Scenery constituted the main focuses of cultural tourism in the early republic, but Ticonderoga improved that formula by adding historical associations to the motivations for travel. "There are few sites in our country," guidebook author Theodore Dwight noted, "that can be compared with this for a combination of natural and moral interest."[67] Dwight's guidebooks, and the many others that emerged after the 1820s, featured detailed and lengthy accounts of battles and events from the Revolution and Seven Years' War. He and other New England conservatives sought to create an "epic history" of the American past that would "reinforce the hierarchical and deferential society that the elite preferred."[68] They borrowed their battle narratives and history from published recollections such as General James Wilkinson's *Memoirs* that eschewed sentiment in favor of bland facts and military maneuvers.[69] An 1849 travel journal sounded much like Dwight's guidebook, and may even have imitated its words: Lake Champlain "is a classic lake in American history and he who passes through its extent with interest should acquaint himself minutely with its stirring scenes."[70] Battlefield ruins offered stimuli to musings about valor and warfare and "the great important results arising from them."[71] Yet despite reminders that a visit to Ticonderoga "will amply reward the patriotic tourist who loves to visit the places consecrated by the blood of his fathers," most tourists eschewed these more formal histories.[72] Abigail May self deprecatingly recommended the dull military detail of Heath's *Memoirs* as an antidote to her own supposedly inadequate prose, claiming, "I know of no other work, equally flat and insipid." By comparison, her emotional diary entries stirred the heart and were the kind of literature preferred by most tourists.[73]

Still, during the early republic, Ticonderoga was one of those places that evoked images of past valor, glory, and patriotism when its name appeared on the page or passed someone's lips, much as "Normandy" or "Gettysburg" or "Ground Zero" does today. Many accounts skipped the details, as did one article that simply stated, "The military history of this memorable spot, which has been rendered almost sacred by the valor of Americans, must be familiar to most of our readers." Everyone knew that Ticonderoga's 1775 "capture was one of those auspicious successes which ushered in the dawn of the revolution."[74] Private accounts also remembered Ticonderoga as a place where "many a freeman fell [and] there some of the best of Britain's soldiers surrendered to American valor in the 'times that tried men's souls.'"[75] Yet such knowledge gleaned from primers and generals' memoirs constituted something altogether different from what visitors gained when they walked the ground where independence was won. "All my reading had failed to give me a correct idea of this place," New Englander Alexander Bliss wrote from Ticonderoga in a deceptively simple sentence.[76]

Upon viewing Ticonderoga's ruins, most tourists mustered little more than generic responses to the past that could apply to almost any battlefield. Despite magazine articles claiming that the ruins seemed "calculated to inspire the mind with serious and devout meditations," few diarists differentiated between the 1758 British assault, 1775 American capture, or 1777 American evacuation in their writings.[77] After visiting Ticonderoga, Timothy Dwight could only describe the combat as something "which would have done honour to the soldiers of Caesar, and an exhibition of courage, which rivalled the most romantic days of chivalry."[78] Elkanah Watson, without discussing the justness of their causes, mused about "how many hundred poor dogs have bit the dust in attacking and defending this fortress." He "could not contemplate this pile of ruins, without appreciating the most painful recollections, that several of the companions of my youth...here lie mouldering in the dirt. A'way—a'way says I to myself."[79] Constructing memory involved direct interaction with place and meant more than the details of a particular battle. In 1825 two travelers and an older man who had fought with Abercromby strolled up from the lake and walked Ticonderoga's French lines "with emotion." The former soldier broke down in tears at the spot where his father and brother had fallen in the disastrous 1758 assault.[80] Ideology or the causes of war remained secondary in these highly personal and very painful rememberings, emblematic of an age when "a great many Americans wished to carry little or nothing of the past with them."[81] Like James Kirke Paulding concluded after a long conversation with an old general that revealed "the contradictions in historical records," instead of studying history tourists preferred "reading romances, as more amusing, and at least as true."[82]

The fort's history composed a part, but not the central subject, of the scene and visitors' personal responses to it. They desired the kind of romantic interactions with place depicted in Thomas Cole's painting *Gelyna: A View near Ticonderoga* (1826). In 1829 Cole modified it to align with the story "Gelyna: A Tale of Albany and Ticonderoga

**Figure 4.** Thomas Cole, *Gelyna: A View Near Ticonderoga* (1826, 1829). The painting depicts the dramatic moment when an American officer rushes to the aid of his friend and fellow officer, who had been wounded at Ticonderoga during the Seven Years' War. Viewing historical scenes, whether paintings or actual landscapes, elicited emotional responses from most early-nineteenth century Americans. Collection of the Fort Ticonderoga Museum.

Seventy Years Ago," published by his acquaintance Giulian C. Verplanck in *The Talisman for 1830,* a handsomely illustrated and lavishly produced Christmas annual popular among wealthy readers. In the tale the beautiful Gelyna Vandyke falls in love with Major Edward Rutledge. His Royal American regiment marches on Ticonderoga during the disastrous 1758 campaign. Wounded in the fighting, Rutledge is carried from the battlefield by his friend Herman Cuyler, Geylna's brother-in-law. Atop a rocky cliff Rutledge asks the day; "The eighth of July," Cuyler replies. Rutledge's parting words to Gelyna had been the same, marking the date when he would resign his commission and marry his beloved. Seeing that Rutledge is severely wounded, Cuyler rushes to the French lines for the military courtesy of aid to a fellow officer, but returns to find only a bloody track to "a bare open space of high and open rock," which "commanded a view of Lake George." Alas, Rutledge lies dead.[83] Cole's painting captured this tragic moment.

By the 1830s this kind of sentimental response dominated visitors' reactions to Ticonderoga. One diarist described the "romantic" scene thus: "The dilapidated walls and half fallen barracks, now grown black by the pass of time, [stand] on elevated ground, by frowning over the surrounding scenery it presents a very imposing, and striking appearance." Yet with only the ruins to view, one "could scarcely imagine, that at one period, formidable armies had arranged... descriptions of "bare stone walls" and "subterranean apartments" at "the once important but now harmless fortress." Even though the diarist included lengthy discussions of British, French, and American campaigns to take the fort, as well as its significance in the struggles for empire and independence, those descriptions served only to highlight

> the feelings it excites. When we stood upon its fallen and deserted walls, and reflected upon the quietness and solitude, that reigned around the ruins, it naturally excited like comparisons between its present situation and the time when it exhibited all the formidable appearance, and preparation of war; when its beautiful plains sounded with the confusion of clustered armies, the noise of battle, the shout of victory, or the feeling which defeat generally produces.

While published memory reminded Americans of the Revolution's causes and ideals, enacted memory remained focused on landscape and melancholy. "You must stand upon their ruins, if you wish to realize them, and reflect upon the various scenes they have witnessed," wrote one tourist.[84] In visiting and responding to battlefields, Americans constructed memory through personal, performative nationalism.

Edifying appeals to historic grandeur and patriotic connections failed to sway private diarists and published travel writers from contemplating romantic landscapes at the expense of history. The "old Ti" appealed to tourists because "its mounds and trenches remain undisturbed, as they should ever be by the desecrating plow."[85] Well into the 1850s, visitors would rather spend their time "sketching and wandering about the fortifications" of the "beautiful site" than rehearse the fort's battles.[86] The Southern diarist Jane Caroline North was typical. She reached Ticonderoga on a Lake Champlain steamboat from Canada in September 1852. "We passed the afternoon walking over the hills, examining the Ruins & enjoying the pretty prospects all around." Intrigued by "the trees just beginning to change their foliage," she spent the afternoon "seated on a stone of the Old Fort. I thought of the days gone by, of the Indians, the French, the English, & lastly ourselves." Only the fort's outer walls remained, but the "heaps of stones in every direction" created historic ambience. "Walking among the ruins made one solemn, the martial deeds of the Past embodied in the crumbling Wall! The masses of broken stone while the Peace of the Present was betoken by grass covered battlements [which may] have been a 'soldiers sepulcher,' and the cultivated fields extending around." Summing up her experience, North wrote, "The evening was delightful, the air just cool enough, & the rich green carpet of Nature's handiwork softer than any velvet. It is a walk & afternoon to be remembered!"[87] History played a secondary role in her encounter with Ticonderoga. Something other than written accounts would have to prompt tourists to remember the patriotic struggles more explicitly. They continued to seek scenery and romantic allusions, favoring sentimental remembrances over gore and ideology. The moment when the tourist gazed about the ruins and surrounding scenery, memory began.

## Veterans, Tour Guides, and Personal Memory

Among the central agents in the emergence of romantic memory were the aged veterans serving as tour guides at the ruins. Long before guide-books were published, travelers had relied on local knowledge to comprehend battlefield. At Ticonderoga one wagon driver and innkeeper's son was "a shrewd young man [who] satisfied our curiosity as to 'what's that' and 'what's this.'" During an 1800 visit he pointed out overgrown fortifications, crumbling barracks, and various rooms among the stone ruins. Although the driver may have been "perfectly acquainted with the spot, [and] conducted us sedulously to every thing which we wished to see," he lacked more than "imperfect information," in another tourist's opinion. "I wanted to know all, every particular, of a spot that interested my feelings so much."[88] Likewise, well-connected visitors to Saratoga could call on General Philip Schuyler, who had commanded an earlier portion of the northern campaign and supported the American army later in 1777. In December 1780 Schuyler hosted the Marquis de Chastellux in his manor house and escorted the Frenchman around the battlefield. Schuyler impressed his guest: "We could not have had a better guide, but he was absolutely necessary for us in every respect, for besides that this event happened before his eyes, and that he was better able than anybody to give us an account of it, no person but the proprietor of the ground himself was able to conduct us safely through the woods; the fences and entrenchments being covered a foot deep with snow."[89]

But Schuyler died in 1804, to be replaced by less-refined guides. Benjamin Silliman hired Ezra Buel, a seventy-five-year-old veteran and Saratoga resident since before the war, to guide him around the battlefield in 1819. Buel had provided similar assistance to the American army in 1777, frequently "in the post of danger; and he was therefore, admirable qualified from my purpose." The two men scrambled over fences, fallen logs, and stone walls, crashed through bogs, thickets, and ravines, and clambered up and down hills. "In short, through many places where I alone would not have ventured; but it would have been shameful for me not to follow where a man of seventy-five would lead, and to reluctate at going, *in peace,* over ground which the defenders of their country and their foes once trod in steps of blood."[90] Two years later the attorney and politician William Wirt also toured the Saratoga battlefield with a still-vigorous Buel—"his usual gait of riding is twelve miles *per* hour on a very hard riding horse." Buel had just finished guiding "another traveler" around the battlefield, but "not at all fatigued with the excursion from which he had just returned, [Buel] wheeled about again and accompanied us with the most alacrity." As another traveler noted, "the old Gentleman's face beamed and eyes sparkled with pleasure" as he showed his guests around the battlefield. "Retracing the steps of battle with one who had been there "enabled me to imagine at times that I saw and heard all the tumult, agitation, shouting, thunder and fury of a long and well-contested field."[91]

When, on the Saratoga battlefield with Silliman, Buel "bared his aged breast, and shewed me where a bullet had raked along, superficially cutting the outer integuments of the thorax, and carrying with it into the wound portions of his clothes," Silliman had come as close to witnessing the Revolution as one could without traveling back through time to smell the powder burn and hear the balls whistle.[92] Buel provided a walking monument that complemented the romantic past of decaying ruins and bucolic scenery. Encountering the past in the person of this old soldier enabled Silliman to reenact the history he had only read about in memoirs or guidebooks. He gained a personal understanding of what most knew as a mythic event.[93] Tour guides like Buel offered personal interaction, anecdotes, and individual memories that imbued a battlefield visit with more meaning than any guidebook could transmit. They provided another prompt to sentiment and melancholy, as well as an individual link to the noble struggle of the Revolution.

Problematically, by the late 1820s the "race of men" who fought the Revolution had "now become few: decimated, over and over again, by the ravages of sixty years, their ranks, once so full and so irresistible, have been closed and closed again, to supply many a lamented vacancy; and now present only a few greyheads and feeble frames, supported by tottering knees." The men who had fought for freedom and liberty served as "objects of veneration to one generation after another: a sort of living monuments, exalted like columns of antiquity, and bearing the inscription of many a virtue." Such self-sacrificing Revolutionary War veterans represented "the principal symbol of civic virtue" in a nation riven by individualism and avarice. Their service, whether in the unsuccessful defense of Ticonderoga or during the dismal 1777–78 winter at Valley Forge, was "transformed into an inspiring legend in which virtue had triumphed after sacrifices had been made." Americans owed a "debt of gratitude" to these impoverished, hobbled "suffering soldiers." Congress had passed the 1818 Pension Act that provided financial support to Revolutionary War veterans, but tightened the qualifications two years later amid spiraling costs and charges of false claims.[94] Instead of receiving government support, ex-soldiers often were dependent on public charity, like the "old man, bent down by age and infirmities, [who] was almost daily seen with a small paper which he occasionally handed to some of the passengers" on the Brooklyn ferry in 1836. The slip told how at Fort Griswold he "had lost a leg and received thirteen bayonet wounds. He worked the ferry passengers, "soliciting a trifle from the benevolent to cheer the evening of his days."[95]

Too few of these men remained fifty years after the Revolution, just as battlefield tourism began to grow. Many Saratoga visitors failed to realize that Philip Schuyler's son "was living on the ground," or they would have "found means to pay him... respects" as part of a battlefield visit.[96] They settled for "the son of the innkeeper," at Saratoga, "who was himself one of our revolutionary warriors," for interpretation of the site's history. "The young man had acquired a perfect knowledge of every part of the ground... not only from the descriptions of his father, and other venerable soldiers, but also from an attentive perusal of the histories of the war."[97] Instead of seeking out the few remaining soldiers, by the 1830s tourists could consult the increasingly popular guidebooks and travel accounts that featured long histories of key Revolutionary War sites, especially those places where the United States scored a major victory, such as Saratoga or Ticonderoga. Many guidebooks pirated Wilkinson's memoirs, Timothy Dwight's comments, or Silliman's travelogue verbatim and without apology. The popularity of traveling and the low cost of books made the veteran-as-tour-guide a luxury or quaint diversion. He no longer constituted the main interpreter of, and intermediary for, the nation's past.

Yet the veteran remained an honored part of a battlefield's scenic landscape. Nathaniel Hawthorne disliked his 1835 visit to Ticonderoga because "a young lieutenant of engineers, recently graduated from West Point," chattered in his ear about military geometry and strategy, as well as the specific movements of various armies. Hawthorne's place of poetry, "where armies had struggled so long ago that the bones of the slain are mouldered," lost its passion. Instead, he wrote, "I should have been glad of a hoary veteran to totter by my side, and tell me, perhaps, of the French garrisons and their Indian allies, of Abercrombie, Lord Howe and Amherst; of Ethan Allen's triumph and St. Clair's surrender. The old soldier and the old fortress would be emblems of each other." Hawthorne viewed the veteran not just as a guide and interpreter, but also as integral to the experience, a part of the landscape. Talking to a veteran conveyed as much meaning as walking the lines or stepping into the barracks; it was more immediate yet also oddly impersonal. Hawthorne desired not the veteran as individual person, but the veteran as totem and interlocutor of the past. His "hoary veteran... might have mustered his dead chiefs and comrades, some from Westminster Abbey, and the English church-yards and battle-fields in Europe, others from their graves here in America; others, not few, who lie sleeping round the fortress; he might have mustered them all, and bid them march through the ruined gateway, turning their old historick faces on me as they passed."[98] History and personal narrative mattered little to Hawthorne here; he preferred a generic emotional, almost ahistorical yet firmly sentimental encounter with history. Hawthorne's distance from the past allowed him to define history as he preferred it; in identifying with the "dead chiefs and comrades," he gained a position of privilege, a mastery of history.[99] Hawthorne further reduced the guide to a relic, an innocuous medium to the ghosts of Ticonderoga. History had been replaced "with a kind of domestic timelessness" as nostalgia supplanted partisan rancor and ideological recitals.[100] The nationalism Hawthorne and other tourists discovered on battlefields lacked the Revolution's ideological passion, even if it was intensely emotional and personal.

Visitors such as Hawthorne might still happen upon an aged veteran strolling the grounds, but it was the exception rather than the norm. The diminishment of the veteran's interpretive role reversed itself by the late 1840s, when political veneration of Revolutionary War veterans had lost its punch.[101] By then the rare existence and advanced age of Revolutionary soldiers—a veteran who enlisted in 1780 at age fifteen would have been seventy-five in 1840—created nostalgia for those who had experienced the nation's making. One ancient warrior remained at Ticonderoga in the late 1840s, when several different visitors "wandered about some time with an old Revolutionary soldier" who lived near the ruins. After he recounted tales and pointed out where Ethan Allen had entered the fort, "we gave him a pittance for his courtesy as all visitors do."[102]

This figure was almost certainly Isaac Rice, the soldier Benson Lossing portrayed in his influential 1850 work, *Pictorial Field-Book of the Revolution*. "Kind and intelligent," Rice guided Lossing and his party about the ruins, answering questions and identifying features. The white-haired, octogenarian Rice depended "upon the cold friendship of the world for sustenance...obtaining a precarious support for himself from the free will offerings of visitors to the ruins of the fortress where he was garrisoned when it stood in the pride of its strength." As Rice related to Lossing, a technicality had deprived him of his due pension, and death the members of his immediate family, but he remained optimistic. According to Rice, he had "heard that the old man who lived here, to show visitors about, was dead, and so I came down to take his place and die also." Rice hoped to clear away the brush from a small room, "arrange a sleeping place in the rear, erect a rude counter in front, and there, during the summer, sell cakes beer and fruit to

**Figure 5.** Isaac Rice, from Benson Lossing, *Pictorial Field-Book of the Revolution* (1850). Lossing met Rice while touring Fort Ticonderoga's ruins. The old soldier claimed to have fought at Ticonderoga and Saratoga, and eked out a meager existence telling tales of the Revolution amid the fort's ruins. He was buried at Fort Ticonderoga in 1852. Author's collection.

visitors." Fate cast him close to poverty and left him "to feel the practical ingratitude of a people reveling in the enjoyment which his privations in early manhood contributed to secure." Yet Rice did not despair and provided Lossing and his readers an object lesson in the nation's highest values, "for this poor, friendless, aged man had bright visions of a better earthly condition even in the midst of his poverty and loneliness."[103] Rice served as a direct, living link to a nearly dead past for a nation contemplating history and sentiment simultaneously, without contradiction. Lossing revived interest in the Revolution, remembering the past, and visiting historic sites, as well as boosted sales of his own book, which included a sketch of Rice. Both Lossing and Rice manipulated and profited from the idealized image of the Revolutionary War veteran, as well as tourists' anticipated battlefield experiences. Rice eked out a meager existence among the ruins, even if modern research reveals that he had never actually fought in the Revolution. But in Lossing's time, when few veterans remained alive, such details were irrelevant: Isaac Rice looked like an old soldier and he could tell a good story.[104]

By the 1850s attempts to commemorate Revolutionary War sites along the Northern Tour relied on personal interactions with landscape and a solitary veteran like Rice. Tourists' personal memories emphasized scenery and romanticism, often informed by the accounts they had read of the sites. Yet even the few historic sites with significant extant ruins, such as Ticonderoga, failed to become major tourist attractions, because the typical tourist sustained multiple interests in social display, amusement, and dissipation at places such as Saratoga Springs and Niagara Falls. With only intermittent steamboat service and a sole hotel, Ticonderoga lacked the infrastructure to support heavy tourist traffic; Old Saratoga served only as a day trip from Saratoga Springs and its massive hotels, and tourists rarely did more than look at the lower Hudson River Valley's fortifications from fast-moving steamboat decks. The battlefields remained secondary stops on the Northern Tour. Tourists enjoyed seeing Sam Patch jump from a platform above Niagara Falls just as much as, or perhaps more than, hearing an old soldier recount his glory days on the old battlefield, without detecting any cognitive dissonance.[105] Both experiences emphasized a personal interaction with a place and event, whether modern or historical.

Isaac Rice united amusement and memory because he offered an opportunity to reanimate Ticonderoga's crumbling walls. Lossing's musings on Ticonderoga's history were shaped by

> the old patriot, who came and sat beside me. . . . He has no companions of the present, and the sight of the old walls kept sluggish memory awake to the recollections of light and love of other days. "I am alone in the world," he said, "poor and friendless; none for me to care for, and none to care for me. Father, mother, brothers, sisters, wife, and children have all passed away, and the busy world has forgotten *me.*"

On that "pleasant moonlight evening" Lossing and Rice performed their parts in an emotional play of past and present. But even such personal encounters with a "suffering soldier" offering only a fleeting glimpse of the past. Rice, Lossing recounted, regaled him for "more than an hour with a relation of his own and his father's adventures, and it was late in the evening when I bade him a final adieu. 'God bless you, my son,' he said, as he grasped my hand at parting. 'We may never meet here again, but I hope we may in heaven!'" Once Rice died in 1852, no walking monument remained to interpret the fort's past, and Americans now relied on the scarcely visible remains at Revolutionary War battlefields to interpret the past. Lossing lamented, "Year after year the ruins thus dwindle, and, unless government shall prohibit the robbery, this venerable landmark of history will soon have no abiding-place among us."[106] He was writing about the fort, but his words applied equally well to Rice. When either disappeared, Americans would no longer enjoy a direct connection to their past. Personal interactions with place constructed impermanent memories, a problem that Americans were slow to address.

# CHAPTER THREE

# Retrieved Relics and New Monuments

## Lafayette in Yorktown

Americans thrilled at the triumphant return of the Marquis de Lafayette. He visited the United States in 1824–25, welcomed by dignitaries and enthusiastic crowds across the nation. Gilbert du Motier de Lafayette had earned fame fighting as a young major general alongside George Washington during the Revolutionary War, as well as for his later defense of republicanism during the French Revolution. His visit marked an opportunity for the United States to reconnect with its past and to celebrate one of the last living heroes of their nation's birth. Among the hallmarks of Lafayette's tour were his stops at the battlefields where he won glory and helped the nation achieve its independence from Great Britain. Yorktown appeared on his itinerary for October 19–20, 1824, the siege's forty-third anniversary, on which occasion Lafayette "was received with great demonstrations of respect and joy."[1] Speeches, parades, and dinners celebrated the surrender of British forces under General Cornwallis and the effective conclusion of large-scale fighting. On the second day of his visit Lafayette and other dignitaries marched onto the battlefield to view "two obelisks; one erected on the spot which was stormed by Viomenil the other where the sword of Cornwallis was delivered up. They were twenty six feet in height, and surmounted by a Fasces, and Battle axe, of ten feet." This effort to formally commemorate the battle of Yorktown might be seen as an important step in erecting monuments to the Revolution in a nation that possessed few such structures. But the obelisks lacked the permanence that would make them fixed reminders of the American victory. Presumably made of wood, they were "painted to resemble stone."[2]

Yorktown belonged to the overwhelming majority of Revolutionary War battlefields that lacked any type of permanent, physical commemoration of the events that had taken place there. Lafayette visited several battlefields and helped to encourage greater interest in remembering the Revolution, but his 1824–25 tour did not result in a sizable number of monuments being erected on the nation's battlefields. Though tens of thousands of Americans flocked to see the nation's hero, decaying fortifications and half-buried bones remained the only battlefield reminders of the past on these sites until decades after Lafayette sailed home to France one last time. The slow pace of monument building, and perhaps even the neglect of Revolutionary War battlefields, indicate Americans' hesitancy to commemorate their past and their uncertain relationship with place. Even Lafayette's spectacular commemoration of Yorktown's anniversary left behind few visible reminders of that important military event.

## Yorktown in Ruin

Beginning in August 1781 Yorktown residents discovered war's impact in what one resident called "one of the greatest calamities of my life." British and German troops occupied the town, erected fortifications, and dug entrenchments. American and French soldiers lay siege to Yorktown on September 28. Once encircled, Yorktown felt the brutal force of eighteenth-century siege warfare. Over fifteen thousand artillery rounds, an average of seventy-one shells per hour, fell during the nine-day bombardment.[3] Secretary Thomas Nelson's large two-story brick house barely stood, "with one of the Corners broke off, & many large holes thro the Roof & Walls part of which seem'd tottering with their Weight," which "afforded a striking Instance of the Destruction occasioned by War." The once-thriving harbor now contained British "ships sunk down to the Waters Edge—further out in the Channel the Masts, Yards & even the top gallant Masts of some might be seen, without any vestige of the hulls," casualties of American and French artillery or British scuttling.[4] Baron Ludwig von Closen, an aide with the French army, viewed the "frightful and disturbing" scene inside Yorktown the day after the British surrender. "One could not take three steps without running into some great holes made by bombs, some splinters, some balls, some half covered trenches, with scattered white or negro arms or legs, [and] some bits of uniforms."[5] The town seemed riddled with "carcasses of men and horses, half covered with dirt, whose moldering limbs, while they poisoned the air, struck dread and horror to the soul." Yorktown, once noted for its fine buildings, was ruined. A French chaplain "saw many elegant houses shot through and through in a thousand places, and ready to crumble to pieces; rich household furniture crushed under the ruins, or broken by the brutal English soldier." Even the books of the town's gentry lay "piled in heaps, and scattered among the ruins of the buildings."[6]

Residents hoped that the return to peace would restore their town. Shortly after the October 1781 British surrender, Washington's army began to demolish the earthworks surrounding the village. Washington feared that the British, who still controlled a sizable army in New York, might attempt to retake the position. Once the immediate threat passed, French and American troops made desultory efforts to remove the siege trenches that fall. When French units departed in the spring, the works remained. Virginia governor Benjamin Harrison ordered the state militia to complete the job, but county officials refused to send their delegations because of inadequate lodging in Yorktown.[7] Frustrated at the lack of progress, the town's residents appealed to Congress in 1783, requesting that the entrenchments be filled and earthworks removed so that they could farm the land. But neither the Continental army nor the Virginia government took action. Residents also feared the costs of stationing troops at Yorktown to complete the demolition, having suffered the consequences of idle soldiers on garrison duty during the year after the battle: "Very few nights passed without Robbery or gross insult being committed by them." One local resident proposed hiring slaves to perform the work, at a much lower cost than soldiers' salary and rations, but Congress refused the money, saying it lacked funding and that other states had paid for such work themselves.[8] The effort was too great for a town almost completely destroyed by bombardment and the hard use of two armies. A decade later New England merchants applied Yankee ingenuity to the remnants of the fifteen thousand artillery rounds fired at Yorktown. They "dug them up, and carried them away in their ships" to sell as scrap iron.[9]

But Yorktown continued to languish. Some of the redoubts and fortifications remained on the bluffs above the river, but major ones had been leveled. "The plough has passed over some of them, and groves of pine trees sprung up about others." Townspeople quickly resumed agricultural pursuits while simultaneously preserving the signs of damage to their homes. They refused to "suffer the holes perforated by the cannon balls to be repaired on the outside."[10] As one observer noted in 1796, "none of the ravages of war have been repaired."[11] Yorktown's fortunes revived briefly when the War of 1812 brought American troops to the town. But the remaining 1781 entrenchments made preparing the town for defense from the more powerful modern artillery difficult, and the town remained a minor post. One soldier described "not more than 40 dwellings at present which mostly have an ancient appearance." What few improvements had been made vanished in an 1814 fire that dealt Yorktown another blow. The following year "Not Less than 50 or 60 naked chimnies are to be Seen Standing the houses of which have been consumed by fire."[12]

Little had changed by the time of Lafayette's October 1824 visit to "much dilapidated" Yorktown.[13] The battlefield "seems to have lain entirely forgotten and neglected," and the village of York itself "had almost been lost in weeds of mourning for its declining situation, and buried in its forgetfulness."[14] Simply put, Yorktown "never recovered from the disasters of the revolutionary war."[15] Yet this kind of devastation and neglect provided much of Yorktown's allure during the 1824 celebration. Lafayette's assistant and personal secretary, Auguste Levasseur, enjoyed visiting the nearby ruins, rising at dawn the day after the grand events and walking "the ruins of the ancient entrenchments of the town." He carried a map of the military engagement as he traced the old lines.[16] "A few yards beyond the edge of the town to the East, you see the nearest British lines; the mounds of the entrenchments, and the ditch: the mound, considerably sunk from the tread of cattle, and the washing of the rains; and the ditch rapidly filling up." But Levasseur's encounter with history at Yorktown proved fleeting.[17] On the morning of October 20 he reported that the "temporary encampment...has already been abandoned."[18] This kind of impermanent memory and lack of commemoration occurred at many other battlefields that Lafayette visited across the United States.

## The Nation's Guest

Perhaps no other event during the 1820s sparked interest in the nation's past as much as Lafayette's triumphant return to the United States. He had visited once before, in 1784, when "he was received with an affectionate welcome." Lafayette's most valued moments took place not in the halls of Congress and state legislatures, or at formal dinners, but among his former Continental army fellow officers. At a Massachusetts dinner hosted by General Henry Knox, Lafayette remarked, "During my absence, gentlemen, my heart has been constantly with you. As an army, we are separated. But forever, I hope, shall unite in a brotherly affection."[19] The 1784 connection between Lafayette and Revolutionary War veterans lasted forty years until his next visit. Throughout his successes and failures in French politics, imprisonment in Germany, and financial difficulties chronicled in the numerous biographies and reports of his travels published in 1824–25, Lafayette's relationship with the United States had never soured. He had become "an integral part of the national creation story."[20]

Lafayette garnered his fame fighting during the Revolution, first as an unpaid nineteen-year-old volunteer at Charleston, South Carolina, in January 1777, where he used his own funds to purchase "clothing and arms" for the troops. Commissioned a major general by Congress later that year, he served with distinction at Brandywine, outside Philadelphia; at Monmouth; and during the retreat from Rhode Island. Lafayette commanded divisions and departments before sailing to France in 1778 to aid his home country, which by then was also at war with Great Britain. He led French troops in battle and helped to secure French ships and troops for the American theater before his return to the colonies in 1780, where he assisted in the victory at Yorktown. As "the last surviving Major General of the American revolutionary army," Lafayette was seen by Americans as their greatest living war hero.[21]

Lafayette had expressed his desire to return to the United States before old age prevented it. President James Monroe invited him to make an official visit, and offered a ship to carry him across the Atlantic. He arrived in New York City on August 14, 1824, accompanied by his son, George Washington Lafayette, and Levasseur.

> At an early hour, the whole city was in motion; almost every man, woman and child was preparing to witness the landing of their much respected guest. The shops and stores were closed, and all business was suspended for the day. The ringing of bells, the roar of cannon, and the display of the national flag, at all public places and on board the shipping, proclaimed that it was a day of joy, in which all were anxious to partake.[22]

This enthusiastic reception was imitated in almost every city, town, hamlet, or crossroads visited by Lafayette's party.

A delegation of local elected officials greeted the "nation's guest" at each town or county border, with a more prestigious group, which often included the governor, meeting Lafayette when he crossed into a new state. Many towns flew banners emblazoned with the hero's name or erected triumphal arches festooned with flowers under which Lafayette obligingly processed. Military escorts of state militia or cavalry, and occasionally national troops, marched beside Lafayette's carriage as it rolled through town, usually stopping long enough for a few gracious remarks. Federal installations carried out President Monroe's orders that Lafayette "be received by the military officers of the nation, at all public posts, with the salutes and honors due to one of the highest rank in the army."[23] Speeches and public dinners, private balls, receptions at city hall, meetings with the Freemasons or the Society of the Cincinnati, as well a delegation of local women, rounded out the formal events. As Lafayette's traveling secretary recorded, "We could not pass a hamlet without being detained some moments by collections of people from more than 20 miles around."[24] Each town repeated the scene: "To describe the brilliant parades, the triumphal processions, the costly fetes, the balls, the parties, which made his long journey an uninterrupted gala day of excitement and display, would be to repeat a thousand times, with variations, the same gorgeous and imposing scene." The speeches alone "would require a volume."[25]

Artists painted nearly twenty portraits and made countless engravings of Lafayette, and his image graced scores of everyday articles, including sheet music, plates, embroidery, tobacco pipes, and currency.[26]

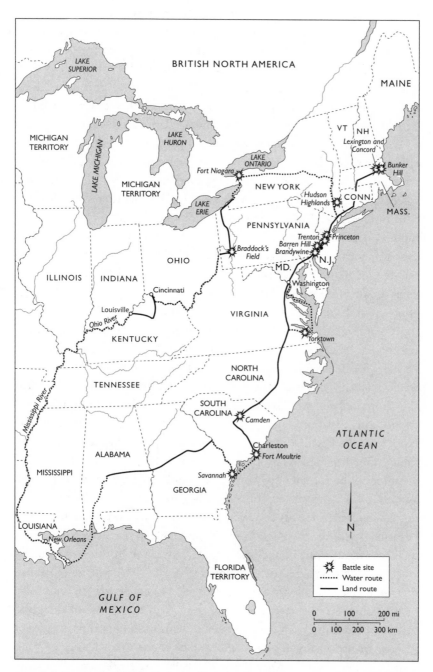

**Map 4.** Lafayette's tour, 1824–25. During his national tour, Lafayette visited several battle-fields, including those marked here.

One Charleston mother even dressed her infant son in "a little Beaver hat with a La Fayette cockade upon it & a pair of blue shoes with the head of La Fayette on the front part of them."[27] This overwhelming interest made Lafayette's initial plan to honor invitations from New York City and Boston, before traveling to Washington at President Monroe's request, increasingly difficult to follow. Other cities wanted to extend their welcome as well. Richmond planned to "take some steps to honor their old political father who is about to visit them." Virginia claimed to have been "principally the theatre of La Fayette's military services in America. She will certainly therefore, not be behind her sister states in paying him due honors."[28] Dozens of other towns formed committees of leading citizens to invite Lafayette and his party to visit them. So great was the volume of requests that Lafayette could agree to visit a major city like Philadelphia only after he had completed "previous engagements toward the eastern part of the Union" several weeks later.[29] Baltimore would have to wait to receive him, wrote Lafayette, "pressed as I am with pre-engagements and a sense of duty towards the members of both houses of Congress." He had already committed to visit "Orange Court House, Fredericsburg, and Washington."[30] Perhaps feeling guilty for limiting his time in Baltimore, as his tour wound down Lafayette lamented, "It grieves me to the heart to leave this shore before I have paid one more visit to my Baltimore friends. I expect to hear from you."[31] Smaller cities with less connection to Lafayette such as Petersburg, Virginia, increased their chances of fulfilling their "contemplated plan" of hosting Lafayette by paying for several prominent townsmen "to wait upon Genl. La Fayette at York, and ascertain when it will be convenient for him to visit Petersburg, and to provide means for his conveyance thence, and also to give him their personal attention."[32] Their "pressing invitation" persuaded Lafayette to pass "twenty-four hours" there shortly after the Yorktown event.[33]

In hosting Lafayette, towns sought legitimacy. The citizens of Petersburg must have thrilled when the general apologized for "the necessity in the course of military operations, to disturb the repose of the good town of Petersburg, while it had been a British headquarters" in 1781.[34] The town had changed considerably since then. What had once been a small collection of "miserable wooden houses...now are very large well built brick buildings, in which we can offer you all the comforts of life."[35] In the transformed town, now an example of American progress,

Lafayette "found new opportunities to witness her patriotism."[36] Such visits were civic events meant to demonstrate a community's values. John Peck of Fredericksburg claimed that during Lafayette's visit, "everything was much better managed here" than at Richmond or Yorktown, which spoke well of his town.[37]

Towns sought to outdo each other in welcoming Lafayette. When U.S. Senator James Lloyd of Boston sought to house Lafayette in his residence, the City Council interceded, insisting that Lafayette "should be considered as a guest of the public...he should be considered as the guest of the City; and are making arrangements accordingly."[38] The city would pay for the entertainment and lodging as an expression of its civic virtue, which could not be expropriated by any one individual. The Commonwealth of Virginia proclaimed its patriotic commitment by paying not only the $10,178.04 in costs related to the Yorktown celebration, but any other funds "actually expended, or necessary to be expended, in the reception and entertainment, and for the travelling expenses of General Lafayette."[39] "A nation's gratitude has been his passport through our Country," wrote one of George Washington's relatives, who might have added free transportation and room and board to the items provided to Lafayette. "All ages, sexes & conditions welcomed the defender of our rights with every demonstration of joy."[40]

## Historic Relics

Totems of the past appeared at nearly every stop along the itinerary, as Americans searched their attics and barns for relics. Towns saluted Lafayette with cannon "taken from the British, at Bennington, Saratoga, and Yorktown."[41] Lacking artillery, Fredericktown, Maryland, displayed a candleholder made from "an enormous fragment of a bomb shell used at the siege of Yorktown."[42] Better yet, an aged veteran of Lexington produced a musket he claimed was used to wound the first British soldier in that battle, perhaps the very gun that fired "the shot heard 'round the world."[43] Old muskets, swords, bomb fragments, or the "raggard standard...under which Pulaski died at Savannah" provided the touchstones of memory that Americans required. The Pulaski flag had "never been displayed" since the Revolution, but "the arrival of Lafayette was a sufficiently glorious occasion for bringing it to light."[44] A direct connection between an object and the honored guest, such as the "standard of [Colonel Peter] Gansevoort's regiment, which had waved at Yorktown, under the command of La Fayette," brought greater authenticity to the moment. That many of the old soldiers greeting Lafayette at Albany, New York, had served in Gansevoort's unit further added to the flag's nostalgic appeal. The mere sight of light infantry company uniforms, a group Lafayette once commanded, "deeply affected the general, he could not keep his eyes off it, and exclaimed every moment, 'my brave light infantry! Such was their uniform! What courage! What resignation! How much I loved them!'"[45] The citizens of Hartford, Connecticut, exhibited the most sacred relic of all: "A sash and pair of epaulets...which were worn by La Fayette when he entered the American army. The *sash was stained with blood* from his wound received in the battle of Brandywine."[46] Seeing the patriot's blood, as well as the man who had once shed it, connected the object and the individual to the past in a way that speeches or processions could not.

Lafayette also represented a living link to the nation's departed patriarch, George Washington, which brought forth a whole new category of historic relics. At Newark, New Jersey, Lafayette "was presented...with a cane made from an apple tree, under which he had dined in company with general Washington during the war of the rebellion."[47] The mayor of Trenton, New Jersey, praised Lafayette under "a civic arch, rendered to us deeply interesting by being the same, which five and thirty years ago, served to evince our attachment to the beloved and revered Washington"—it was the same "triumphal arch under which General Washington passed, on his journey to New-York, to be inaugurated as President."[48] Whether the cane was really carved from that specific tree or if the arch miraculously retained the original 1789 evergreens and flowers mattered little. They were physical reminders of the great men and great deeds that had made the nation. One item possessed more significance than any other souvenir: first appearing in Baltimore in early October 1824, "the venerable Tent of Washington" hosted banquets during Lafayette's visit. It was to be carried to Yorktown, where "within its ancient walls, and impressed with its great and heroic recollections, the last of the Generals of the Army of Independence, will hold his military levee." Perhaps the moldering forty-eight-year-old canvas might reanimate the Revolution. Because the tent still belonged to the Washington family, "this venerable relic" possessed legitimacy that no other totem could match. Such object reverence for Washington's tent and other relics gained a central role in Americans' understanding of their past and national identity.[49] Its walls, pieces of the true cross, had witnessed the Revolution and the father of his country making the nation. As a foreign observer noted, "Every thing which recalls this glorious epoch, is to them a precious relic, which they regard almost with religious reverence."[50] Lafayette, who had witnessed and participated in many of those scenes, connected past and present.

## Old Soldiers

His compatriots, the cadre of Continental army officers, dominated the official ceremonies at Lafayette's various stops, and the Society of the Cincinnati often organized the proceedings or hosted a separate celebration restricted to its members. Some cities took the lead from the society and issued invitations "for the surviving officers of the revolutionary army to meet him."[51] These were mostly junior officers, though, as "not a single individual of the General Staff of the army of the American Revolution now survives to participate in the joy that your presence in the United States has awakened."[52] Instead of a roll call of former soldiers, Lafayette would be greeted by whatever "old companion in arms" could be found in each town.[53] Age constituted a significant problem during these encounters. The delegation "of several field officers of the revolutionary army" at Staten Island consisted of men "upwards of eighty years of age."[54] Lafayette's advancement to field grade officer while still in his teens meant that many of his peers, at least in terms of rank, were either quite elderly or already dead in 1824, when he was sixty-seven and but a decade away from death. As one observer of his visit noted, "There, indeed, Lafayette was in the midst of posterity; a living monument of the valour and wisdom of other days."[55] His old age rendered encounters with the few surviving, often older veterans all the more poignant.

Lafayette's reunions with "his old revolutionary companions" resulted in emotions and recollections that no official program of speeches and parades could script.[56] At Cambridge, Massachusetts, several old veterans crowded Lafayette's official residence, uninvited, to tell tales of their service in war. "Some were on crutches, and others bared their arms to show the honorable scars occasioned by the bayonet or ball of the enemy, in the 'glorious fight' for freedom."[57] This kind of impromptu encounter with ordinary soldiers, like the "one decrepid veteran...recognized by the General as a companion in arms at the memorable onset at Yorktown," produced embraces of genuine feeling.[58] "Not a dry eye was to be found among the throng of spectators" when Lafayette met men with whom he had fought and bled. "He was so eager to meet them, that he very generally first seized them, and clung to them with all the affection of a brother."[59] As one newspaper declared, "these mutual recognitions were sometimes deeply affecting and very gratifying to all present."[60]

Lafayette seemed to have an amazing power to recall the faces and names of men he had not seen in decades. Colonel Marinus Willet was one of the first soldiers to greet Lafayette in New York City. "'Do you remember,' said he to the marquis, 'at the battle of Monmouth, I was volunteer aid to general Scott? I saw you in the heat of battle. You were but a boy, but you were a serious, sedate lad.'" Lafayette replied, "Aye, aye, I remember well. And on the Mohawk, I sent you fifty Indians, and you wrote to me that they set up such a yell that they frightened the British horse, and they ran one way and the Indians another."[61] Being able to recall such detail indicates the formative nature of the Revolution in Lafayette's and other veterans' minds, as well as the intense personal connections they made. The soldiers themselves, not Lafayette, the Society of the Cincinnati, or the organizing committees in various towns, initiated these meetings. They "now came forward (some of them from a distance), to greet their old commander with tears in their eyes." One ninety-six-year-old veteran walked 115 miles to meet Lafayette, claiming "I have always marched, and I can march still."[62] These individual veterans were reconnecting with their past through the person of Lafayette in much the same way that their nation revived memory of the Revolution through him, as they had during President James Monroe's 1817 tour of Northern states. Monroe, who had fought in the New Jersey campaigns and risen to the rank of major, "sought after his revolutionary compatriots." The president "laid his hands on the traces of their wounds...the scars which bore honorable testimony to their valour, and their suffering."[63] The "suffering soldier" continued to provide a powerful icon in American memory, especially if he appeared where he had fought and bled.[64]

## Encountering Yorktown

During this tour Lafayette visited more than twenty battlefields or forts dating from the Revolutionary War, including several where he had fought, such as Brandywine, Yorktown, and several minor sites from the 1781 Virginia campaign. Skipping the 1778 Rhode Island campaign battlefield pained Lafayette enough that his aide remarked, "He would have enjoyed much the pleasure of revisiting places, which recalled so many of his youthful recollections."[65] But a battle like Barren Hill, where Lafayette's effective rearguard action "laid the foundation of his fame in military tactics," merited no stop as the party rode "within sight" of the battlefield.[66] Instead, more storied scenes such as Bunker Hill, Lexington and Concord, the Hudson Highlands, Princeton, Camden, and Fort Moultrie received Lafayette with elaborate ceremonies. But no battlefield featured as sustained an encounter between Lafayette and Revolutionary War soldiers, or captured as much of the nation's imagination, as did Yorktown. The site of one of Lafayette's bravest deeds and the place of America's climactic victory over the British resonated with Americans. Lafayette had led Continental army and Virginia militia troops in the Old Dominion since March 1781, first attempting to thwart General Benedict Arnold (now fighting for the British) in his raids across the countryside from a base at Portsmouth. Lord Cornwallis's main army arrived from North Carolina by early spring, having failed in its attempts to conquer the South, and moved inland, thrusting as far west as Charlottesville. Never able to fully engage or defeat the Americans under Lafayette, Cornwallis withdrew eastward, eventually encamping at Yorktown while he waited for expected reinforcements to arrive by ship. Instead, a Franco-American army besieged Yorktown, and a French fleet controlled access to Chesapeake Bay, blocking British resupply. Lafayette had participated in a nighttime assault on key British redoubts whose capture had sealed the fate of the British defenders. Shortly thereafter, Lord Cornwallis surrendered his command.[67] Lafayette received praise then and in years to come for his role in the 1781 campaign. "Perhaps no general in the siege," wrote one observer of the 1824 visit, "under Washington was more active and useful."[68]

Virginians planned to honor that glorious moment and its surviving hero at a gala celebration at Yorktown on October 19, 1824, the forty-third anniversary of Cornwallis's surrender. "I hear of nothing but La Fayette," wrote one Richmond resident; "all the inhabitants of the city have gone now to York, great parade there for La Fayette."[69] They anticipated a "glorious" celebration that would elicit "national feeling."[70] The day exceeded even these lofty expectations. The general's steamship left Alexandria on October 16, stopped at Mount Vernon for an emotional visit to Washington's tomb, and by noon on the eighteenth had proceeded up the York River to the old battlefield. In addition to Secretary of War John C. Calhoun, who had accompanied Lafayette from Washington, Supreme Court chief justice John Marshall, the governor of Virginia, various local politicians, and a host of military officers greeted the honored guest.[71] The Virginia militia had been encamped at Yorktown for three days, preparing the grounds and practicing their formations and salutes. No detail, even "the uniforms of the companies," escaped the planners' eyes.[72] Disembarking from a temporary wharf erected below the town, the party could see that "crowds of free people, of all ages and sexes, loaded all the heights, and stretched along the beach below for a considerable distance, teeming with life and the fulness of joy, to behold and welcome the gallant stranger who had risked his all in their cause."[73] Among these "anxious spectators...the anticipation was intense." Boats on the river and an artillery company on the bluffs above fired their cannon in salute while a band played a fanfare. The procession, led by another military band, "passed through the long lines of citizens and old revolutionary soldiers arranged in two columns. It wound up the hill, and finally terminated at the General's quarters" at General Nelson's house. Once the honor guard received its salute, the band followed orders to "*immediately* cease playing." With the military pomp and circumstance over, Lafayette "was cheered by a crowd of citizens."[74] In a delicious inversion of historical events, he allegedly stayed at "the very house that Cornwallis inhabited during the siege of Yorktown."[75]

The first day's events were largely civic, with flowery speeches from the organizing committee, the governor of Virginia, and Lafayette himself. Delegations of ladies and ordinary citizens greeted the general, who shook hands with anyone who approached, including yet another Revolutionary War veteran. The old soldier "advanced, seized the General by the hand, exclaiming, 'I was with you at Yorktown. I entered yonder redoubt at your side. I too was at the side of the gallant De Kalb, our associate in arms, when he fell in the field' [at the battle of Camden, South Carolina]. The tears streamed down from the veteran's eyes; and La Fayette showed by his countenance the sympathy he felt. 'Yes, my brave soldier, I am happy to have lived, to meet you once more.'" This exchange, coupled with a small dinner under a tent for twenty to thirty former Continental army officers, produced "a scene which no man who saw it will ever forget.... The moral effects of this spectacle were sublime. There was an effect in it, which no words can describe. Tears streamed from an hundred eyes. The sentiments it diffused through several thousands of spectators, were of the loftiest character."[76] As emotional and jubilant as that first day of celebration was, it paled in comparison with the intense nostalgia and sincere gratitude that followed on October 19.

Artillery fire awakened the company at dawn on what was to be a perfect day. "The sun rose gloriously; and the azure arched sky, looked pure as the Spirit who made it," recalled one attendee.[77] Lafayette and his party proceeded to Washington's much-traveled marquee, said to cover "the same ground which it had occupied on that memorable occasion when Cornwallis bowed to the superiority of the republican chief."[78] A review of troops outside Washington's tent brought a familiar scene: "two old revolutionary soldiers fainted away in shaking hands with the general."[79] Militia companies from surrounding cities and towns made the gathering "the largest crowd of persons collected together I ever saw at one time."[80] At eleven that morning Lafayette's procession passed through two columns of soldiers en route to "a triumphal arch erected over the situation of the English redoubt which he formerly carried."[81] At the Rock Redoubt, just a few yards from the riverbank, Lafayette "advanced up the hillock...limping and supported by the Governor" of Virginia. Under the arch "erected atop the ruins" of the redoubt, Virginia militia general Robert Barraud Taylor "saluted him with profound respect, and addressed him."[82] Taylor praised Lafayette for his service to the Revolutionary cause and to republicanism more broadly. Several times in his speech, however, Taylor mentioned the importance of "this spot, consecrated by successful valor." Place evoked more powerful memories than the date or the man. "Can we be here and forget?" Taylor asked rhetorically. "On yonder hillock, the last scene of blood was closed by the surrender of an army; and the liberty of our nation permanently secured. With what resistless eloquence does it persuade our gratitude and admiration for the gallant heroes, for whose noble exertions we owe the countless blessings which our free institutions have conferred upon us?" He concluded his speech by declaring, "On this redoubt, which his valor wrested from the enemy at the point of the bayonet; I place on the head of Major General La Fayette this wreathe of double triumph."[83] Lafayette modestly and gallantly brushed aside the wreath before it reached his head and gave it to another officer, Colonel Fish, who had assisted in the assault. He then thanked the assembled crowd for receiving him "on the very place where" American and French arms joined together "in favour of independence."[84]

Rock Redoubt and its triumphal arch was only the first stop on a tour of Yorktown's sacred places. Two other "temporary works" marked spots of historic significance: "An obelisk at the site of the Redoubt, which Viomenil stormed...; and farther to the south, another obelisk on the famous spot where General O'Hara offered to deliver up his sword to General Washington."[85] Lafayette reviewed the troops at each redoubt before riding in his carriage to the next site, a battalion of politicians and officers trailing behind. Only at one of these sites was the ceremony's formality broken. A "rare old soldier of about seventy" mounted a redoubt ahead of Lafayette's company, "shouldered a cornstalk, and mounted guard," demanding sign and countersign before he would let anyone pass. Eventually another veteran recalled the passwords, and "in a moment the joke was discovered, the old soldier grasped by the hand, when a hearty laugh ensued, which no one enjoyed more heartily than Lafayette."[86] This was perhaps the only instance on Lafayette's entire tour where place and people combined in an attempt to reenact, not just remember, the past.

Later that evening the party retired to Washington's tent, where the dancing of "our old revolutionary soldiers" lasted long into the night. A box of old candles discovered in storage around Yorktown that had once belonged to Cornwallis during the siege so invigorated the veterans "that notwithstanding their great age, and the fatigues of the day, most of them were unwilling to retire until the candles were entirely consumed."[87] Antiquities such as these candles or the flags, muskets, and canes produced by veterans and citizens provided powerful prompts to memory, especially when contemplated at the place where the objects made history.

After a fireworks display late that night, the next day Lafayette reviewed more troops and shook the hand of every well-wisher before departing for Williamsburg that afternoon. He stopped at Green Spring—where he had commanded troops in a battle preliminary to Yorktown—and at Jamestown and Norfolk before continuing his journey around the United States.[88] The Yorktown celebration brought together the battle's key patriot actors at the place and on the anniversary of an event that helped shape the nation. It produced a scene that "baffled all description. The feelings were too acute to be expressed by words."[89] As one account attempted to explain, "Here were the fields, which forty-three years ago, had witnessed the tread of a conquering enemy!"[90]

Those unable to attend felt the need to explain their absence lest others consider them "devoid of patriotism." George Fayette Washington, the great-nephew of President Washington, cited fatigue from his "participation in the celebration at Washington and Alexandria" as the reason for his missing Yorktown.[91] But at least he had attended some of the events honoring his namesake. St. George Tucker, the Virginia jurist and Yorktown siege veteran from nearby Williamsburg, declined the repeated invitations to attend various celebrations because he spent the summer and fall of 1824 at mineral springs resorts in Virginia's mountains, where his wife struggled with a grave illness.[92] His absence meant one fewer witness to the British surrender would recount those events in October 1824, that one fewer witness was left to help stage commemorations to "make the fire of youth return" to the republic. Americans took Lafayette's visit seriously and remembered the event fondly as a moment when, as the general recalled, "my feelings of patriotism were wrought up to the highest pitch. . . . That day forms a bright oasis in my recollections."[93] The challenge was to maintain that enthusiasm once Lafayette left and veterans died. Americans did little to permanently commemorate Yorktown as the scene of their climactic victory in the war for independence. As Auguste Levasseur discovered on the morning of October 20, the "temporary encampment . . . had already been abandoned."[94] Yorktown returned to obscurity soon after Lafayette's departure.

The nearby ruins and the town's dilapidated condition persisted, and actually added to its historic ambience. Levasseur felt that Yorktown "appeared from its actual condition very properly adapted to the celebration." His eye was drawn to the "houses in ruins, blackened by fire, or pierced by bullets; the ground covered with fragments of arms, the broken shells, and overturned gun carriages; tents grouped or scattered according to the nature of the ground; small platoons of soldiers placed at various points, all in a word, conveyed the idea of a camp hastily formed near a village taken and occupied after an obstinate battle."[95] Most of the anniversary celebrations took place on portions of the battlefield outside the town proper, providing the perfect backdrop for remembering the past. General Taylor had lauded the setting in his speech to Lafayette: "These plains, where the peaceful ploughshare has not yet effaced the traces of military operations; these half-decayed ramparts, this ruined village, in which the bombs' havoc is still every where visible, tells us of past warfare; and remind us of that long, arduous, and doubtful struggle, on the issue of which depended the emancipation of our country."[96] The contrast between the enthusiastic reception of Lafayette "on this day, associated with so many thrilling recollections; on this spot, consecrated by successful valour," and the dilapidated condition of Yorktown and its temporary monuments at the scene of his greatest triumph was striking.[97] Only "a small pyramid...inscribed in large letters, [with] the names of Viomenil, Rochambeau, Lauzun, St. Simon, Dumas," and other French officers who had fought at Yorktown existed after 1824.[98]

## Generals Memorialized

If the Yorktown battlefield remained largely uncommemorated, its key players did not go completely unremembered. In 1783 Congress had proposed an equestrian statue to celebrate George Washington's military triumphs. The following year Virginia commissioned French sculptor Jean-Antoine Houdon to create a statue of Washington and a bust of Lafayette for its new capitol building. Lafayette's bust arrived in 1789, and Washington's full statue was delivered in 1796. Both marble sculptures graced the building's rotunda.[99] Washington's statue proved particularly popular, and his relatives "always insisted that if any one wished to have his illustrious ancestor called up before their mind, he should go and stand in the presence of this remarkable statue—that it represented Washington as he <u>appeared</u>."[100] Yet even if these statues constituted "a good likeness," they lacked "the classic dignity which would have been given to this statue by an artist who [had] ever studied the sublime monuments left us by the ancients."[101]

Washington remained prominent in the national imagination even if relatively few monuments testified to his accomplishments. He embodied the Revolutionary struggle, the justness of its cause, and the disinterested sacrifice that many Americans saw as the basis of republicanism. His death in 1799 triggered a sixty-nine-day period of national mourning and over four hundred funeral events laden with contemporary political and cultural agendas. Most significantly, the ceremonies renewed interest in the military valor of Revolutionary War soldiers and officers. The Society of the Cincinnati revived its flagging status and claimed the role of chief mourner at many public Washington funerals, helping to "reinforce the national memory of the glorious cause."[102] Congress revisited architect Pierre-Charles L'Enfant's plans to erect an equestrian statue of Washington at the geographic center of his designed capital city, where it could be seen from both Congress and the Executive Mansion. The statue would provide a physical moral compass, the ideological and geographic core of the capital city that lawmakers and the executive would see daily. But the fledgling city's uncleared scrubland and general lack of residential development made such an undertaking impractical, and Congress instead proposed erecting a public tomb to Washington in the Capitol building. Controversy erupted once Federalist politicians revised the initial proposal into an outdoor mausoleum featuring a 100-foot-high pyramid. The monument smacked of royalist worship of the ruler over the people and exposed conflicting views of republicanism. Democratic-Republicans proposed a simple tablet where citizens could record their thoughts about Washington, thus eliminating any distinction between historic figure and common man. Mired in the electoral controversy of 1800–1801, the proposal died in Congress shortly before Thomas Jefferson became president. Although no politician openly questioned the legitimacy of commemorating Washington, the utility of erecting public monuments was not yet fully part of American conceptions of how to commemorate the past.[103]

Individual cities and states took the lead in elevating Washington to an icon preserved in stone. Baltimore raised perhaps the first large Revolutionary War monument, a 178-foot column proposed in 1809 and completed twenty years later. Protests from downtown residents that the pillar might fall on their houses delayed the erection until one of Washington's officers, Colonel John Howard, donated his own land in what was then countryside to serve as the monument's home. Travelers to Baltimore "visited Washington's monument" while on business, and the column became a popular destination.[104] Another marble statue of Washington graced the North Carolina capitol by 1820, which Levasseur considered "one of the most precious monuments" in Raleigh.[105]

Attempts to commemorate the father of his nation in the town that bore his name, including the 1799 pyramid proposal, proved less successful. The promised equestrian statue in the nation's capital remained unfinished until 1853, despite repeated efforts by Congress to provide funding. It belonged to a broader movement in the 1850s to erect equestrian monuments to military heroes, including the 1853 Andrew Jackson statue in Lafayette Square. Only the 1832 centennial of Washington's birth prompted Congress to authorize that a portrait and sculpture of Washington be installed in the Capitol Rotunda. Horatio Greenough completed the "unlucky affair" in 1841, but citizens objected to the Roman theme because the toga revealed too much of Washington's skin. David Hunter Strother saw this Washington as "a half-naked Olympian, shivering in a climate where nudity is not, and never can be, respectable," and doubted "that the American people will tolerate the nudity of Greenough's statue of Washington five more centuries hence." Greenough's attempt to depict Washington "in the costume and position of a Heathen God, a Jupiter, etc. was unfortunate for the artist." The "pitiful heathen divinity set up to be scoffed at by the children" quickly became "the butt and laughing stock of the public" and resided in the Capitol Rotunda for just two years before being relegated to the grounds.[106]

Private citizens responded to Washington's birthday centennial by forming the National Monument Society in 1832. They slowly raised funds and called for a design competition, eventually adopting architect Robert Mills's model in 1845. Mills drew on the traditions of ancient

Egypt, Persia, Greece, and Rome in arguing for monuments to "he that daring for his country or his friends to die, has signalized himself in arms, and broken the bondage of tyranny." Such a man "deserves that his name be recorded in a public and durable manner." A monument's permanence "recommends it as a means of conveying to succeeding generations, the knowledge of memorable actions and occurrences." Mills articulated a splendid idea that he found difficult to put into action. His initial design, which included statues of thirty Revolutionary War generals and politicians around a six-hundred-foot-tall obelisk, was modified due to lack of funds before President James K. Polk finally laid the cornerstone on July 4, 1848. Insufficient fund-raising and the anti-Catholic Know Nothing Party's takeover of the Washington National Monument Society halted construction in 1858, with only just over 150 vertical feet completed. The Revolution's centennial and federal assumption of construction led to the monument's completion in 1888, with a far more abstract design based more on the Bunker Hill Monument than Robert Mills's original drawings.[107]

In the meantime, a proper statue of Washington in the nation's capital still had to wait. In the decades following his death, Washington's military legacy faded, to be replaced by his residence at Mount Vernon as the primary locus of his memory. The bucolic landscape there, carefully maintained by Washington's heirs, evoked a simpler time of happy slaves and genteel masters. Any association with the plantation and its master elicited patriotic memory, even for P. T. Barnum's first humbug, the 161-year-old Joice Heth, who claimed to have nursed and raised the father of his nation. The veracity of Heth's account mattered far less than her association with Washington and Mount Vernon, both paragons of Revolutionary simplicity. Mount Vernon seemed separate from the modern world, although it could be reached by steamship from the nation's capital in a few hours. It became a premier tourist destination, and pilgrimages to Washington's tomb were an obligatory stop for any patriotic traveler.[108] Lafayette's tearful visits, including his descent into Washington's tomb, reflected the nation's reverence for the imagined past. Lafayette's son, George Washington Lafayette, who had spent several years living at Mount Vernon, "assured us that every thing in the house was as he saw it twenty-eight years ago" when Washington was still alive.[109] Such continuity validated the nostalgia that so many visitors felt. The buildings and landscape of Mount Vernon, as well as

**Figure 6.** John Trumbull, *Surrender of Lord Cornwallis* (1820). One of four Trumbull paintings depicting scenes from the American Revolution that` hang in the Capitol Rotunda, this scene shows American and French troops, the latter assembled under the white Bourbon flag, receiving the British surrender. Trumbull places American General Benjamin Lincoln at the painting's center and keeps General George Washington in the background, chronicling the British commander Lord Cornwallis's absence from the surrender ceremony, purportedly because of illness. Architect of the Capitol.

Washington's tomb, had become a monument to the man and his times. Place evoked more powerful memories than did stone memorials.

On the national level, the Continental Congress had marked important military victories with gold medals awarded to commanding generals. Yorktown was not among the eight battle medals officially struck by Congress, but American envoy to France Benjamin Franklin commissioned a medallion depicting the victories at Saratoga and Yorktown. It served "as a lasting monument of the events described on it; and to immortalize the gratitude of the united states towards their great & generous benefactor." Franklin, sensing a opportunity to further his nation's diplomatic goals, presented the medal to various French officials, as well as to Secretary of Foreign Affairs Robert Livingston and some members of Congress.[110] But Congress took no further action on the medals, instead commissioning painter John Trumbull to execute four historical mural paintings in the Capitol Rotunda, including *The Surrender of Cornwallis*. Trumbull completed the work in 1820, and

Congress installed it in 1826. Later viewers considered these "battle pieces his finest productions," in part because Trumbull was "a man of those times and a spectator and assistant at some of the scenes."[111] The space hosted Lafayette's 1824 visit, when Congress lauded the general and granted him $200,000 and a "township of land" amid the swell of patriotic enthusiasm.[112] These commemorative efforts demonstrated the many ways in which Americans physically remembered their past, even if few of them occurred on the fields of battle.

## Unmarked Battlefields

Interest in the Revolution and celebrating its key figures pervaded early republic America, especially if it centered on prominent heroes such as Washington or Lafayette. Yet commemorating the places where patriots bled to win independence failed to reach the same level of enthusiasm or success. As one patriot declared, "No spot on earth is more honoured than the grave of a soldier,"[113] yet few monuments commemorated such spaces, and whitened bones poked up from the ground at more than one battlefield. Place seemed less important than individual heroes in American memory. Still, at least twice during his travels Lafayette was overcome by the powerful associations of place. Near Orange Court House, Virginia, a triumphal arch marked the spot past which he had led a forced march to surprise Cornwallis at Michunk Creek, a turning point in the Yorktown campaign. Young women strew flowers across the path, moving the general "almost to tears" with "the honourable recollection in which the Americans held all his actions." The spot itself, where a bold move "would have been fatal, if unsuccessful," held special importance for Lafayette—it was where, he said, Cornwallis's entrapment had begun.[114] More powerful still was the site of Lafayette's first wound. While riding toward the Brandywine battlefield, Lafayette corrected his escort as they planned to cross the creek near "the point at which, as we had been informed, the army had passed" in 1777. They had come to the wrong spot: "It must be a little higher up the stream," he told them. Lafayette's memory proved correct, and his "vivid recollection excited in a high degree the admiration of the numerous witnesses."[115] On the battlefield itself, he pointed out where the armies had maneuvered and fought, until, when he arrived at the spot "where he had been wounded, he paused a moment." The militia and veterans gathered around his carriage to shout Lafayette's praises; he could only deflect the "profound emotion on his part" by lauding Washington and the troops who had fought on that September 11. The crowd preferred to idolize Lafayette himself and replied by "pointing him to the soil on which he had spilled his blood," calling it "this indestructible monument."[116] The place itself was a monument to Lafayette, and in identifying material reference points he gave meaning to place. In moving across the landscape, Lafayette gave Brandywine a narrative.[117]

His attempts to help erect traditional monuments at several battlefields proved less successful. At Camden, South Carolina, "the occasion of Lafayette's arrival was embraced by the citizens of South Carolina to lay the corner stone" of a monument to Baron Johann DeKalb, who fell on the battlefield on August 16, 1780, as British troops overwhelmed the Continental line. A procession including Masons, elected officials, and a delegation of ladies marched to military music until it reached the appointed location. "The monument" consisted of DeKalb's "remains, which had been carefully preserved," over which "the stone which was to cover them was laid by General Lafayette." Most stirring to those present was how "bending with deep humility and great emotion," Lafayette rested his hand "upon the stone, followed it as it slowly and gradually descended." Like the German DeKalb, Lafayette had left his own country to fight for liberty across the Atlantic "in a land which they both had moistened with their blood." The physical reminders—place, a stone marker, and especially DeKalb's bones—combined to elicit "many glorious and painful recollections...in the mind of Lafayette." Yet besides Bunker Hill, this was the only battlefield dedication that Lafayette attended, and DeKalb's marker was only a gravestone to a single general, not a monument to an entire battle. Yet it was "seated on classic ground. Its haunts are consecrated by the shades of heroes: its plains honored by their dust. Monuments of the revolution, on all sides remind us, of the deeds of our fathers."[118] DeKalb's burial on the field itself conferred greater significance to the stone memorial above his remains. But Lafayette had few other battlefield monuments to choose from.

In point of fact, besides the "pyramid which indicates the place where the first martyrs of liberty fell, and now repose" at Lexington, only Bunker Hill and Yorktown featured completed battlefield monuments that Lafayette visited during his trip up, down, and around the United States.[119] That one of the Revolution's great military heroes encountered so few monuments in any state of progress is surprising. That one of these monuments was inconspicuous, another wooden, and the third temporary reveals the relatively weak American interest in erecting permanent monuments to the places where their independence was won. Lafayette's tour did create enthusiasm for reclaiming the Revolution through erecting monuments, though. Shortly after his arrival, Philadelphia's citizens began a subscription campaign for a George Washington memorial in the city, and national efforts again called for a Washington tomb in the nation's capital. But Philadelphia failed to raise sufficient funds to build the statue, and Washington's family objected to moving their patriarch's remains from Mount Vernon.[120] Lafayette skipped a ceremony to lay the cornerstone for Baron von Steuben's monument near Rome, New York, because of his harried schedule, but he did manage to lay the cornerstones for two "funeral monuments" to generals Nathanael Greene and Casimir Pulaski, "which the citizens of Savannah were about to rear." The Georgians "thought that the presence of General Lafayette would add to the solemnity of the occasion." He "accepted with the more readiness and ardour" the duty of laying the cornerstone, "as he was gratified to have an occasion of publicly testifying his esteem for" the generals. Portraits of Revolutionary heroes, coin and paper money, and a medal stating that Lafayette had laid the stone were placed in "the foundation" at "the bottom of the excavation."[121] These monuments, like the DeKalb marker at Camden, were not yet complete and commemorated individual officers, not the battles in which they fought.

Patriots beyond the lower South preferred to commemorate great men as well, again far from the sites of military valor. By the 1790s stone markers commemorated the lives of Generals Joseph Warren, Israel Putnam, Richard Montgomery, and Anthony Wayne.[122] But even these few successful commemorations quickly escaped the public's imagination. Warren's 1794 wooden pillar at Bunker Hill began to rot, Putnam's Connecticut gravestone deteriorated, and the pyramid above Montgomery's repatriated remains became an innocuous object passed by on the way to services in New York City's St. Paul's Chapel. One 1824 observer noted the "considerable dilapidation going on among the monuments" at the church. Wayne's simple obelisk in an eastern Pennsylvania churchyard covered his bones, but his organs and rendered flesh remained buried hundreds of miles west in Erie, where he had died.[123]

Less famous soldiers fared far more poorly, even amid a culture that believed citizen-soldiers, not regular Continental army troops, had won the Revolution. The people of Lexington, Massachusetts, erected perhaps the only successful monument to ordinary soldiers. They dedicated a simple obelisk on the town green in 1799, on the very spot where the Revolution began. By the time that Lafayette viewed the monument it constituted "hallowed ground, consecrated by the blood of the first martyrs to liberty."[124] Efforts to erect a monument at Wallabout Bay, Brooklyn, to remember the roughly eleven thousand patriots who died in dank British prison ships there began in 1802, yet no monument was raised until 1844, and it remained incomplete until 1908. An 1826 pamphleteer attributed such indifference to "Ingratitude! Ingratitude to the memory of those who suffered, who bled, who died in their cause!"[125]

Before 1830, only three monuments to Revolutionary War soldiers rose at the places they fought: in 1817 the citizens of Chester County, Pennsylvania, reinterred the bones of several American soldiers resting under a cairn. A marble obelisk now marked the site of the "Paoli Massacre."[126] Leading men in New London, Connecticut, proposed construction of the Fort Griswold monument in 1825, perhaps motivated by Lafayette's visit the previous year. The soldiers who were "*massacred, after the Fort was surrendered: not shot, but killed with the sword, the bayonet, and the butt of the musket,*" deserved commemoration. Both the Paoli and Fort Griswold monuments honored soldiers as victims of, not participants in, violence. Their innocence proclaimed the justness of the patriot cause and the treacherousness of British tyranny. Local pride and community activism succeeded in building monuments to remember the "debt of Honor, to the estates of soldiers, who died in its service."[127] But that only Paoli, Fort Griswold, and Lexington did so indicates the difficulty involved in erecting battlefield monuments.

## Attempts at Battlefield Commemoration

Despite a handful of gravestones and obelisks, Americans erected few monuments during the early republic. Lafayette's 1824–25 national tour belongs to a triumvirate of events, also including the fiftieth anniversary of the Declaration of Independence and the nearly simultaneous deaths of Thomas Jefferson and John Adams on July 4, 1826, that sparked Americans' interest in their past and increased patriotism. It was a moment when "Americans were explaining themselves to one another and to the world." It was not, however, the genesis of widespread and effective monument building in the 1820s and 1830s. Expert at staging parades, giving toasts, firing artillery salutes, and making speeches, Americans equivocated about how best to permanently commemorate the Revolution.[128]

The series of events around the jubilee may have initiated a flurry of American monument *planning,* but effected only lethargic monument *building.* One "hoary veteran," Colonel Allen McLann, returned to Norfolk, Virginia, during Lafayette's visit and swapped tales of the nearby battle of Great Bridge with his fellow veterans. "'And yet,' he added, after a pause, 'no monumental marble has been raised to perpetuate its recollection! It must not be so. Old as I am, I will try if I cannot excite this brave and patriotic people to erect a MONUMENT commemorative of an achievement of which Virginia may well boast, and which the nation may contemplate with pride and pleasure.'" McLann endeavored to organize a committee and to raise funds for a monument. As a matter of civic pride and patriotism, Great Bridge "ought to be more honored in our memory.... Who will—who *can* refuse to cooperate with this venerable patriot in an undertaking which cannot fail to enlist the best feelings and wishes of the nation, and to reflect lasting honor on our patriotism and liberality?" But no obelisk rose above the Great Bridge battlefield for another seventy-five years.[129]

Even at Lafayette's most famous battlefield dedication, Bunker Hill, progress in erecting a monument was slow. Early in his tour Lafayette "inspected the works" at Charlestown and "ascended Bunker Hill...the spot where [General Warren's] blood stained the soil."[130] Lafayette called the site "holy ground."[131] He even promised to return for a monument dedication on the battle's fiftieth anniversary, just ten months later, and subscribed to the monument fund.[132] As his secretary put it, "His answer was received by the acclamations of the multitude and the roar of the artillery."[133] Lafayette provided the first celebrity endorsement for a historic commemoration.

Forty-five thousand citizens attended the June 17, 1825, ceremony during Lafayette's visit. Over seven thousand marchers, including military officials and politicians, two hundred Revolutionary War veterans, and forty Bunker Hill survivors carrying their cartridge boxes, preceded Lafayette's "superb calash drawn by six white horses." Music and artillery hailed the procession, and one Bunker Hill veteran displayed the drum he had beaten at the celebrated battle. One token of the Revolution, "the modest pyramid" commemorating Warren, "had disappeared." The Masons transformed the wooden base of the monument into "a cane" with a gold head inscribed to Lafayette. He "accepted it as one of the most precious relics of the American revolution." All that remained was a large hole in the ground where the new monument would rise. Lafayette, Daniel Webster, and the monument's architect laid the cornerstone in the gap, and Masons enacted their rituals before proclaiming the ceremony complete. The crowd moved to an amphitheater on the northeast side of the hill, where Daniel Webster held forth on the battle and its patriotic significance. General Lafayette sat in a chair at the front of his fellow veterans "as the only surviving general of the Revolution." Songs and prayers completed the event, which was followed by more artillery salutes and a banquet under a temporary wooden pavilion. "Four thousand four hundred plates were set and not one was unoccupied." Lafayette concluded the evening with a toast to freedom that "was enthusiastically received."[134] But it would be another eighteen years before the association secured sufficient funds to complete the monument. Parades, speeches, artillery salutes, and banquets captured American interest more than did completing monuments. Webster delivered yet another stirring speech upon the monument's completion, but Lafayette could not hear or see the celebration. By 1843 he had been dead for almost nine years.[135]

The many battlefields located far from cities like Boston remained unremembered or barely commemorated. At Saratoga in 1795, the Duke de la Rochefoucauld-Liancourt expressed "astonishment that neither Congress nor the Legislature of New York should have erected a monument on this spot."[136] Thirty years later no monument had been erected, and another visitor worried that "future generations may in vain seek for the scenes of these important events, unless they are marked by some durable memorial."[137] No less sacred a spot than Valley Forge, which "must necessarily awaken in our minds the recollection

of the gloomy seasons of the revolution," lacked commemorative architecture in 1811, despite a magazine's insistence that there "should be
erected a monument" on the battlefield.[138] At Kings Mountain in rural
South Carolina, a small 1815 stone marked the grave of Major William
Chronicle, but the majority of soldiers from both sides received no formal commemoration, as their bones littered the surrounding hillsides
before eventually disintegrating.[139] Well after Lafayette's national tour
such laments continued.

In 1838 Southern advocates of Colonel James Williams invoked
"family pride...to induce his numerous, wealthy, and respectable
grandchildren, to do that which his country has not yet done,—erect
a monument to his memory." They never answered the call.[140] Most
veterans remained like the hero of Huck's Defeat, Colonel William
Bratton: "His monument is neither brass nor marble, column or tablet, but his own heroic deeds enshrined in the hearts of his admiring
countrymen." For the ordinary soldiers of that battle, "No sculptural
marble or monumental stone, points us to this battlefield, and tells of
the exploits and triumphs of the men, who gained this glorious victory."[141] Too many men "sleep in unhonored graves" with "no monument erected" to their sacrifice.[142] The *Freemason's Magazine* declared,
"The backwardness of our nation, in erecting monuments to those
who trode the fields of danger in the revolutionary war, is universally reprobated."[143] But opinions could not quarry, carve, and dedicate
stone memorials. Little help was forthcoming from governmental or
private sources.[144]

Despite Lafayette's cornerstone-laying at several sites and other
plans to erect monuments, calling 1826 "a year when granite or marble
monuments to Revolutionary greatness were being erected" or a time
of a "wave of monument building" emphasizes intention over completion.[145] A comprehensive survey of the seventy-three Revolutionary
War battlefields categorized as Class A and B "Principal Sites" by the
National Park Service identifies only three battlefield monuments that
were initiated around the time of Lafayette's visit, plus the two statues
to fallen generals.[146] And not one of these monuments stood complete
before 1843. Only the Fort Griswold monument, begun in 1826 and
dedicated in 1830, stood as an example of successful, rapid monument
building that resulted from the nation's jubilee—pushing the start of
effective monument building to later in the nineteenth century.[147]

**Table 1.** Pre-1860 monuments

| Battlefield | State | First commemorative effort | Monument erected |
|---|---|---|---|
| Yorktown | VA | 1781 | 1884 |
| Lexington | MA | 1799 | 1799 |
| Kings Mountain | SC | 1814 | 1815 |
| Bunker Hill | MA | 1823 | 1843 |
| Camden | SC | 1825 | 1909 |
| Wyoming Valley | PA | 1826 | 1843 |
| Concord | MA | 1836 | 1837 |
| Trenton | NJ | 1843 | 1893 |
| Waxhaws | SC | 1845 | 1860 |
| Monmouth | NJ | 1846 | 1884 |
| Bennington | NY/VT | 1854 | 1891 |
| Fort Ticonderoga | NY | 1854 | 1909 |
| Cowpens | SC | 1856 | 1856 |
| Guilford Courthouse | NC | 1857 | 1887 |
| Moore's Creek | NC | 1857 | 1907 |
| Hubbardton | VT | 1859 | 1859 |

Americans proposed only sixteen battlefield monuments at "Principal Sites" before 1860, and completed just eight of them by that date. The average time required to complete a Revolutionary War monument exceeded thirty-one years in the pre-1860 period. Wait times shortened to almost eight years around the Revolution's centennial and were quite rapid around the turn of the twentieth century and in the years that followed. By the mid-twentieth century, most monuments were completed shortly after civic organizations or governments announced their plans. But thirty-one battlefields never raised a formal monument and either settled for a state historical marker or, as with many New York City battlefields, became part of the urban environment. The rise of memorial architecture came several years after 1826, with rural cemeteries such as Mount Auburn (1831), Laurel Hill (1836), and Greenwood (1837) attracting tourists who contemplated the elaborate statues and obelisks memorializing the worthies of Boston, Philadelphia, and Brooklyn, respectively. Until those sites showed Americans what memorial architecture could look like, and transformed death from an event associated with gloom to one promising hope in the afterlife, commemorating the dead played a limited role in American culture.[148] Not commemorating battlefields set

**Table 2.** Time required for battlefield monument completion

| Year begun | Average years to completion | Number of monuments |
|---|---|---|
| 1781–1826 | 31.1 | 6 |
| 1827–35 | n/a | 0 |
| 1836–59 | 27.5 | 10 |
| 1860–70 | n/a | 0 |
| 1871–79 | 7.9 | 6 |
| 1880–95 | n/a | 0 |
| 1896–1912 | 2.0 | 11 |
| 1913–24 | n/a | 0 |
| 1925–76 | 1.0 | 8 |

*Sources*: American Battlefield Protection Program, National Park Service, Department of the Interior, *Report to Congress on the Historic Preservation of Revolutionary War and War of 1812 Sites in the United States* (Washington, DC, 2007); websites for the National Park Service, state and local government agencies, individual battlefield preservation organizations; the Historical Marker Database (www.hmdb.org). I exclude the 1860 Yorktown marker from this analysis. See pages 179–81.

the norm for the republic's first century, mirroring the chronology of European sites.[149]

## Congressional Dithering

One of the most obvious candidates for commemoration and preservation, Yorktown, repeatedly faced disappointment. In 1781, just ten days after the British surrender there, and five days after news of the victory reached Philadelphia, the Continental Congress authorized "to be erected at York, in Virginia, a marble column, adorned with emblems of the alliance between the United States and his Most Christian Majesty; and inscribed with a succinct narrative of the surrender of Earl Cornwallis to the allied" American and French forces.[150] The resolution remained unfulfilled when Lafayette walked the battlefield in 1824, although in 1834 the citizens of Yorktown and nearby communities reminded Congress of its earlier promise.[151] A select committee considered the matter and agreed that "no event in our history is more worthy of commemoration than that which crowned the American revolution with success and triumph," but a proposed bill never passed.[152] The next Congress considered funding a Yorktown monument; limited financial resources and Congress's commitment to the

Washington Monument doomed that effort as well. Virginia congressmen attempted to fund the monument in 1838 and 1848, again without success beyond congressional pledges that the monument "be carried into effect."[153]

The 1838 effort to complete the monument discovered a larger problem. Between 1776 and 1786, Congress had promised to construct twelve different Revolutionary War monuments, eleven to generals, and the Yorktown battlefield obelisk. But only one, an equestrian statue to George Washington, was "under execution" by 1838, and it was never completed with that design.[154] The Committee on Military Affairs reported that none of the ten other monuments to important generals had been completed, "and that no money has been paid from the treasury for that purpose." Resolutions to construct monuments that once "contributed to stimulate the exertions of those who achieved our independence" lacked urgency decades after their passage. In 1838 "it might not be expedient to erect the monuments," the committee noted. Yet Congress had "pledged the nation's faith" and promised that the memorials to Generals Montgomery, Warren, Mercer, Wooster, Herkimer, Nash, DeKalb, Davidson, Scriven, and Greene "be carried into effect." With regard to the single national monument to a Revolutionary War battle, Yorktown, the committee reminded Congress of the need "to appreciate the importance of an event that terminated the struggle of our fathers for liberty and independence." And it should not be done cheaply, but "in a style corresponding with the importance of the event." Yet nothing happened at Yorktown.[155] The grand designs of the nation's capital and its ornate Washington Monument took precedence over individual battlefields. "Democracy," Alexis de Tocqueville wrote, "not only encourages the making of a lot of trivial things but also inspires the erection of a few very large monuments."[156] A plain obelisk to fallen soldiers on a battlefield would have to wait; the six-hundred-foot monument near the halls of power came first. No permanent "marble column" commemorated Yorktown until 1884.

The 1824 celebrations surrounding Lafayette's visit resulted in few long-term changes to Yorktown's appearance. The town and battlefield continued to offer a canvas upon which visitors painted their own memories. Former governor and U.S. senator John Tyler, in his 1837 address to the Virginia militia at Yorktown, felt the need to point out various redoubts, "traces of which are now scarcely discernible." Before comparing the valor of Lafayette and Washington to heroes of the ancient world, he self-consciously defended the gathering at ruined Yorktown. He wondered "why stand we here, my countrymen, on this almost deserted spot, this day? Have we come but to pass an idle hour, in gazing on these mounds of earth—this village in decay—that noble river, and yon more distant sea?" Yorktown lacked distinction in comparison with "other lands more fair—other mounds more lofty—other ruins more splendid," and especially in terms of scenery. There were "other prospects which, to the mere lover of the picturesque, are equally captivating." Rejecting the kind of scenic tourism that made sites such as Ticonderoga and the Hudson Highlands famous, Tyler declared, "we are here for a far nobler purpose." The ruins themselves provided reason enough to visit Yorktown. "Each object which this scene presents to the sight, is consecrated in the memory as a proud memento of a glorious past: they speak to us of other times, and of other men. They tell us a tale of heroic fortitude—of patriotic devotion—and of majestic triumph." For a visitor, "the ground on which he treads, is hallowed; and the ennobling objects around him, picture to his mind deeds there enacted in days long gone by, for the good of mankind.... There is yet a voice proceeding from each ruin—it speaks from each broken stone—from each crumbling mound."[157]

Yorktown attracted traveler Charles Campbell precisely because it lacked carefully designed and manicured monuments. "The spot is consecrated by the ashes of the illustrious dead, the charms of nature, its antique recollections and the classic associations of the siege and surrender." Its ruins provided the allure. The Nelson house, once the dwelling of Virginia governor and militia general Thomas Nelson Jr., still stood at Yorktown's center, where it had suffered from the American bombardment during the siege. It offered an ideal relic for contemplation, "traces of the damages being yet visible." Inside the brick structure "a panel in the wainscoat is still loose, from the effects of a cannon-ball, or bomb-shell."[158] The persistence of Yorktown's damaged structures—whether military or civilian—supplied much of its charm. Described by one visitor as "a pretty little town" and "this little locality," Yorktown, in its simplicity, belied its own historic significance. Moore's house, where British officers met their American and French counterparts and agreed to surrender terms, still stood nearby.

MOORE'S HOUSE—Yorktown, Va.
In which Lord Cornwallis signed Articles of Capitulation to the Combined American and French forces, Oct 19th, 1781.

**Figure 7.** *Moore's House at York Town,* from the *Family Magazine* (1835). Just a few years after Lafayette's triumphant return to Yorktown, the town had once again fallen into decay. Moore's House, where the surrender terms had been negotiated, now attracted livestock instead of generals. The bucolic scene allowed travelers to ruminate on the contrast wrought by time. Virginia Historical Society (F234 Y6 M641 1835).

The *Family Magazine* published a pastoral engraving of the building, including two cows lazing in its yard. "There it is, in its primitive simplicity, invested as it is with all its glorious associations, precisely as it stands at this very moment, just as it was then. The same house— the same windows—the same clapboards—the same dormer roof—the same old kitchen—the same green pasture in front—and the identical beautiful York river, stretching off with its mirrored surface in the distance." The accompanying text lauded the American victory and criticized British arrogance, but the scenic beauty and ordinariness of the setting were most noteworthy. Because great events took place in such humble surroundings, they were all the more important.[159] Still, both the *Family Magazine* and John Tyler wondered why Congress had not yet completed the monument they originally had promised in 1781. Even Lafayette could not prompt its construction.

# CHAPTER FOUR

# Memory without Tourism

## Traces of the Southern Campaigns

When Robert Gilmor tried to visit "the celebrated field of battle" at Eutaw Springs, in South Carolina, in 1806, he got stuck on a swampy road en route and found "the accommodations at Richboro very bad." He "gave up my plan of visiting" and continued on his journey to Charleston, never reaching the battlefield. Later Gilmor managed to visit "the celebrated field where the battle of Camden was fought at Hobkirk's Hill," perhaps because he did so during "my morning ride" from a friend's nearby house.[1] A quarter century later Rowland Gibson Hazard managed a quick carriage ride from a friend's nearby home to "the Eutaw Spgs and battle ground." But instead of commenting on the battlefield, he noted that "the Springs are the handsomest I ever saw and I enjoyed the day tho it rained all the afternoon and we returned in a violent storm."[2] The two travelers' accounts represent the limited interactions with Southern Revolutionary War battlefields that Americans experienced, as well as the relative indifference many held toward those places. With little tourist infrastructure and neglected or abandoned battlefields, the American South grappled with what to make of the Revolutionary War. Most chose to look away from the bone-strewn battlefields and eroding earthworks. Battlefields across the American South provided too many reminders of bloodshed, defeat, and painful internal divisions that were best ignored or at least neglected. Isolated rural locales such as Guilford Courthouse, Camden, Ninety-Six, Cowpens, or Kings Mountain proved difficult to reach, and the busy ports of Charleston and Savannah obliterated their battlefields. Even Yorktown, left behind by transportation innovations, remained a backwater. The reality of place made preserving battlefields, erecting monuments, or engaging in battlefield tourism difficult in the post–Revolutionary War South. That region cultivated interest in ruined landscapes much later than the North, preferring to construct Southern Revolutionary War memory from relics and legends. Joseph Johnson captured the essence of Southern memory when he visited the Eutaw Springs battlefield. Johnson "heard many exciting stories of it, of the dead, and even of their ghosts."[3]

## Guilford Courthouse

Among the stops on George Washington's 1791 tour of the South was Guilford Courthouse, in North Carolina, where "a considerable gathering of people . . . came to satisfy their curiosity" and view the president and former general, if not the field of battle. Washington "examined the ground" with his usual military eye, but could only ride "over that where their lines were formed and the scene closed in the retreat of the American forces."[4] General Nathanael Greene had skillfully employed American militia and the Continental line in confronting General Charles Cornwallis's British regulars across mostly open ground. The March 1781 battle, a nominal defeat but strategic victory for the Americans, was fought on the run, and neither army erected massive entrenchments or built extensive fortifications, leaving few remnants of the engagement to guide Washington's investigation of the battlefield.[5]

The area around Guilford Courthouse failed to thrive, perhaps because of reports by local residents of "foul odors and the presence of spirits." Several nearby residents later told a local historian "that they were on the ground the next day . . . and saw the British burying their dead. They said that they buried a *great many* in the field where Mr. Hoskins now lives and not very far from his house, perhaps, a little to the west, where they dug two large pits and laid in the men one on top of another." With this and many other grisly remnants of war nearby,

Guilford Courthouse ceased to exist as a municipality in 1785. Alexander Martin attempted to develop a town named Martinsville, but in 1809 county courts ceased to meet there and farmers concentrated on cultivating the littered battlefield's one thousand acres and clearing the remaining forest. Guilford Courthouse literally vanished from the map.[6]

Anyone intrepid enough to visit the battlefield would have encountered a "very disagreeable road" toward Guilford Courthouse made of "a soft clay badly cut up by wagons, numberless stumps, some steep hills, the ascent obstructed by large stones." To make matters worse, "There is no good tavern in the whole of this distance."[7] Traveling on a still "road bad" in 1835, George Rogers "passed by the old iron work where the American[s] retreated to after the battle."[8] The site itself revealed little about the battle. "The court-house is gone; [and] the village is wasted to a house."[9]

The battlefield remained difficult to reach and neglected when David Hunter Strother, writing under the pseudonym Porte Crayon, visited in the late 1850s, while traveling by train across North Carolina. At "Greensborough" he felt the need to "tarry to visit the battle-field, which is but a few miles distant." Without Guilford Courthouse's attraction he would likely have passed by, since "there is nothing about [Greensboro's] exterior either to prepossess or interest the passing traveler."[10] Five miles on horseback "through muddy lanes" brought Strother to "this interesting locality" of the battlefield. His interest mingled with "something of awe" when he arrived "in the midst of a group of ruined chimneys and decayed wooden houses, all, save one, ruined and deserted....I knew instinctively that I was upon the field of Guilford." Steeped in "the descriptions I had read," from military histories, Strother recognized the battlefield's topographical landmarks, the spot having experienced "so little change since the day of the battle." He approached a farmer tilling a nearby field who "indicated the different points where the hardest fighting had been, showed an old tree which had been struck by a cannon-shot, and said that in plowing, even at this day, he frequently turned up bullets, bayonets, and portions of arms and accoutrements that had withstood the tooth of time." One day the farmer's harvest yielded "a complete musket-lock, much rusted and standing at full cock." No other object amid the farmer's assortment of war memorabilia garnered more of Strother's attention.

VIEW OF THE BATTLE-GROUND.[2]

**Figure 8.** *View of the Battle-Ground* (Guilford Courthouse), from Benson Lossing, *Pictorial Field-Book of the Revolution* (1850). When Lossing visited the scene of one of the United States's key strategic victories, on a windy, snowy January day in 1849, he found only "a few dilapidated and deserted buildings" and one inhabitant, a farmer. Most rural Southern battlefields suffered from similar neglect. Author's collection.

The farmer told Strother, "'It looked more like fighting. The man that cocked that gun was killed perhaps before he had time to pull the trigger. Many a time, Sir, when I am idle, I take that lock in my hand and look at it, until I feel curious like, as though the battle that was fought so many years ago was somehow brought nearer to us.'" Sophisticated readers might expect such an emotional reaction from "the unlettered plowman," but Porte Crayon assured his readers that the "quaint talisman...might even set more learned men to thinking."[11]

Strother represented a new kind of traveler, the roving reporter who sent back illustrated catalogs of his adventures to readers who shared his pleasure in observing the curiosities of American life outside the more refined eastern cities. He wrote in the same style as Benson Lossing, whose *Pictorial Field-Book of the Revolution* revived the young nation's interest in its old battlefields. Strother went so far as to quote Lossing and to reproduce his sketch of Guilford Courthouse. This type of travel writing featured glances at historic sites from a tourist constantly on the move. Strother spent just a few hours at Guilford Courthouse and only one night in nearby Greensboro. His tour followed the course of the North Carolina Railroad, allowing him to "hear the old familiar names of Revolutionary memory…as we pass along." Names such as Guilford Courthouse or Haw River "make the heart leap in recalling the wild, romantic details of the Southern war, all the more thrilling that they have escaped the varnish of spiritless limners, and are not heard in the common babblings of fame."[12]

The very obscurity of the South's Revolutionary War battlefields, at least from the tourist's gaze, provided much of their allure. As one visitor noted, "Taking your stand on this highest ground, where the court-house stood, you may look over the whole battlefield."[13] Compared with a memorialized landscape like Bunker Hill or decaying ruins like Ticonderoga, Guilford Courthouse's relatively intact scenery provided a blank slate upon which to sketch memory. Those unable to interpret this barren landscape relied on living monuments they met along the way to comprehend the soldiers' sacrifices and struggle for independence. Near Guilford Courthouse George Rogers "stopped at the house of an old revolutionary soldier who told me all about it."[14] The Marquis de Chastellux encountered another Guilford Courthouse veteran immediately after the war. Traveling through Virginia's Shenandoah Valley in 1782, he sought lodging at David Steele's home and mill. The twenty-two-year-old possessed a "charming face, fine teeth, red lips, and rosy cheeks," yet "appeared sluggish and inactive." When asked about his condition, Steele replied that "he had been in a languished state ever since the battle of Guilford Courthouse, where he had received fifteen or sixteen sword wounds." He provided an object lesson in British tyranny, as it was after he "was made prisoner, that he had been thus cruelly slashed." While on the ground, "beaten down and bathed in blood, he had still had presence of mind enough to think that his cruel enemies would not want to leave any witness or victim of their barbarity, and that there remained to him no other way of saving his life than to pretend to have lost it." By playing dead Steele survived the battle and returned to Virginia, where he and his "young and pretty" wife offered Chastellux a simple but filling meal. Their company "made us pass agreeably the time," aided in large part by "the interest with which Mr. Steel inspired us." Besides relating tales of his sufferings in battle, "he had a piece of his own skull, which his wife brought out to show me."[15] Apparently the fragment came from "a wound above his left eye. His skull bone had been cut through and the severed bone was hanging just by the skin. That piece of bone was

**Figure 9.** Bone fragment from the skull of David Steele. Wounded by a British sword at Guilford Courthouse on March 15, 1781, Steele recovered and lived until 1840, wearing a silver plate over his wound. He operated a tavern and grist mill in western Virginia and on occasion would produce the skull fragment for curious travelers. Special Collections, University of Virginia Library.

removed and a silver plate was put in its place and worn by him for the rest of his life." Also wounded severely in the shoulder, Steele belonged to a company of Virginia militia that suffered heavy casualties at Guilford Courthouse. He lived to be eighty-four years old, his "sandy-red, curly hair" concealing "his disfigurement." Steele continued to operate the flour mill visited by Chastellux, made rifle stocks and furniture, and ran a tavern. "He kept this piece of bone, which is elliptical in shape and about the size of a silver dollar, to show his friends" and perhaps visitors to his tavern. Steele said "it was the only medal he had to show."[16]

This kind of relic, whether a human remain or physical object, constituted much of the Revolutionary War memory in the South. With the passage of time such mementos lost their power to enliven the past. David Hunter Strother's 1857 visit to Guilford Courthouse relied instead on his imagination: "There was not a human being in sight of whom to make inquiry" among the abandoned town. "Unmarred by monuments, uncontaminated by improvements, the view of the silent, lonely fields and woods brought the old times back, so fresh, so real, so near." Calling upon "wizard fancy" to "fling me a picture of the fight," Strother reanimated the scene. "The hills are again crowned with armed battalions. The rolling of drums, the startling bugle call, the voice of command, break the silence of the budding forest." He recounted the "lines of the grim Continentals, men of reliable mettle" who stood patient and calm as the militia fled past them, the thunder of cannons, "the long scarlet lines" of British infantry, and the cavalry charge that halted the British advance. When, in his imagined battle, as part of William Washington's American cavalry, "with hoof and sabre, trampled I the dust!" Strother/Crayon exulted: "I rose up in my stirrups, and gave a shout that made old Guilford's echoes ring again."[17] His highly personal reenactment of the battle occurred because Guilford Courthouse remained largely unchanged. The blank landscape, punctuated by a few half-ruined buildings, allowed Strother to interact with place without the guidance of reconstructed lines or newly erected monuments.

## Travel to Southern Battlefields

Battlefields like Guilford Courthouse remained undeveloped in part because they were very difficult to reach. In general, traveling in the post-Revolution South involved uncertainty and risk. British merchant Robert Hunter found it exceedingly difficult to obtain "satisfactory information" regarding stagecoach travel from Virginia into the Carolinas in 1786. The prospect of traveling to Charleston made him "almost frightened at the dreadful account that a gentleman has given me who has lately traveled through North Carolina." Hunter encountered flooded creeks that delayed crossings over rickety bridges, or tippy "canoes" and ferries, "miserable" inns, irregular schedules, and indifferent scenery.[18] To make matters worse, most battles of the southern campaigns had been fought in the backcountry, far from major population centers and transportation hubs. The largely rural, small-town character of the American South, at least outside the major port cities, limited the interaction that Americans could have with important battlefields such as Guilford Courthouse, Cowpens, or Kings Mountain.

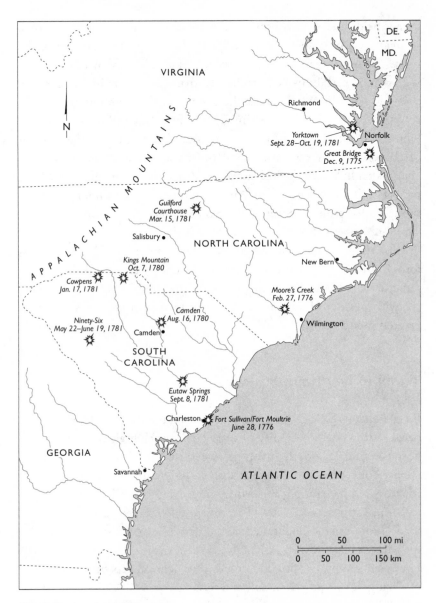

**Map 5.** Southern battlefields.

George Washington faced challenging road conditions during his goodwill tour of the Southern states in 1791. The president traveled from Virginia through the Carolinas along the coast to Savannah, although he would "return, by an upper road," through the backcountry.[19] His party included an aide, Major William Jackson, and five servants, "a

Chariet & four horses drove in hand—a light baggage Waggon & two horses—four Saddle horses besides a led one for myself."[20] Although he traveled in style, Washington's entourage faced the same perils as other travelers. Moving inland from Savannah, Washington crossed pine barrens "of the worst sort, being hilly as well as poor." The road to Augusta was "more uneven than I had been accustomed to since leavg. Petersburgh in Virginia." The wretched roads and heat near Columbia, South Carolina, "foundered one of my horses very badly."[21] For less affluent travelers in all parts of the South, stagecoaches left before dawn each morning, paused for a brief breakfast after more than a dozen miles of travel, and rode another twenty or more miles before dinner, sometimes totaling eighteen hours of travel. Muddy roads bogged the coaches down to the point where passengers "were obliged to get out and clap our shoulders to the wheels, to assist a restive horse." On hot days passengers "walked several miles to ease the horses."[22] The typical road consisted of "trunks of trees laid parallel, the interstices filled up with earth, sand or any material near at hand."[23] In general, Washington criticized "the abominably Sandy & heavy" roads just beyond the port cities. By his estimate, from Savannah he faced "150 or 200 miles of heavy sand to pass before I fairly get into the upper, & firmer roads."[24] Yet even there, travelers "got stuck in the mud" and their carriage springs "were broke" by the rough ride. George Rogers considered the route "so bad that I could not get along at any rate." In frustration the traveling salesman recorded, "roads this day as bad as ever."[25]

Roadside lodgings offered little improvement. Robert Hunter "retired to a most disagreeable bed, where I got no sleep for the bugs and mosquitoes."[26] Even a distinguished traveler like Washington discovered that "the only Inn short of Hallifax having...no Rooms or beds which appeared tolerable, & every thing else having a dirty appearance, I was compelled to keep on" until finding suitable accommodations.[27] According to another traveler, "along many of the Roads in our more Southern States, the Stranger in vain looks for the comfortable Inns" that might be found farther north. When a traveler did manage to find "small taverns," the inns were "destitute of the means of well kept Hotels."[28] If a stagecoach or later railway car stopped at "a log hotel...the weary passengers desired rest, but could not find it. Men, women, and children, as they best could, composed themselves on the floor, some took to the benches, and some to the few rickety chairs which had survived their more useful days."[29] Forced to improvise bedding from her cloak and a chair, Ann Maury spent the night "much disturbed with the fiddling and dancing" at one North Carolina inn.[30] While teamsters or traveling salesmen may have been content to spend a night in such meager accommodations, they "would not be very attractive to northerners."[31] The tourist class expected better.

Wealthier or better-connected travelers could find more tolerable accommodations. Southerners felt obliged to entertain travelers of sufficient social standing with food, drink, and lodging if they knocked on the door. Robert Gilmor stopped at the plantation of "Col. [John] Chesnutt...one of the richest cotton planters in Carolina," in 1806 and "was received with a great deal of hospitality, and offered a bed in the house." Once he left the Chesnut plantation, Gilmor, a wealthy Baltimore merchant traveling south for his health, employed his friendships within the DeSaussure and Gilchrist families to gain entry into Charleston society. He even met and eventually married Sarah Ladron, "daughter of James Ladron, an old revolutionary officer."[32] Such personal connections eased the burden of travel and provided comfortable accommodations, but applied only to the most privileged travelers. For those who lacked letters of introduction, travel in the South remained a haphazard affair. As Washington wrote, "It is not easy to say on which road—the one I went or the one I came—the entertainment is most indifferent—but with truth it may be added, that both are bad."[33]

Scenic landscapes—which might compensate for bumpy roads and wretched taverns—were also lacking in most of the South. Travelers considered the region between Charleston and South Carolina's upland "one of the most dreary I ever beheld; it appeared to be nothing but one immense *pine-barren,* extending for thirty or forty miles."[34] William Blandford dismissed the region as having "no particular interest, being only slightly diversified by woods and hills with few houses and generally poor soil."[35] By the 1850s railroads increased the speed of travel across the "dark wilderness of pines."[36] Yet one passenger complained that she had "never traveled through such an uninteresting country. You don't know anything about gloominess until you travel through that country."[37] Southern roads, scenery, and accommodations continued to provide few amenities for travelers who might have tried to reach the upcountry battlefields. "In America," wrote English traveler

Basil Hall while in North Carolina, "where the labour of a journey must not be measured by its length, we were never sure how we were likely to be off as to roads or accommodation, till we came to try."[38]

Even in 1850, when sectional tensions led to an increase in Southern travel, the region "was completely unprepared." Destinations emerged that "had scarcely ever been indicated on the maps. The means for reaching them were rude and hastily provided. The roads were rough.... The craziest carriages were hastily put in requisition, to run upon the wildest highways." Railroads hauled passengers in "long and massive frames of timber, set on wheels, with unplaned benches, an interminable range, crowded with the living multitudes, wedged affectionately together, like herrings in boxes." Where the railroads ended, "Paths, only just blazed from the woods, conducted you to habitations scarcely less wild." Even genteel planters could be found lodged in "frames covered with clapboards,—queer-looking log tenements, unplastered chambers, and little uncouth cabins, eight by twelve."[39] Accommodations for travelers, wherever they hailed from, were far from adequate, even at mineral springs resorts. Getting around the South was no pleasure trip, and most Southern tourists chose to visit Northern resorts and cities, or Europe. With relatively little transportation infrastructure, tourism was slow to develop in the American South.[40]

## Coastal Fortifications

Yet even in easily reached coastal cities, tourists found few Revolutionary War fortifications to interpret and commemorate. Many travelers, whether on business or pleasure, visited the bustling ports of Charleston and Savannah, where key battles had raged in both the early and later stages of the war. Just west of Charleston lay the landward defenses, which were quickly being overtaken by the city's growth. In 1791 George Washington "visited and examined the lines of Attack & defence of the City" from the Spring 1780 siege by British forces. Washington's inspection of the lines on Charleston Neck left him "satisfied that the defence was noble & honorable altho the measure was undertaken upon wrong principles and impolitic."[41] Washington emphasized military strategy and the necessity of fortifying Charleston's barrier islands, where General William Moultrie had successfully defended

**Figure 10.** John Blake White, *Battle of Fort Moultrie* (1826). South Carolina lawyer and painter White depicted the battle from within the American fort, as British ships bombarded its palmetto log walls. On the left, holding the South Carolina flag, is William Jasper, who famously rallied the troops during the battle and later became an icon of Southern nationalism. U.S. Senate Collection.

against an amphibious British attack in 1776. The day after his tour of the landward trenches Washington "visited the Works of Fort Johnson on James's Island, and Fort Moultree on Sullivans Island." He hoped to find an explanation for American general Benjamin Lincoln's surrender of Charleston's five thousand troops in 1780, but these important posts both stood "in ruins, and scarcely a trace of the latter left—the former quite fallen."[42] Charleston's decaying forts provided few lessons for the commander in chief. "Only three or four batteries, part good, part bad" remained shortly after his visit. The fortifications were "very injudiciously constructed," leading to their rapid decay.[43]

A less martial visitor to Charleston might find it "rich in historical recollections relating to the days of the American Revolution." But one Northern traveler felt no need to visit those sites, terming Charleston's Revolutionary War history a subject "with which every intelligent American citizen is familiar."[44] Fort Sullivan became a curiosity, having been "built in great haste from trunks of the cabbage-tree." This building material was "highly recommended for entrenchments, as the balls of the enemy cannot splinter it."[45] After 1809 visitors saw the third fort on Sullivan's Island, the earlier versions having fallen into the sea or been destroyed by a hurricane. No remains of the original palmetto and sand fort existed after the mid-1790s.[46] Charleston's prominent families built simple summer houses on the barrier island within sight of the latest Fort Moultrie, and attended receptions with United States officers stationed there.[47] The small community of Moultrieville never contained more than a few hundred houses and served mainly as an escape from the "extreme heat and desolating pestilence" of Charleston's summers.[48] Still, an 1810 visitor passing Fort Moultrie on his way into Charleston Harbor noted, "It will be ever memorable for the successful attack made by it against a British Squadron under Sir Peter Parker in June 1776."[49] South Carolina, and particularly Charleston, remembered and celebrated the fort's June 28, 1776, victorious defense as Palmetto Day, in honor of the stalwart building material. The event began in 1777 and ran for several years until the British occupation of Charleston. Revived after the War of 1812, the event quickly transformed from a military commemoration into a festival of all things patriotic, indistinguishable from a Fourth of July celebration in any other part of America during the early republic. The ceremonies took place in the center of Charleston, though, with only an evening salute from the Sullivan's Island fort, as well as other harbor batteries, involving the battlefield. June 28 eclipsed July 4 as the main patriotic event on Charleston's calendar and became central to the way many residents viewed their city's role in the Revolution.[50] In later years Charleston even boasted a "Display of Fire Works...in commemoration of the Battle of Fort Sullivan."[51] As much as Charlestonians valued Palmetto Day, holding the event on the battlefield itself would have been nearly impossible, since by 1829 the "spot on which the achievements of that day were acted is now submerged beneath the wave that then kissed its feet."[52]

As he headed down the coast, Washington's keen military eye viewed Savannah in much the same way as he had studied Charleston. Once again accompanied by military officers, the mayor, and "principal Gentlemen of the City," Washington toured sites of "the attack & defence of [Savannah] in the year 1779, under the combined forces of France and the United States." He sought evidence to evaluate American commander General Benjamin Lincoln's shortcomings, this time for failing to successfully capture Savannah. But "to form an opinion of the attack at this distance of time, and the change which has taken place in the appearance of the ground by the cutting away of the woods, &ca., is hardly to be done with justice to the subject; especially as there is remaining scarcely any of the defences." Local militia saluted him at Spring Hill, the site of a bloody battle that broke the siege and kept Savannah in British hands, yet again few traces of the contested redoubt remained.[53]

Even where such ruins existed, they posed interpretive challenges, and their future was precarious. Visitors to important sites in Florida found "Spiked cannon on St. Roses," the "Old f[or]ts at Pensa[cola] blown up by Spanish."[54] Even the Spanish fort at St. Augustine, "more than a century old," stood atop the "foundation" of "an old one of much earlier date," confusing Ralph Waldo Emerson's 1827 attempts to understand the site's history. He noticed that "over the gate of the Fort is an inscription which being in Spanish & in an abbreviated character I was unable to read."[55] The South possessed relatively few extant coastal fortifications capable of transmitting the Revolution's history. By the mid-nineteenth century, Charlestonians rediscovered the Revolutionary War sites in their midst. Writing in 1851 to remind his children and grandchildren of the sacrifices his generation made, seventy-seven-year-old Joseph Johnson sought out historic remains in his city. He went beyond the occasional "bullet marks [that] may be seen in the house" to identify the city's landward defenses. Johnson sketched the old earthwork lines across Charleston Neck, naming the houses of prominent residents and the area "long known as the fresh water pond" as familiar reference points. The fortifications once ran "on the ridge of land where St. Paul's Church, the Orphan House, the Citadel and the Second Presbyterian Church now stand." Traces of the tabby wall from the "strong elevated fortress or citadel" on either side of King Street were "still visible on the east side of it, about forty yards from the street, on a vacant lot, between the picket guard-house and Dr. Boylston's, owned by Mordecai Cohen." Old armories still dotted the city, including one on the eponymous "Magazine-street" and another at the Medical College, which had been "converted into a kitchen." Johnson's effort to uncover Charleston's forgotten past proved difficult, as most of the historic structures had either decayed or been built over. Rather than preserve their Revolutionary past, Charlestonians put the "extreme right of our lines" to better use. Those fortifications once stood "on the south-east part of the old race course, where the nine pin alley and club kitchen are now erected."[56]

## Inland Battlefields

Once George Washington had been feted in the South's main coastal cities, he turned inland along the Savannah River. Along this route were the battlefields where the Revolution became a civil war, as loyalist and patriot partisans fought each other in backcountry skirmishes, sometimes joining with British troops or Continental soldiers in larger battles. British strategy had shifted to the South after Burgoyne's surrender at Saratoga in 1777 made defeating the Continental army in the North impractical. The Crown focused its efforts on retaining the southern colonies and their valuable potential for trade and taxation. The king's ministers believed the less-populous region would be more easily conquered than the North, especially considering what they thought was significant loyalist and Indian support in the backcountry. In 1780 and 1781, Lord Cornwallis occupied Charleston and moved inland, laying waste to patriot strongholds and inciting further partisan warfare.[57]

Washington's journey took him past several key cities and battlefields from that campaign for the first time, and he again made a point of studying the sites' military tactics. At one of his first stops he found only "the ruins, or rather small remns. of the Works which had been erected by the British during the War and taken by the Americans" at Augusta in 1781.[58] At another stop the "british works about Cambden" revealed little about military strategy because they had been erected after the August 1780 battle, during the British occupation of the town. Only well outside of town at Hobkirk's Hill, the site of an April 1781 battle, could Washington find the kind of military landscape that he desired. He referred to "the ground on wch. Genl. Green & Lord Rawdon had their action" and "the ground where Genl. Gates & Lord Cornwallis had their engagement" near Camden, not forts or ruins.[59]

Such unimproved terrain allowed Washington to picture regiments marching and cavalry charging, the tactical maneuvers that interested his eighteenth-century military mind. He recounted how the August 1780 battle of Camden had "terminated so unfavorably" for the Americans.

The "level & open" ground Washington saw allowed neither side a tactical advantage. If only Horatio Gates had moved forward one-half mile, "an impenitrable Swamp would have prevented the attack which was made on him by the British Army, and afforded him time to have formed his own plans; but having no information of Lord Cornwallis's designs, and perhaps not being apprised of this advantage it was not seized by him." Gates's replacement as Southern Department commander, Nathanael Greene, took better advantage of the ground where he fought. In Washington's opinion Greene's position at Hobkirk's Hill "was well chosen—but he not well established in it before he was attacked...in some measure by surprize."[60] Washington's interaction with place focused on the effect of terrain on tactics and helped him to confirm his opinion of Gates and Greene. At Camden and Hobkirk's Hill, as well as most other Southern battlefields, no stone walls or collapsing fortresses stood to structure Washington's view. Instead, he imagined history by investigating the fields where British and American soldiers fought.

Another 1791 traveler, William Loughton Smith, followed much the same route and called "the country about here well known in the history of the war, particularly for the actions of Hanging Rock and Camden: I passed over the spot where both were fought." Landscape provided the main evidence of the battle, for when Smith "saw the traces of the famous battle of Camden," the only specific evidence he noted was "the marks of balls against the trees."[61] Only "shattered trees, and the unburied bones of horses and men" remained, but few visible structures existed.[62] Besides the grave of the Continental army's fallen hero, Baron DeKalb, which Washington had visited for "a few minutes" at the Camden battlefield, there was little to see.[63] The town, one of the few fortified British garrisons in the region, subsequently suffered the wrath of a defeated army when the British abandoned Camden and retreated to the coast. "They burnt the Court House, Gaol, and the greatest Part of the best Houses. They cut down all the Fruit Trees; and destory'd all the Furniture, which they could not carry away." A 1784 traveler noted "evident Proofs of their wanton Barbarity and Desolation" among "the stacks of chimnies, that appear'd along the Road."[64] Only "the old start redoubt," a fortification dating to the 1780–81 occupation of Camden, remained when soldiers fired "a national salute" to greet Lafayette during his 1825 visit.[65]

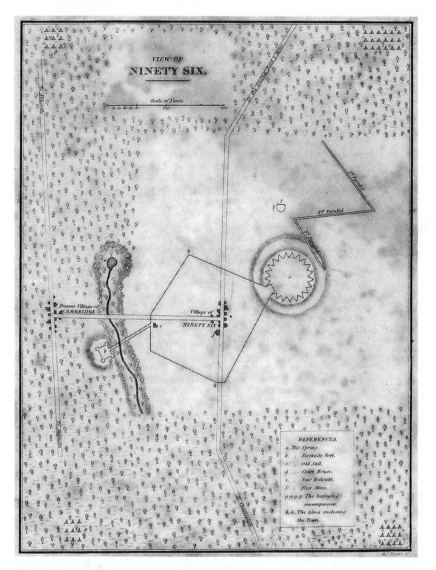

**Figure 11.** View of Ninety-Six map (1822), engraved by H. S. Tanner. One of the largest fortifications in the South, Ninety-Six quickly fell into decay after the British evacuated it in June, 1781, after a lengthy, but unsuccessful, American siege. The tiny town of Cambridge grew up nearby, but the remote site never became a significant tourist destination, despite its ruins. Courtesy of the South Caroliniana Library, University of South Carolina.

Few extant landmarks to the Revolutionary War existed across the South. Even the British fort in Augusta, Georgia, on the town's east side, one of the larger garrison structures in the South, had disappeared, identified only by its former location "a little to the west of the bridge, on the lot where the Episcopal Church is now built."[66] And the area between Augusta and the settlement of Ninety-Six, South Carolina, "the theatre of active and important operations during" the war, attracted few visitors, despite its ruins.[67] A failed 1776 loyalist uprising centered on Ninety-Six, and in 1781 patriots unsuccessfully laid siege to the newly constructed star-shaped fort. The village of Ninety-Six never recovered after the war. "On evacuating it," the British "burnt all the Public and private buildings in the Place." Three years later, one traveler noted that "the inhabitants are just now beginning to rebuild" a short distance from their village's original location. Isolated from all but a trickle of trade with mountaineers to the west, the area stagnated economically and lost its hope of economic revival, Cambridge College, in 1825. Stagecoach service ended in 1845, and an 1852 railroad bypassed what little remained of the village.[68] An 1857 traveler briefly noted "a place called Ninety Six where the old Fort used to stand, signs of which remain to be seen." But the earthwork served only as a local attraction, and few tourists reached it.[69]

Other remote sites, like Cowpens, where in January 1781 American cavalry routed the much-hated British lieutenant colonel Banastre Tarleton's British and loyalist troops, reverted to farmland, tilled from 1826 to 1840 by Revolutionary War veteran Nathan Byers, whose grave and perhaps house remain near the battlefield.[70] When the historian Benjamin Franklin Perry visited in 1835 he discovered "a beautiful and almost perfect plain, with a fine growth of tall pine, oaks and chestnuts." He toured the battlefield with "one of the few surviving gallant [patriot] officers" and observed "places of burying." Near one spot "the dead were found in straight lines across the field," providing "a most singular appearance when seen at a distance." But "the only vestige of the Battle now to be seen are the trees which have been cut by bullets," some high off the ground, "evidence of bad shooting." Perry "procured" several bullets from the tree trunks during his visit. The field of battle had changed, though: "bushes and saplings have grown up, and destroyed in a great measure the beauty of the forest." With "the whole of the battle ground yet in woods," Perry had difficulty imagining the

1781 appearance of Cowpens, when cavalry charged across the grassy plain.[71] When a local militia gathered on the field in 1835 to mark the battle's fifty-fourth anniversary, they relied on the orator's "sublime and eloquent" history of the engagement, as well as "a stand, erected near the centre of the battle ground," to frame their understanding of the battle. Besides the occasional military encampments positioned on the field "imitative of their fathers on the night previous to that memorable battle," few physical reminders of the fighting remained.[72]

Similarly, Kings Mountain, in South Carolina, served as farmland and forest throughout most of the nineteenth century as the surrounding area pursued a mixed agricultural and industrial economy. Immediately after the October 1780 battle, where backcountry patriot militia from as far away as Virginia and Tennessee overwhelmed loyalist troops, the two sides "each buried their own." When this proved cumbersome, the soldiers "dug large pits and put a Number of them in together and threw their Blanket over them." After receiving news that Tarleton "was in pursuit of us to rescue the prisoners," the patriots "left the mountain in...haste before burying the dead."[73] Soon wolves "found some bodies overlooked and unburied, while they easily scratched the others out of the shallow graves. Vultures joined them and for weeks they feasted on the bodies of the slain soldiers, leaving the bones to be polished by the rains and air." Some of the scattered remains were gathered and reburied beneath a "humble monument" in 1815, but the majority of soldiers' bones littered the surrounding hillsides before eventually disintegrating, the battlefield becoming overgrown. The attendees at a massive 1855 monument dedication ceremony discovered the battlefield returned to "mountain forest" and undeveloped; the fifteen thousand attendees had to clear the land and pitch a thousand tents for the event.[74] Most Southern battlefields lacked the physical landmarks that acted as narrative links and punctuation marks in people's interpretation of the scene.

## Reviving Yorktown

The series of battles across the Carolinas broke Cornwallis's army, which retreated to the coast at Wilmington, North Carolina, before marching into Virginia later that spring, eventually meeting defeat at Yorktown. In the battle for that once quiet port, Yorktown suffered comparatively more damage to its infrastructure and long-term prospects than perhaps any other town in the American South, or indeed the nation, suffered throughout the war. Its ruins might have been used to remake Yorktown into what would now be considered a heritage tourism site, but the town continued to wither. The prominent Nelson family saw its fortunes decline precipitously. Thomas Nelson Jr. served Virginia in politics and war, commanding the militia during the Yorktown campaign. He likely even ordered that his own house inside the village be shelled, because its brick walls might provide safe haven for British officers. After the war General Nelson moved back into his home, which had been battered but was damaged less than others in town. The general offered one traveler a personal tour of "the different works that were raised." This kind of genteel, old-fashioned tourism based on personal relationships belied the fact that Yorktown consisted of only "a few scattered houses; some of them have been elegant, but a good deal battered during the siege."[75]

When Nelson died in 1789, most likely because of ill health brought on by service in the military, his family of eleven children that "had been accustomed to all the Luxuries of life, [was] reduced by his immense expenditures for his country to abject poverty." Nelson claimed to have expended over a half million dollars toward the Revolutionary cause, but Virginia was slow to reimburse him. "The very beds on which the Widow and Orphans pillowed their heads, were sold to pay that debt, which he had contracted for this ungrateful country."[76] By the 1840s one of Nelson's daughters looked back on the Revolution bitterly, lamenting a government "for years hesitating and doubting whether his children had a right to claim any thing." The valiant general's "heirs...are worse than neglected, for their claim is doubted by many."[77] The war had damaged not just Nelson's house, which his widow occupied for another thirty years, but the family's long-term financial status as well. Yorktown fared much the same.

One 1796 traveler estimated Yorktown at "one third of the size it was before the war," with few prospects of recovering its lost glory.[78] Around that time Benjamin Henry Latrobe characterized the town as "half deserted. Trade has almost entirely left this once flourishing place." Very little tobacco flowed through the port, largely because local farmers grew wheat instead. The "excellent harbor" was clear enough of sunken ships for shipping to resume, "but of what use is a harbor without trade?"[79] In particular, Secretary Nelson's house stood as a symbol of the town's suffering and defiance. Just over ten years after the battle, legends of Nelson's slave being beheaded by a cannon-ball (which finally convinced the owner, who had remained inside his home during the early stages of the British occupation, to evacuate his home) and the ability of American gunners to repeatedly hit only the structure's fascia on a bet, emerged. These kinds of tales, coupled with the building's ragged appearance—"the walls and roof are pierced in innumerable places, and at one corner a large piece of the wall is torn away"—transformed the Nelson house from a dilapidated building into a historic relic.[80] As a ruin it provided interest, the kind of histori-cal associations that gave landscapes meaning. But few people noticed. When Benjamin Henry Latrobe painted the scene in 1789, he found the subject "wholly destitute of merit." Without trees and "works of fancy," the vista constituted a mere "accurate representation of a scene of great political importance." Latrobe did his best with what he con-sidered the poor light contrast and insufficient coloring at Yorktown but produced an image that "has nothing of what the painters call *pit-toresque*."[81] In one observer's opinion "the whole Country around here has a dreary barren appearance mostly Marshy."[82]

According to some observers, Yorktown lacked sufficient scenery to qualify as picturesque. Because it still showed the consequences of warfare, Yorktown qualified as neither a tourist stop nor a bustling port. The town boasted few prospects, and its residents knew it. So they took up the cause of revitalizing the town that the Nelsons had helped to build. The tens of thousands of visitors who viewed Lafayette's 1824 return to the battlefield prompted more Virginians to imagine new possibilities for Yorktown. Some boosters even stubbornly clung to the idea that their port could be renewed and would become "the grand central depot of western produce."[83] Two different state-chartered rail-road corporations hoped that "we will soon recover our former wealth and power," but only one track was completed by 1859, and it ter-minated over twenty miles upriver at West Point. Plans to launch a steamboat company appeared in the 1850s with limited results, and one of the many ventures' main organizers invested instead in the James River Steamboat Company, which ran two boats up and down the

**Figure 12.** Benjamin Henry Latrobe, *The Nelson House* (1789). The home of one of York-town's most prominent families, the Secretary Nelson House suffered severe damage from American bombardment during the 1781 siege of Yorktown. Latrobe's watercolor was part of a larger "Essay on Landscape, explained in tinted drawings." Historic ruins were only beginning to gain acceptance as subjects of artistic study and national memory. The Library of Virginia (Lab # Latrobe Vol. 1-15 1J.T.F.).

opposite side of Yorktown's peninsula, cutting the once-proud town off from another path to prosperity.[84] The York River did not connect Virginia's two largest cities, Norfolk and Richmond, as the James River did. Instead of developing as a tourism site catering to patriotic Americans, Yorktown stagnated, and no regular steamboat or railroad service reached its ruins.

Scenic tourism extended to the Virginia tidewater only in the 1850s, when steamships carried tourists down the Potomac River from Washington, with an obligatory stop at Mount Vernon to view Washington's tomb. The ride followed "a noble and beautiful river, without any highlands or bold promontories, yet its fine expanse of blue water studded with sails and covered with sea fowl, fill the mind continually with agreeable sensations." But the lines stopped at Norfolk, forcing travelers to take either a stagecoach or wind-powered shallop to Yorktown. There tourists could still walk the British lines "on a green plateau overlooking the York River."[85] Yorktown's flaw during the early-nineteenth century—its lack of economic development—provided an attractive scene for some observers. Gazing across the water to Gloucester, one traveler imagined Cornwallis's attempted retreat, "prevented by the winds." The "water scenery" was "very fine—the wide rippling clear and blue in the splendor of the morning sun," a perfect setting for contemplating past events.[86] Somehow, Yorktown never fully capitalized on this potential for scenic tourism and remained behind the times.

One traveler put it bluntly: "The country appears to be in a state of decay; every thing, like the ponds, is stagnant." General Nelson's house still bore the scars of American artillery, bombshell fragments lay on the ground inside the British defenses, and all that marked the spot where Cornwallis surrendered was "a stake, erected on a rising ground."[87] Little changed before the Civil War, as visitors continued to take note of Nelson's house and the entrenchments. Still, the most remarkable aspect of Yorktown was its decline from what was once "a flourishing village," with "considerable commerce.... There are now only about 40 dwellings, many of which are dilapidated."[88] David Hunter Strother went further, criticizing Yorktown as "a most desolate and apparently deserted village." He claimed that most of the inhabitants remained asleep late in the morning, including the obese village clerk dressed "in slippers and shirtsleeves, sitting in an arm chair with his feet on another." At the river's shore "an old negro servant" dug oysters, but proved "sleepy and inane." After gathering seashells Strother and his companion rode back to Williamsburg, "scarcely meeting a soul by the way, going or returning."[89] Problematically, "the whole Country around here has a dreary barren appearance mostly Marshy untilable," and provided little for the scenic traveler to enjoy.[90]

According to Strother, besides lacking an interesting landscape, the town offered little in the way of accommodation. One chimney wafted smoke in what appeared to be "a house of entertainment." When Strother entered the structure, the rooms were empty until he reached "the kitchen where we found an old black woman, the cook. Master, she said, was at home, but asleep upstairs and she didn't dare to arouse him." This was likely the Swan Tavern, Yorktown's main public house and reputedly "the oldest in Virginia."[91] The "Sleepy Tavern" received little business around the time of Strother's visit. Between February and

**Figure 13.** Benjamin Henry Latrobe, *View at Little York in Virginia* (1789). Below the village of Yorktown, a small cave on the shoreline was allegedly used by British General Cornwallis as shelter during the siege. Local entrepreneurs sought to capitalize on this story and erected a fence at the cave's entrance, charging admission to view the interior. The Library of Virginia.

July 1852, only 337 visitors stepped through its doors, and only six, or 2 percent, stayed more than a single day. The business remained largely unchanged from the 1810s and 1820s, when visitors stayed for about one night to refresh their horses, eat supper, and drink copious amounts of liquor. Almost all the 1852 registrants came alone and hailed from within Virginia. The ledger reveals that bar tabs on "C[ircuit] Court days" constituted the overwhelming majority of the Swan Tavern's business. Yorktown functioned as a quiet shire town, not a busy tourist destination.[92]

Yet Yorktown tried, however feebly, to create objects of interest. As early as 1796 visitors walked down the bluff from the village to the riverbank to see "a cave... described by the people here as having been the head-quarters during the siege." In 1781 an American soldier had recorded, "Lord Cornwallis has built a kind of Grotto at the foot of the secretary's Garden where he lives under Ground," and the legend grew. The idea that Cornwallis occupied such a tiny dwelling, of less than sixteen square feet, seemed preposterous to Benjamin Henry Latrobe, who insisted that the general "shared the dangers of his army in the town."[93] Few believed the tale, saying that a gentleman such as Cornwallis would never crawl into a cave. Instead, the space either housed an officer's wife or served as a powder magazine and storage area. Cornwallis may have used the cave for staff meetings, but the structure's exact provenance and wartime use became irrelevant. The legend mattered more.[94] A Virginia militiaman visiting during the War of 1812 called the cave "the greatest of Curiositys I saw" and repeated the tale that Cornwallis "Concealed himself from his Enemys during the Siege."[95] Yet even this potentially attractive historical legend faltered. By 1837 one traveler termed his visit to the cave "one step from the sublime to the ridiculous—Cornwallis's cave is converted to a hog pen!"[96]

Someone capitalized on the cave's legend and "placed a door at the entrance, secured it by lock and key, and demand[ed] a Virginia ninepence... entrance fee from the curious." In 1850 Benson Lossing "paid the penalty of curiosity, knowing that I was submitting to imposition."[97] The visitor may have paid "an old negro named Billy," the slave of the cave's owner, for "showing us around." Billy invented a tale of Washington jumping from behind a bush and collaring Cornwallis, proclaiming, "'Ah, you blamed old rascal, I've caught you at last!'"[98] Lossing participated in a ruse designed to fleece tourists of their money willingly. He ultimately cared little about the cave's veracity or the cost of admission; simply seeing the place because of its historic connection mattered. Such a "fake" historic site attained mythic status, despite the dubious tale behind it. The only way to determine the cave's authenticity was to see it for yourself. In this context place provided meaning.

When Bushrod Washington visited the cave in 1798 he asked his "conductor, a white boy of about 16, when that Cave had been dug? 'During the War,' said the boy. 'And pray,' said Mr. Washington, 'didn't a General, or somebody of the Kind live in it?'" Not knowing the visitor's identity, for Washington had assumed "an air of ignorance," the boy replied that "it was General Washington, or some such Man!" The general's nephew knew the tale was false, as Washington obviously had remained outside Yorktown's defensive lines during the siege. Yet the actual facts did not matter. As Washington's companion Latrobe stated, "Of such materials is traditionary history made up."[99] By 1857 Virginians debunked the cave's history, identifying it as "a mere cellar... for liquors and molasses, dug out of the side of the bank" by a local grocer long before the Revolution. "Cornwallis was probably never in it in his life." One observer complained, "It is a gross imposition to pretend to point out to unsuspicious & curious travelers, the hole in the bank now to be seen at York as Cornwallis's Cave."[100] In his opinion, more than tall tales was required to render a battlefield attractive to tourists. However, tourists visited for reasons other than authenticity.

Yorktown's location on the water offered one incentive to visit. Latrobe's 1796 complaint that his view of the Secretary Nelson house was "wholly destitute of merit" might have had more to do with his early unsuccessful efforts as a painter than the actual landscape. By the mid-nineteenth century writers lauded the prospect: "The water scenery at Yorktown is very fine—the waves of the wide river rippling clear and blue in the splendor of the morning sun." From atop Yorktown's bluff the river "is seen stretching far away until it merges into Chesapeake Bay—an object of beauty when rolling in the morning light, . . . or when its broad bosom is tinged with the cloud-reflected hues of an autumnal sunset."[101] One of Betsey Ambler's most vivid recollections of her childhood in Yorktown focused on "this noble and never to be forgotten river." Its historical associations as an early point of resistance to British tyranny and later with the conclusion of the Revolutionary War made Yorktown special, but in Ambler's opinion the town stood "unrivaled in its commanding view, its vast expanse of water prospect, its excellent harbor, together with the beautiful neighboring country, which in early times rendered it a delightful residence for persons of all descriptions resorted to by travelers from every part of the world."[102] Lossing called the prospect "very charming, looking out upon the York stretching away toward the broad Chesapeake." The combination of such "charm" and historical interest might make Yorktown prosper again.[103]

It was the latter quality, in the shape of actual artifacts in the very places where Americans made history, that still attracted a small number of travelers to Yorktown. And although visitors repeatedly mentioned the old entrenchments, it was not until the late 1840s that these became an object of specific tourist interest. Lossing's *Pictorial Field-Book of the Revolution* helped to spark such visits, although he used battlefields as an opportunity to instruct. Yorktown's redoubts and siege parallels "may be better understood after receiving the lessons of history," he insisted. He provided page after page of troop maneuvers, military tactics, and officers' personalities. His much briefer passages on the physical remains of one British redoubt or the tulip poplars that marked the surrender field, placed there along with ballast stones from Lafayette's 1824 ship by Thomas Nelson's son in 1847, appear more frequently in tourist accounts.[104] Lossing sought to instruct where others wanted to explore. More thrilling than reading Lossing's tome was walking the very ground that Lafayette and Washington once trod at Yorktown.

Yorktown's allure rested in the fact that its environs remained "as they were in 1781, nearly seventy years ago." In addition to viewing artillery-pocked houses and weed-overgrown earthworks, one intrepid tourist at Yorktown "picked up bullets and bones" from the battle-field. Near the army surgeon's headquarters there were "still quantities of bones and skulls, and iron bullets."[105] The contrast between such a "dull, silent and monotonous place" and 1781's momentous events intrigued tourists. How could a village "of between twenty and thirty houses, half of them uninhabited," have once been "the scene of a con-test, more portentous to the welfare of the human race than any that has occurred since the dawn of the Christian era?" Only by visiting the place and walking the battlefield could one understand the past. York-town possessed both historic structures that showed damage, especially General Nelson's house, and earthworks "in excellent keeping." Being able to view the same ground where General O'Hara had surrendered his sword and his commander's army, as well as to see the poplar trees that marked the spot, connected people to the past, and specifically to place, in a way that Lossing's books could not.[106]

Yorktown also possessed enough aged residents with a connection to the past to verify its legitimacy. There may not have been an old sol-dier alive in 1849 to show Lossing about the works, but "the authority of an old lady who resided at Yorktown at the time of the siege" per-suaded him to part with his coins to view Cornwallis's cave. Likewise, Robert Anderson, "who was born during the siege," received visitors amicably and generously. His private collection included "the only contemporaneous plot of the field now extant," a belt-plate, a dra-goon's saber, the end of a wax candle that once belonged to Cornwallis, "and a cart load of cannon-shot and bomb-shells."[107] Yorktown's relics and Anderson's wealth of information pleased the new kind of visi-tor, an amateur historian who sought to learn about the past firsthand, through landscapes, documents, or objects. Yet Anderson represented just one side of Yorktown's face to the traveling public. The county clerk showed David Hunter Strother several old documents and "gave us a sight of the plan" of the town and works, "but evidently thinking he had something valuable, he declined to allow us to copy it."[108] Here the Virginian's fierce local pride limited Yorktown's ability to attract and accommodate tourists. By claiming Yorktown's history as his own, and limiting what he was willing to share with an outsider, the clerk made Yorktown a tale owned by the commonwealth, not the nation. Yorktown had struggled for over seventy years to reestablish itself as a prominent town and to reclaim some of its past prosperity. The decaying ramparts, scattered shells, and burned-out houses constituted an ideal place for tourists seeking the picturesque. Its residents tried to promote Yorktown and secure the necessary transportation routes, but failed to sustain a viable economy. They never succeeded in making their village, like the many other Revolutionary War battlefields below the Potomac River, a major stop on the southern tour, such as it was.

# CHAPTER FIVE

# American Antiquities Are So Rare

## Remembering the War of 1812 on the Niagara Frontier

Before she became a famous novelist, Catharine Maria Sedgwick toured battlefields. In particular, Sedgwick visited key War of 1812 sites in New York State and Canada during the summer of 1821, noting at Ogdensburg, "American antiquities are so rare that we all felt some emotion as we stood under the shadow of these leaning walls."[1] The fort's decaying ramparts, the site of a humbling American defeat, provided the ideal combination of history and sensibility that Sedgwick and others used to begin creating a distinctive memory of the War of 1812. Much of her journey and writing focused on the Niagara River region, the thirty-five miles between Lake Erie and Lake Ontario called "a tract where armies had marched, camps had been pitched, and feats of valour accomplished." In this regard, encountering history and place at War of 1812 battlefields followed many of the same practices and cultural assumptions as did visitor interactions with Revolutionary War sites. Differences in geography and chronology seemed insignificant when tourists interacted with place, and the fact that both wars featured a common foe, Great Britain, reduced the sense of historical difference in many travelers' minds. But the War of 1812 battlefields that Sedgwick and others engaged featured one major difference. These battlefields surrounded the preeminent tourist attraction of early nineteenth-century America, Niagara Falls, located halfway along the river's length. Tourism constructed memory on "[battle]grounds which, like the Grand Falls themselves, have attracted visitors from distant quarters."[2] In the Niagara region the confluence of tourism and memory elevated place to a primary role in understanding the War of 1812, a relatively rare arrangement at Revolutionary War sites. Along the Niagara River, touristic imperatives dominated encounters with historic battlefields, even relegating memories of the war to ambience.

Sedgwick's journey along the Northern Tour route enabled her to ponder the progress of American history and culture. The daughter of a prominent Massachusetts Federalist family, she sought evidence during her travels of America's accomplishments and character, whether "the novelty of mechanical rising and falling" along the Erie Canal or the sublime power of Niagara's prodigious falls.[3] Battlefields where Americans had fought to win and maintain their independence, whether in 1776 or 1812, provided an ideal venue for reflecting on not just valiant struggle and martial glory, but also emotional responses to landscape and memory. At the ruins of Fort Erie, Fort George, and Fort Niagara, or the battlefields of Queenston Heights, Chippawa, and Lundy's Lane, Americans such as Sedgwick rekindled nationalism, even if they had yet to formally commemorate these battlefields. That all but one lay in Canada further complicated attempts to emphasize American nationalism. Remembering the War of 1812 along the Niagara River echoed the sentimental and landscape-based commemorations at Revolutionary War battlefields, but with less patriotic fervor.

The battles mentioned above proved especially resonant with Americans for reasons other than their military significance. The Americans unsuccessfully attacked Fort Erie in 1812 before capturing it in July 1814. After a British siege later that summer and fall, which included an ill-conceived nighttime bayonet attack, in November American forces exploded and burned the remaining fortifications and withdrew across the river to Buffalo. Thirty-five miles north at the river's entrance into Lake Ontario, Fort Niagara and Fort George guarded the American and Canadian shore, respectively. Americans bombarded and captured Fort George in May 1813, then blundered across the Ontario peninsula before retreating within the fort's protective walls. The disastrous 1813 campaign in Upper Canada resulted in the abandonment of Fort George in December, but not before militia burned the nearby town of

Newark (the present-day Niagara-on-the-Lake). When British troops crossed the river into the United States on December 18, they surprised the Fort Niagara garrison and took the fort; to avenge the destruction of Newark, they burned American settlements south to Buffalo. Halfway between the two forts, on the western shore near Niagara Falls, the Americans held their ground at Chippawa in 1814, earning Winfield Scott fame as an American general who could confront British regulars and accept hundreds of casualties as the cost of martial valor. After twenty days of maneuvering up and down the Niagara River's shores, the two armies once again clashed, just a few miles from Chippawa, at Lundy's Lane. They inflicted significant casualties on each other in one of the war's bloodiest battles. The British held the field the following morning and claimed victory. Further downriver at Queenston Heights, where the Niagara Escarpment dropped several hundred feet and the river calmed after miles of rapids, the first American invasion across the Niagara River had ended in surrender on October 11, 1812, when New York militia refused to cross the river in support of regular troops. Fighting along the Niagara River provided few decisive victories that Americans could cheer, and other than the British outpost at Fort Niagara, neither side held new territory at the war's conclusion. As the aggressors who had first invaded Upper Canada, the Americans might be said to have been the losers. At the end of 1814, "the British celebrated victory, for Americans had no territory in the Niagara District to show for their long, bloody, and expensive campaign."[4] Americans would have to find something other than great military successes to commemorate the War of 1812.[5]

What made each of these battles the site of so many touristic responses to history was its proximity to the paragon of nineteenth-century tourism, Niagara Falls. Just a decade after the fighting concluded, an important guidebook reminded readers that the Niagara River "frontier was the theatre of many important events during the late war."[6] Tourists bored by the hotels and scenery of Niagara Falls, or the novelty of crossing the river just below the falls in a hand-rowed ferryboat, discovered that "in the immediate vicinity of the Falls many incidents have occurred to impart an additional interest." The curious reader learned that nearby "was the scene of a number of battles fought during the last war with Great Britain; those at Fort Erie, Chippewa, and Lundy's Lane, were among the most bloody and hard-fought, that

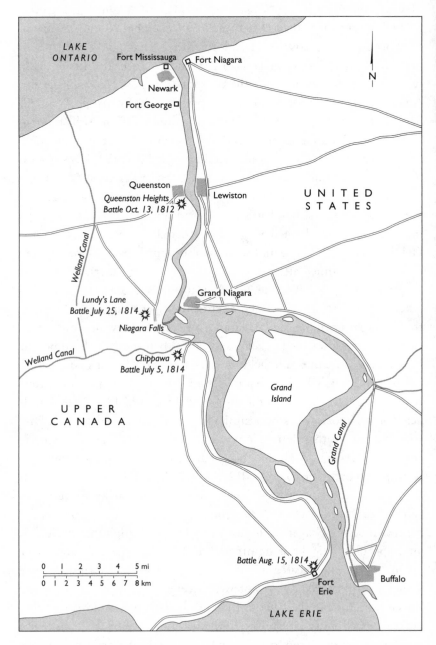

**Map 6.** War of 1812 sites along the Niagara River, ca. 1840.

are recorded in history."[7] Such "historical scenes," noted one guide-book, "are among the objects which should be included in a visit to the Falls."[8] History complemented the tourist's routine. What remained of and on the battlefields guided the memories tourists constructed at the War of 1812's historic places.

## Ruined Forts

At the Niagara River's beginning, the outlet of Lake Erie at the north-eastern tip of the lake, Buffalo was a bustling city only a few years after its destruction by the British, who reportedly left only three structures standing in the wake of their December 1814 attack. Catharine Maria Sedgwick wrote a friend who had visited Buffalo when "the havoc was recent" that she "would be surprised by the phoenix resurrection." What Sedgwick termed "the devastation of the last War, during which every habitation save one was burnt," quickly faded: "now, but few vestiges of it remain." Grass had grown over the graves of those soldiers or civilians who had died during the war, their remains "mostly in-closed in fruitful fields." The city was expanding too quickly to dwell on its past, and Sedgwick only "traced the impression of one Marquee" in Buffalo. The small settlement of Seneca Indians just south of the city, along the banks of Buffalo Creek, provided "the only objects" of the past; the chief and famous orator Red Jacket attracted many visitors. Few people came to see the scenes of fighting, though. By 1821, "the memorials of the War are nearly effaced and all is dressed in the smiles of prosperity."[9] In the eyes of United States Army officer Roger Jones, "the expensive stile of many of the dwellings, much beyond the first means of the occupants," indicated that Buffalo had recovered nicely from the war.[10] When the Marquis de Lafayette visited in 1825, his sec-retary was "struck with its air of prosperity, and the bustle in its port." Once Erie's "grand canal" stretched from Albany to Buffalo, the war's destruction seemed a distant memory.[11]

Across the narrow Niagara River, however, lay "the ruins of the memorable *Fort Erie*," its entrenchments and stone walls providing ample evidence of war's destruction.[12] It was, wrote one guidebook, "during the late war, the scene of some of the most memorable exploits of the Republican army."[13] Facing a delay in his steamboat's departure,

**Figure 14.** Philip John Bainbrigge, *Ruins of Fort Erie and the City of Buffalo* (1838). Directly across the Niagara River from the booming city of Buffalo, New York (visible in the background), Fort Erie's stone ruins and earthen ramparts provided a reminder of the bloodshed along the border just twenty-five years earlier. Many travelers heading westward visited Fort Erie while waiting for their steamboats to leave Buffalo. Library and Archives Canada, accession number 1983-047, item number 83, reproduction copy number C-011869.

Jones "availed myself of the opportunity" to visit. He and several other officers "examined the field works of both armies, some of which are demolished, whilst others are quite in a perfect state." They found signs of the July and August 1814 battles: "The surrounding wood still bears evidence of the duration and severity of the cannonade, by the destruction, yet visible, of some of the largest houses and trees. In some instances, they are entirely prostrated by cannon shot, as tho' they had yielded to the hand of the axman."[14] They and the "little hillocks that dot the plain below, each marking a soldier's grave, attest the obstinacy with which the attack was urged, and the assault repulsed."[15]

Unlike most other battlefields along the Niagara River, Fort Erie was "a fortress of great consequence in the late war. There was a strong wall surrounded with intrenchments reaching to the lake."[16] Although the fort had been abandoned after the war and existed "entirely in ruins, deserted and desolate," in 1845 "its ancient defences may still be traced out."[17] Such remains, even if they were "wholly dilapidated," became what tourists called "a spot of particular interest."[18] Fort Erie allowed tourists to encounter not just a battlefield, but also physical reminders of the past. Augustus Silliman and a "Major" who had been at Fort Erie rode over the battleground where "generous and gallant blood has deeply stained it soil." The ramparts, trenches, bastions, lines, and earthworks were "now all sinking to their original level," yet sparked poignant memories for the veteran. Atop one "decaying mound" where Lieutenant Colonel Wood had led a charge, the major paused. "'Here he fell; he was bayoneted to death on the ground, on this spot.' The Major's voice quivered, and he turned his face from me, for the cruel death of his dear friend was too much for his manhood."[19] To encounter the place where death had occurred or where relatives and friends had suffered constituted one of the main attractions for battlefield tourists. Sedgwick sought out the spots where soldiers she knew had fought, and she identified a popular spot, "the very Bastion where [Lieutenant Colonel William] Drummond fell when he was exclaiming 'Give no quarter to the damned Yankees'" during the August 1814 attack on Fort Erie. Her reaction extended beyond celebrating military valor, though. Inside Drummond's bastion "was a beautiful sweet briar in full bloom. I broke a branch with three roses on the same stem.... How beautiful are the peaceful triumphs of nature. I wish all the Forts in the world were in the condition of Fort Erie."[20] Like so many other decaying ruins, Fort Erie served as a prompt for sentimental reflections.

Peter Porter, the American general who helped lead attacks on Fort Erie and the defense of Buffalo during the war, enjoyed the most opportunities to view the ruins. His mansion sat just north of Buffalo, "handsomely situated immediately on the Niagara, in full view of the ruin of Fort Erie, and the adjacent fields."[21] A British surprise attack forced him to flee his home in 1813, and the following year the British burned his house to the ground, along with most of the surrounding community. Porter responded by constructing a grander edifice in 1816, situated on "high lands" that provided a good view of Fort Erie. Influential politicians and famous visitors, including John Quincy Adams, Daniel Webster, and the Marquis de Lafayette, called on Porter and likely heard the general recount his exploits across the river. In the years that followed, Porter sold off portions of his land to the settlers in the growing communities of Black Rock and Buffalo before relocating to Niagara Falls in 1837. One of the purchasers included the United States government, which erected a military barracks nearby in the early 1840s. Their location, "nearly opposite to the site of Fort Erie, on the Canada side," provided a vista for visitors to interpret a fort "made memorable by the sortie of Gen. Porter...in the glorious campaign of 1814." In looking upon those ruins from a newly built military site designed to "secure the command of the river," Americans could construct memories of the war that depicted themselves as victors.[22] Their visual superiority, as well as the improved physical condition of the American fortification in comparison with the dilapidated Fort Erie, meant that their cause had triumphed. Fort Erie stood as a sentimental landscape, not as a contemporary threat to invade and burn the bustling city of Buffalo. It had lost much of its military allure.

At the river's terminus at Lake Ontario thirty-five miles north, British Fort George and American Fort Niagara seemed "to frown defiance across the water" at each other.[23] The garrison that American armies bombarded in 1812, captured in 1813, and evacuated the same year quickly fell into disuse by 1821: "It hardly deserves the name of a Fort, being merely an embankment, surrounded by a palisade."[24] After the war the earthworks were supplanted by Fort Mississauga, located just over a mile north at the river's mouth. It controlled navigation and best protected Newark, the former provincial capital. Abandoned by the British in 1826, Fort Mississauga was "rapidly crumbing into dust" by 1833, and six years later Fort George, which had once been "considered of consequence as a military post during the war," stood "deserted and dismantled, and is fast crumbling to ruins."[25] Staffed only by "three privates and a corporal," Fort George was mistaken by one visitor "for a dilapidated brewery."[26] Its decay contrasted with the adjoining village of Newark's "flourishing appearance," even though it had been "entirely destroyed in the fall of 1813." Within a decade the town had "risen more populous than it was before. The merchants are very rich." Blame for Newark's destruction fell on American General George McClure, who had "set the first example of burning" civilian property as he evacuated Fort George and retreated back into the United States. The "Irish Gen'l McClure" was suspect in the early nineteenth century because he was both "of the militia" and of supposedly inferior racial stock. This ungentlemanly soldier burned Newark "out of curiosity."[27] In December 1813, when British troops captured

Fort Niagara, Newark's destruction "was revenged immediately after, by the destruction of every settlement" from Youngstown to Buffalo, "involving every family in misery."[28] The bitter memories of those events quickly faded, however. Guidebooks instructed tourists to overlook past atrocities: "Let no American speak of such acts, no matter from whence they emanate, without bestowing on them that censure, and the full measure of indignation which they so justly deserve."[29] Unpleasant wartime memories were easily forgotten, especially when few structures stood as reminders.

Across the Niagara River from the abandoned Fort George, the American Fort Niagara fared only slightly better. The main three-story stone building erected by the French in 1726 lent an air of permanence, and Fort Niagara remained an active United States military station for well over another century. Yet in 1821, to Catharine Maria Sedgwick "it did not seem to my unpractised eye a place of any strength." Two years earlier, when Roger Jones visited, he noted that work on an expensive seawall designed to protect the shoreline "is stopped, and probably will never be resumed." The fort quickly fell into decline as a sleepy frontier post, featuring only "a single picketed fence, which is no better defence than that around a peaceful garden, which you know is not always a protection against the batteries of pigs and chickens."[30] President James Monroe stopped only briefly at the fort during his 1817 tour of the Northern states, preferring to view Niagara Falls and visit the bustling city of Buffalo. Compared with his much longer stay at Plattsburgh and his address to veterans at Sackets Harbor, two important War of 1812 sites in northern New York, Fort Niagara registered low on the president's commemorative itinerary.[31] The Marquis de Lafayette received a grander reception in 1824, including a twenty-four-gun salute. Yet even with the garrison on full display, Lafayette's party found it "difficult to trace the ravages of war."[32] The fort continued to face neglect. Only the 1837–38 rebellion in Upper Canada "and the critical state of our foreign relations" in following years prompted the United States Army to begin "strengthening [Fort Niagara's] defences." Observers hoped that "in the event of another war, it will be found no easy matter to reduce it either by siege or assault."[33]

The fort's engineer disagreed throughout this period, calling the barracks "not fit to be inhabited and the storehouses are too much dilapidated to be worth repairing." Congress, however, refused to grant his appropriations requests. An 1851 fire destroyed what little work had been accomplished, leaving only "decaying timbers" on the palisade. Seven years later, despite some repairs to decaying timbers and crumbling masonry, it was reported that "the old 'French Castle' is the only building fit for occupancy as quarters, and it is entirely inadequate."[34] Over time "legendary stories" of dungeons, torture, a headless French officer haunting the old castle, and the murder of anti-Mason William Morgan developed around an otherwise "useless and ruinous old fort."[35] Most discerning travelers considered such "dark tales...of inhuman cruelties" to be "much exaggerated," but the stories appealed to tourists trying to make sense of what in 1845 looked like "massive piles of masonry."[36] The historical significance of Fort Niagara grew increasingly distant in the postwar years, perhaps because it continued to house American soldiers, albeit in decrepit conditions. Tourists found the fort "pleasingly desolate, the fortress of a people who are emulous of peace, yet confident in their ability to conquer."[37] Visitors saw romance in the fort's current ramshackle condition and failed to look backward into the past to understand the place's history. An 1860 guidebook expressed the feeling of many travelers hastening to the falls: "Fort Niagara, on the American side, has many historical associations, which we have not space to touch upon."[38] At least "from the ramparts of the Fort there is a beautiful and extensive view of the lake and surrounding country."[39]

## Chippawa and Lundy's Lane

Instead of lingering at old forts, tourists flocked to Niagara Falls and the nearby battlefields. Within sight of the falls on the Niagara River's western shore stood the village of "Chippewa [sic]...noted from its contiguity to the great battle which took place in 1814."[40] Americans spelled the town and the nearby battle with an "e," while Canadians used only "a" in Chippawa. Adding to the confusion, the village had little to do with the battle of the same name, instead having served as the staging ground for American forces before the later battle of Lundy's Lane. Chippawa village included a small inn, whose landlord delighted in showing "the marks his house had received from 'war's artillery,'" a consequence of the American encampment having been "in the rear" of his tavern in the days before Lundy's Lane; he "pointed to a ditch the common sepulcher of the contending parties," just beyond his doors.[41] The 750 men "who died in the action" buried there rested peacefully a mile from the Chippawa battlefield that by 1833 was "a broad plot of flat land upon the bank of the river and is now occupied by a farm."[42] Amid the grass waving "luxuriantly on the sites of [soldiers'] funeral piles," the innkeeper showed a British visitor "a few skulls thrown up by the plough, or found among the underwood." Some of the specimens in the innkeeper's collection "had been gnawed by raccoons, or other wild animals, the marks made by the teeth of the ravenous tenants of the forest being perfectly visible."[43] Such macabre relics reminded American Moses Cleveland that on this "field of blood and carnage...many a poor fellow there lost his life fighting for the liberties we their survivors enjoy."[44] Yet reflections such as his became increasingly difficult without the prompts of perforated skulls and bullet-riddled taverns. By 1840 Chippawa was "a village of considerable consequence," and the nearby "[battle]ground is now undistinguishable in any way except by fields and enclosures."[45] As one guidebook reported, the stagecoach route from Buffalo "passes over the Chippewa battle ground."[46] Yet later in the 1840s and 1850s, "many visitors to the Falls" began seeking out Chippawa's "verdant meadows," which they "regarded with deep interest." Guidebooks advised tourists to "extend your ramble to this plain, hallowed in the remembrance of two nations," especially because the battle "resulted in the triumph of American arms," a rare occasion in this region.[47] Americans celebrated the July 5 battle where "an American force, in fair fight and open field, defeated a British force greatly superior in numbers and drawn from the veterans of Wellington, who had conquered the conquerers of Europe."[48] But Canadians converted the battlefield into farmland, preferring not to commemorate Chippawa, an inglorious moment in their nation's past.

Both nations paid more attention to Lundy's Lane, the battle closest to Niagara Falls. In his 1819 tour of Great Lakes military sites, Roger Jones "walked over this sacred ground" with a soldier's eye: "with a pleasing tho' melancholy satisfaction, I found out, the relative positions of the contending Armies, and all the incidents, as well as I could remember, that occurred during the action." He authenticated the field's military history by viewing "the adjacent trees, and houses [which] still wear the marks of cannon and musket balls."[49] The presence of "the shattered trees everywhere" told "the woeful tale" of battle only partly as well as other relics. Just one year earlier New Yorker Elkanah Watson "picked up on the surface fragments of muskets, bullets, &c., and was shown the calcined bones of Americans, whose bodies had been barbarously burnt in a pile, formed by a layer of rails, and then the corpses of officers and soldiers in succession." He responded bluntly, "My blood chilled at the horrid sight."[50] The type of raw encounter with place and history that Jones and Watson experienced, one based on the physical remains of warfare, failed to appeal to sentimental tourists like Catharine Maria Sedgwick, whose "contempt for war and 'war minions' had like to have led me past 'Lundy's Lane' without a notice."[51]

Her glancing reference to martial matters belied American interest in the war, as tourism to the Falls and nearby battlefields boomed in later decades. Early guidebooks advised tourists to visit Lundy's Lane at least in part because the battle "was fought...near the mighty cataract of Niagara, and within the sound of its thunders."[52] The battlefield itself, although in Canada, "is about a mile from the Falls of Niagara, at an obscure road, called Lundy's Lane." The main American advance took place "across the open level fields seen from Forsyth's Hotel, and about a quarter of a mile to the left." For those travelers seeking to tarry at the battlefield, "comfortable accommodations are offered there, at the inn of Mr. Chysler."[53] Such facility of travel and the placid battlefield's proximity to suitable hotels seemed a contrast to what "in proportion to the numbers engaged" was "the most sanguinary, and decidedly the best fought of any action which ever took place on the American continent."[54] By 1833 one visitor declared, "No one should leave this region before visiting the spots consecrated by the noble efforts of such men." On the "plains of Bridgewater...the gallant [General Jacob] Brown and his brave compeers proved themselves warriors in the service of their country."[55] It would soon become a "must see" destination for Niagara Falls tourists.

Lundy's Lane seemed to become a "sacred place" by 1839, the battle's twenty-fifth anniversary.[56] Relatively few tourists actually visited the site before this year, when a remarkable commemorative event took place. Henry Clay, the American politician contemplating yet another presidential run, visited Lundy's Lane in the company of General Peter B. Porter, a Clay ally from their War Hawk days and an influential congressman and New York politician in his own right. Porter had led New York militia at Lundy's Lane, as well as in an earlier invasion across the Niagara River. Yet on July 25, 1839, a quarter century to the day since the battle, Porter and Clay reviewed the Forty-third Highlanders, one of the most decorated regiments in the British army, "on the trampled sward of the battlefield." One New York newspaper speculated that "as the columns passed [Porter] in review, his thoughts must have reverted to the times when, on this same frontier, and in the very vicinity of the spot where he stood, British columns were displayed before him for far different purposes." Perhaps the fact that the Forty-third had not fought there in 1814 lessened the martial associations. In addition, the twenty-fifth-anniversary event took place in the wake of the 1837–39 rebellion in Upper Canada, when American-born Canadians and other residents outside the ruling faction's patronage, especially those of Irish descent, sought to separate from Great Britain. Their initial December 1837 uprising in Toronto fizzled, and several of the leaders fled to Buffalo. From there they launched cross-border raids with the support of American sympathizers in what became known as the Patriot movement across the U.S.-Canada border.[57] The United States Army, once again commanded along the Niagara River by Winfield Scott, suppressed attempts by Canadian expatriates and American filibusterers to foment war with Great Britain. Motivated by a desire for social order and their obligation as professional soldiers to the federal government, Scott and his officers quashed the Patriot movement in the United States by late 1838. Their Anglophilia and Whiggish view of ordered national expansion motivated them, as it did the U.S. government, to side with British officials and avoid another war. That Scott, the hero of Chippawa, led this effort indicates the transformation of the War of 1812 from something once remembered as a war of nationalistic expansion and defense against British insults. Former adversaries—most of the British officers had fought along the Niagara River decades earlier—now joined together to suppress a rabble-rousing insurgency and to celebrate martial valor, not nationalistic ideology. The rebellion's defeat offered Canadians and Americans a chance to express the values they shared. The valor of Porter and statesmanship of Clay, not their nationality or their role in the events decades ago, mattered. As the report of the 1839 military review stated, "In honoring such men, the gallant 'Forty-Third' honored themselves and the glorious country which they serve, and which is the common mother of us all."[58]

Battlefields now represented shared sacrifice rather than bitter conflict. As an 1844 guidebook stated, "Lundy's Lane is a place much visited; it once being the scene of much bloodshed."[59] It had become a "the celebrated Battle of Niagara," its name moving from a specific to broad binational geography, perhaps in an effort to link the fighting with the famous waterfall. "Most travelers," wrote one promoter, "desire to visit a place so memorable, and it is presumed the reader is not an exception." In just a short jaunt from the Clifton House Hotel, tourists could find "a church, a tavern, and several other buildings" near the "obstinately contested" hill. "One or two [structures] are yet standing, which were there at the date of the conflict," in contrast to the burned and abandoned village of Bridge-water, which travelers passed on their way to the battlefield. The war had left behind "nothing but a name and a few deserted buildings, to show where once they flourished."[60] Further adding to the ruined landscape, some of the structures atop the Lundy's Lane hill "still retain marks of the combat," as did the "burying-ground where many of the slain were buried."[61]

Damaged buildings and soldiers' graves appealed to a kind of visitor different from the military officers who considered it "a soldier's duty to visit [a] battle-ground whenever he is near."[62] Like-minded men such as William T. Coles of Lebanon, Tennessee, walked the grounds because he was the "grandson of W. T. Coles who fought on this battleground."[63] Some travelers thrilled at the opportunity to identify "the very hollow where General Scott tripped his left foot against this stump, when he was leading his men to the charge."[64] After 1840 the stump-finders represented an increasingly smaller portion of visitors to Niagara's battlefield. The new majority of tourists included the genteel readers of *Godey's Lady's Book* who felt that "the few deserted ruins" of Bridgewater "added to the usual horrors of war." Reporting from Lundy's Lane, the *Godey's* correspondent made special mention of the story that on the field itself, "more than a thousand bodies were found the next morning," a fact the author's driver "pointed out to us" as the carriage rattled past the blood-soaked hillside.[65] The typical response, however, lacked outrage at the slaughter or rising patriotism provoked by the soldiers' valor. One traveler opined that "these are certainly the most beautiful, romantic

and picturesque spots to fight battles that the world can afford." The
pleasant country ride was best seen on an afternoon "bright with a few
light, fleecy clouds, occasionally passing over the sun's disk, to moder-
ate his burning beams. It was all peace, quiet, languor, and indolence
around." Even the battlefield itself seemed peaceful. By 1840 the British
had installed a hospital for invalid soldiers near the battlefield, guarded
by "kilted Highlanders laying in the sun like so many New York loafers
on the Battery." Soldiers, whether old or new, belonged to the scenery
as much as "an immense pile of fire wood…on one side of the road, on
the very spot perhaps which the destructive guns formerly occupied."[66]
Scenery, as much as history, appealed to tourists. Battles seemed like the
last thing that could have occurred in such a beautiful place.

Lundy's Lane had achieved sufficient fame and attracted enough visitors by the mid-1840s that "there is generally to be found on the ground,
an old veteran soldier, who was in the action." He guided visitors around
the field, providing "a general description of the whole Battle" and taking "great pride in pointing out the different positions and maneuvering
of the two armies."[67] Of the many named guides, Samuel G. Wiggins
stood out: "he is a soldier and a patriot no mistake you don't fool him."
Such guides certainly provided historical information, but they also ca-
tered to their audience of sentimental tourists.[68] Diligent businessmen
like one "garrulous old Canadian" accosted tourists and "insisted on
telling us all the story of the battle, which we vainly attempted to cut
short."[69] Many veterans appealed to their customers' emotions by clos-
ing their tours at the churchyard graves of their comrades. One stone
and two wooden markers indicated the remains of three British officers.
Two soldiers visiting the site "were much displeased to observe that the
two last monuments had been displaced from their proper positions to
make room for some other graves, but we immediately took steps to
have them replaced over the honored dead."[70] That rare effort stood in
contrast with the Lundy's Lane battlefield itself, where one British officer
failed to locate "some mound or brief monument (of which there was
not even a single vestige), erected to the memory of the numerous brave
who fell."[71] Soldiers and tourists shared a desire to show their respect for
fallen warriors in a sanitized environment devoid of protruding bones.
"A walk through the burying-ground," advised one guidebook, "will
show where rest the remains of many a gallant solider, who lost his life
by the sad chance of war."[72]

The sentimental tone of these responses to place emphasize a more generic engagement with battlefields that paid little attention to the causes and consequences of the war, much less the merits of either side. A visit to the graveyard at Lundy's Lane, "with its drooping willows and flowering locusts," prompted one author to proclaim, "the eternal cataracts roar your requiem." The once smoke-covered plain, now "loaded and bending with the yellow harvest, betrays no human gore—yon hill scathed, scorched and blackened with cannon flame, the very resting place of the deadly battery, shows no relic of the fierce death struggle, as covered with the fragrant clover and wild blue-bell, the bee in monotonous hum banquets o'er it. Nought mars the serenity of nature as she smiles upon us."[73] With reports of "a splendid double rainbow spann[ing] the heavens before us," the battlefield merged with the mist-soaked landscape around the falls. Through a break in the "thick groves of ancient trees," battlefield tourists could glimpse "the vast pillar of cloud rising and waving above the cataract, whose deep voice also falls solemnly on the ear."[74] It was the perfect backdrop for sentimental responses to the past. Lundy's Lane, just like Niagara Falls, provided an opportunity for visitors to reflect on their own place in the world and the frailty of their own lives. Soldiers' graves and thundering water both prompted contemplation of larger forces shaping events.

Yet this moment of introspection lasted only as long as the rainbows fading in and out of the falls' mist. The British troops stationed near the field, as well as the military hospital, gave way to a more pecuniary fixture on the landscape. While visiting Niagara Falls in 1846, Philadelphian J. Warner Irwin "hired a carriage and rode out to Lundy's Lane Battle Ground." His party then "ascended to the top of the Observatory which is 80 feet high, and is erected on the Battle Ground, and near where the dead were buried the day after the action."[75] This "lattice frame staircase," presumably made of wood, literally towered over the landscape, imposing the tourist's desire to observe, regardless of any motivation to preserve the battlefield or the soldiers buried nearby as a sacred place. Irwin responded dispassionately to the battlefield: "neither party gained the victory, both retired from the contested point." The battle itself mattered little to him. However, "from the top of this Observatory you have a fine view of the Rapids, Grand and Navy Islands, Lake Erie, Lake Ontario, Brock's Monument, and many other delightful views and woodland scenery."[76] By 1858 visitors termed a subsequent observatory "one of the finest views, so extended, and over such a beautiful country, it is more like the view from a high mountain."[77]

The vista soon dominated visitors' responses to the battlefield, which became another part of the scenery, an object to be consumed. With tour guides and a viewing platform, Lundy's Lane had been transformed into a tourist attraction, heritage tourism that only tangentially included history. "For this you pay a 'quarter,' as you do for every thing else you see, and almost every time you turn."[78] The stairs on the tower's brick-enclosed first story were lined with shelves of Indian beadwork and bullets gleaned from the battlefield, each available for purchase, as was a booklet offering "an impartial description" of the battle assembled by "the Proprietor of the Observatory."[79] Four different towers sought to

TWO OBSERVATORIES ON LUNDY'S LANE, 1860
Durham Tower in the foreground. The other is the Fralick Tower on the summit of the hill.

**Figure 15.** *Two Observatories on Lundy's Lane* (ca. 1860). Visitors to Niagara Falls made side trips to the Lundy's Lane battlefield, where some of the fiercest fighting during the War of 1812 took place. The observation towers, located atop the hill that American forces sought to capture, provided an excellent view of the battlefield. The towers' owners charged admission to climb their stairs, knowing that the elevated observation platform offered a splendid view of the falls, just over one mile away. Niagara Falls (Ontario) Public Library.

capture tourists' coins, although only two stood at any one time. The fierce competition caused one proprietor to burn down his rival's tower in 1851, hoping to dominate the trade. With insufficient insurance, Donald McKenzie never rebuilt his tower, and his competitor made significant profits. As his daughter recounted years later, "There was a great deal of travel to the battle-ground in those days of long ago. Often there would be five or six carriages filled with visitors going up the Hill one after the other." The trade came largely from Americans, as more of them "visited the battleground than Canadians." Indeed, only 8 percent of observatory tower visitors came from Canada in August 1853. Southerners visiting Niagara Falls stood out for their side trips to Lundy's Lane, bringing with them "plenty of gold, $5 and $1 pieces. They bought souvenirs freely." But they constituted only 20 percent of observatory guests in one sample, vastly outnumbered by their Northern counterparts, who represented 70 percent of Lundy's Lane visitors.[80]

**Table 3.** Visitors to Lundy's Lane by place of origin, 1853

| Origin | Number | % Total |
|---|---|---|
| United States | 628 | 88.3 |
| Northern states | 499 | 70.2 |
| New York | 295 | 41.5 |
| Pennsylvania | 74 | 10.4 |
| Ohio | 46 | 6.5 |
| Massachusetts | 26 | 3.7 |
| Connecticut | 17 | 2.4 |
| Illinois | 12 | 1.7 |
| Maine | 10 | 1.4 |
| New Jersey | 5 | 0.7 |
| Indiana | 3 | 0.4 |
| Rhode Island | 3 | 0.4 |
| California | 2 | 0.3 |
| Michigan | 2 | 0.3 |
| New Hampshire | 2 | 0.3 |
| Delaware | 1 | 0.1 |
| Wisconsin | 1 | 0.1 |
| Southern states | 138 | 19.4 |
| Virginia | 26 | 3.7 |
| Mississippi | 21 | 3.0 |

| Origin | Number | % Total |
| --- | --- | --- |
| Louisiana | 15 | 2.1 |
| Alabama | 13 | 1.8 |
| Georgia | 13 | 1.8 |
| Kentucky | 11 | 1.5 |
| Tennessee | 11 | 1.5 |
| District of Columbia | 8 | 1.1 |
| Missouri | 6 | 0.8 |
| Maryland | 5 | 0.7 |
| South Carolina | 4 | 0.6 |
| Texas | 3 | 0.4 |
| Arkansas | 2 | 0.3 |
| Canada | 58 | 8.2 |
| Canada West | 54 | 7.6 |
| Nova Scotia | 3 | 0.4 |
| Canada East | 1 | 0.1 |
| Unknown | 11 | |
| **Total visitors** | **711** | |

Based on these numbers, Canadians seemed uninterested in the battle, despite its role in their nation's history. Americans came from twenty-seven of the thirty-one United States (as of 1853) and the District of Columbia, and most listed Niagara Falls as their destination. This national audience fits the profile of the emerging traveling class who stopped at sites like Lundy's Lane as tourists, not as nationalistic heritage seekers. As Elkanah Watson declared in 1818, "What a theatre for a mighty battle-field! What a scene for man to exhibit his passions and conflicts,—upon the threshold of such a demonstration of the wonderful, and almighty works of God!"[81]

## Queenston Heights

For a battle that demonstrated American ineptitude on a grander scale than any other engagement along the Niagara frontier, and perhaps during the entire War of 1812, Queenston Heights occupied a central place in regional visitors' accounts of Niagara's historic sites and came to represent much of what Americans, Britons, and Canadians remembered about the war. As with any site seeking to promote itself, location mattered; the battle contested the crest of an escarpment that commanded a spectacular view. American troops had crossed the Niagara River from Lewiston before dawn on October 13, 1812, quickly surprising the small British guard at Queenston landing. They then captured a British battery atop the heights, nearly three hundred feet above the river. Rushing south from his base at Fort George, British general Isaac Brock led a charge that retook a key hillside redoubt and pressed upward, falling shot through the chest before he achieved the summit. Ordered to support their comrades, American militia refused to cross into Canada. When boats carrying severely wounded soldiers returned to Lewiston, New York troops insisted they enlisted only to protect their home state of New York. By late afternoon British reinforcements, including about 160 Grand River Haudenosaunee and 80 Cayuga Indians, overwhelmed the American position on Queenston Heights. The trapped force at the landing surrendered, its boatmen having returned to New York State in fear. Some troops atop the escarpment were so petrified by the prospect of surrendering to Indian warriors that they fled down the hill to the river. Others, surrounded by the Haudenosaunee and British troops, "leapt the precipice and were seen for some time after suspended halfway down in the branches of the trees, where the Savages had shot them from the brow."[82] These dramatic events on the high ground at Queenston gained legendary status. In the decades to come, the space became the Niagara region's most revered site, overcoming the region's initial "bitter memories" of a ruined borderland.[83]

Almost from the moment he fell, mortally wounded, Isaac Brock gained fame and honor and became synonymous with Queenston Heights. His officers staged an elaborate funeral three days after the battle. New York militia general Stephen Van Rensselaer ordered an artillery salute for the fallen general out of respect for his gallant foe. "Even the appearance of hostilities was suspended" as the procession marched seven miles down the river to Fort George. Brock's body "was bedewed with the tears of many affectionate friends" on the way.[84] Brock's legend only grew because he had died in battle without having received word of a knighthood bestowed upon him for his victory at Detroit earlier in the year. Not even a decade after Brock's death, an American tourist anticipated seeing "those celebrated heights" where "the gallant Brock perished." Those looking for a memorial to Brock found only a few "redoubts and breastworks" and a large heap of disappointment, for his body remained at Fort George, "buried under the Flagstaff, without the slightest memorial to remind his Countrymen he perished in their cause." Pausing there to reflect on the man, Catharine Maria Sedgwick "picked a clover stalk from the mound, from a feeling of reverence, we always feel for the deposit of the honored dead."[85] Without Brock's grave or any formal markers to guide their interaction with place, visitors to Queenston Heights could naturally find their attention drawn to the site's other main feature. A military officer on an official inspection tour of western forts described the view: "From this place, Fort Niagara is distinctly seen and the bold Niagara, smooth but rapid in its course, until it empties into Lake Ontario. The great elevation of this position, more than 300 feet higher than the water, enables the spectator to behold a vast extent of county and all beneath, on the left bank, being well cultivated, the whole face of nature, is softened into a beautiful and picturesque landscape."[86] The combination of a dramatic vista and historical associations provided an attractive destination for travelers.

Canadians thought the site should also host a monument to Brock, their fallen hero. The effort began in 1813, when the British Parliament funded a memorial to Brock in St. Paul's Cathedral, London. Two years later the provincial legislature commissioned a much larger, outdoor monument at Queenston Heights, but limited public funds and meager private donations slowed the effort.[87] Work began in 1823, and "after the monument was built, his remains, with those of his aid, Col. McDonald [sic], were deposited here with much pomp, on one of the anniversaries of the battle of Queenston."[88] Specifically, on October 13, 1824, the battle's twelfth anniversary, a "solemn procession" carried the bodies of Brock and MacDonnell up the river from Fort George. A black hearse was drawn by draped horses and accompanied by columns of soldiers and politicians; "to the spectator who had his station on the summit near the monument, nothing could be more finer than the effect of the lengthened column winding slowly up the steep ascent in regular order, surrounded by scenery no where surpassed for romantic beauty." A nineteen-gun salute and a delegation of Grand River Haudenosaunee, who had helped win the battle, honored Brock and MacDonnell. Their "warlike appearance, intrepid aspect, picturesque dress and ornaments, and majestic demeanour, accorded well with the

**Figure 16.** H. Park, *View of Brock's Monument, Queenston Heights,* from Samuel DeVeaux, *The Falls of Niagara* (1839). Dedicated in 1824, this stone monument atop Queenston Heights memorialized Sir Isaac Brock, who died leading a charge to gain the crest. His bones remain entombed under a second monument, completed in 1856. It replaced this 1824 monument, which was damaged in 1840 (see figure 17). Upriver travel ended just below the monument, making it a natural object of curiosity. Courtesy of the Castellani Art Museum of Niagara University Collection. Donation from Dr. Charles Rand Penney, partially funded by the Castellani Purchase Fund, and additional funding from Mr. and Mrs. Thomas A. Lytle, 2006.

solemn pomp and general character of a military procession." The re-mains were then "deposited in the resting place prepared for them in the monument." Beyond the ceremonial grandeur, the condition of Brock's remains proved his saintliness: "Although twelve years had elapsed since the interment, the body of the general had undergone little change, his features being nearly perfect and easily recognised, while that of Lieutenant Colonel McDonell was in a composite mass of decomposition."[89] Brock's original coffin, from his grave at Fort George, was blown up, and veterans present received small pieces as mementos, relics from the saint's life.[90]

Towering from between 350 to 485 feet above the Niagara River (depending on the estimated height of the escarpment) the approxi-mately 125-foot limestone "lofty column" featured an internal spiral staircase that led to an observation deck, circled by an iron railing. Brass telescopes enhanced the "extensive view...over the vast tract of country, including part of Lake Ontario."[91] For those disinclined to ascend the 170 stone steps, "the old park for artillery, and the marks of various works, [could] be observed in different parts of the heights."[92] One British officer who "toiled up the rocky heights" declared that "remains of the British works are plainly visible on the crest of the hill. The position is most formidable; and one cannot but admire the hardihood that prompted the Americans to attack."[93] In addition, near the stone monument were several "double hillocks, marking the silent mansions of many brave fellows sleeping the sleep of death."[94] But the site's allure continued to be the "picturesque lake scenery," visible "for fifty miles" from the monument.[95] In the distance one could see the Niagara River's mouth. At British Fort George "floats the proud banner of England," while on the opposite shore at American Fort Niagara "is beheld wavering in the breeze the standard of liberty." Tourists preferred that tranquil scene at the river's mouth to recollections of wartime bloodshed at Queenston Heights, declaring of the flags, "long may they wave together in peace."[96]

Such paeans to the peaceful landscape seen from Queenston Heights conveniently ignored the fact that Brock "did not fall on the spot where the monument is erected, but down the hill, in a northwesterly direction, about 80 rods distant, near a cherry tree." As late as 1845 it was a spot "still pointed out" to tourists in an effort to authenticate the importance of Queenston Heights the place, not the monument. American tourists focused instead on the "log house" not far from the monument, inside which American troops clustered during their retreat down the heights. With the Americans' ammunition exhausted, "the enemy continued to fire in upon them. This sight, with the piteous cries of our drowning countrymen, who sought to escape the carnage of that day, by endeavoring to swim the Niagara, makes Brock's Monument, to those Americans who were eye witnesses, no object of veneration." For Americans, the site "must cause but one emotion—sorrow for their fellow citizens who fell in that ill-fated battle."[97] American tourists identified the heights as "the theatre of carnage and disaster to our forces." Legend grew "that our unhappy men were driven down the rocks, of which they were ignorant. Many were dashed to pieces, and some pushed into the abyss below." Horrified at such cruel death, Catharine Maria Sedgwick scolded, "Will not Man learn that War is a disgrace to a reasonable Creator!"[98] When the English traveler Frances Trollope asked her guide if American soldiers

S.E.View of Brock's Monument on Queenston
Heights as it appeared May 9ᵗʰ A.D. 1041 .

**Figure 17.** *S.E. view of Brock's Monument on Queenston Heights as It appeared on May 9th A.D. 1841.* Benjamin Lett, part of a movement to gain more autonomy for Upper Canada, detonated explosives beneath Brock's Monument on April 17, 1840. The damage shown here required the demolition of the 1824 structure and the construction of a new monument. It also solidified trans-national memories of the War of 1812 as a valiant contest of brave soldiers, and the war was no longer remembered as a bitter dispute over territory between the United States and Great Britain. Archives of Ontario, Crown copyright Queen's Printer for Ontario.

"had been thrown from the heights into the river," the "British lad" rowing her ferryboat across the river replied, "Why, yes, there was a good many of them; but it was right to show them there was water between us, and you know it might help to keep the rest of them from coming to trouble us on our own ground."[99] During the 1820s and 1830s, Queenston Heights and Brock's Monument held different meanings for American, Canadian, and British observers.

What happened in the spring of 1840 changed American perceptions of the battlefield and reinforced the sentimental view of Queenston Heights articulated by scenic tourists of all three nations. Benjamin Lett, who had initially not participated in the 1837 Upper Canada rebellion but later joined the Patriot cause, detonated explosives under Brock's Monument on April 17, coincidentally Good Friday. A hastily revised 1840 edition of *Steele's Book of Niagara Falls,* presumably issued in time for the summer tourist season, described the column as "very nearly ruined. The key stone, over the door, is thrown out, the inscription stone has a large crack through the centre. A large fissure extends nearly half way up the building, on the side where the door is placed, then forks, and the forks are carried up to nearly two thirds of the height."

Cracks rent the monument's opposite side, and the damage included "the balcony broken, and the iron railing around, bent and disordered." The structure's dome showed several fissures, but luckily "the door at the top leading from the foot of the dome to the balcony, was open, otherwise the dome must have been blown off." In sum the monument "was very nearly ruined."[100] Two years later the structure still stood, "but it is in a shattered and ruined state."[101] By 1845 the dome had collapsed and the railing's base was crumbling, with "scarcely a single part unbroken. The interior is a literal heap of ruins, and the ground for many yards around, covered with the fallen fragments."[102]

Newspapers on both sides of the border condemned the act, yet despite the destruction, observers seemed reluctant to identify the perpetrator. Early reports claimed, "No discovery has yet been made of the perpetrators of the deed nor does any one know what were their motives."[103] Eventually "the ruffian Lett" was roundly condemned, when even mentioned, by American observers.[104] Generic disapproval of what twenty-first-century North Americans would come to call terrorism seemed more appropriate: "The action is certainly deserving of severe censure. Disturbing the monuments raised in honor of the dead, we had thought would not have been attempted by any in this age."[105] Destroying a general's monument was bad enough, but this was *Brock's* Monument, the burial place of a Canadian and British hero. This assault on national honor overcame the political divisions of 1840 Upper Canada. "Wantonly to destroy such a monument, raised in commemoration of such a man, would be base indeed; but there was not wanting some wretch, infamous and despicable enough to be guilty of the outrage." Guidebooks delegitimized Lett's actions and prevented him, instead of the revered hero Sir Isaac Brock, from becoming the object of tourists' interest. "Any wretch, so depraved, as to war against the ashes and honours of the dead is unfit to associate with the living."[106] This was a man, after all, who in 1838 had committed cold-blooded murder in reprisal for events during the rebellion, and had led a foiled 1839 cross-border raid that resulted in his capture and eventual escape. He was both a rebel and a terrorist known for his later arson and bombing efforts. Lett belonged to the kind of lower-class militants that both American and British officials sought to exclude from their arbitration of U.S.-Canada relations. His lack of respectability, both in terms of social status and conduct, disqualified him as a player in attempts to determine the relationship between the two nations.[107] Neither country honored his deed.

The legend of Brock seemed to increase because of Lett's bombing. In Upper Canada, Brock's Monument came to be regarded "with more affectionate veneration than any other structure in the Province." Wartime divisions over profiteering, desertion, and treason, which influenced postwar political quarrels over provincial finances, compensation for wartime losses, and medals and pensions for veterans faded amid "the first strong stirrings of nationalistic emotions."[108] Canadians increased their veneration of Isaac Brock as their national hero, a fallen martyr on the scale of American Revolutionary War general Richard Montgomery, who died assaulting Quebec in 1775 and was later revered by the nation. His body, like Brock's, was exhumed and reburied under an appropriate monument years after his death.[109] Americans even played the role of gracious losers, lamenting the "irreparable loss . . . of General Brock, which no victory could compensate." His monument deserved praise for its "value as a work of art," but more importantly because "it was erected in honour of a good and gallant man, whose name and deeds form a part of the history of the times; and whose uniformly kind treatment of American prisoners—so different from that of too many of his contemporaries—will ever be held in grateful remembrance by the American people." Brock, whose middle names seems to have become "Gallant," gained international respect as a gentleman-officer, even if he had once been America's foe.[110]

Yet by one measure, Lett had succeeded in desecrating Brock's memory. In 1852 one tourist noticed the "desolate-looking pillar erected in memory of General Brock; and it is rent from base to capital, and seems toppling to its fall."[111] Canadians had tried to rebuild the monument, but work progressed slowly, perhaps because some observers felt that "in its partially ruined state it is a noble object in the landscape."[112] One

1844 guidebook reported that the column "is about to be rebuilt," but that estimate proved overly optimistic.[113]

In fact, a few months after the detonation, "a great assemblage of Canadians" had gathered on Queenston Heights to begin the rebuilding. Tents sheltered the dignitaries gathered on the hot August day, while military units provided an honor guard and offered an artillery salute. Public offices in the provincial capital closed in observance of "a solemn holiday," and "thousands flocked from every part of the Province to testify their affection for the memory of one who, nearly thirty years before, had fallen in its defense." "Eight large steamboats" carried Lieutenant Governor Sir George Arthur, his entourage, and the Canadian militia to Queenston landing, where they disembarked to cheers from the riverbank "lined with thousands" and marched up the hill to the monument. When the governor arrived at the site, "a man clambered up the outside of the monument, a height of 126 feet, holding on and hoisting himself by the lightning rod alone." He then unfurled the Union Jack, but not a single person attempted to raise a cheer. Having earlier noted the "very formal" tenor of the gathering that he considered "singularly deficient in enthusiasm," an American observer remarked:

> If such a feat had been performed before an assemblage of Americans, and associated with such deeds as that of Brock's monument, I am perfectly satisfied that one long, spontaneous shout of applause, three times repeated, would have accompanied the unfurling of the banner of the stars and stripes to the free winds of heaven. This is the first great political assemblage I have seen in Canada, and the first characteristic that struck me was its coldness, it formality, its want of all real natural enthusiasm.[114]

The differing American and Canadian interest in commemorating war, or at least in the manner they publicly demonstrated their enthusiasm for such projects, might be too easily attributed to the differences between a republican and a mixed constitutional government. The rebellion that helped spark Lett's attack claimed the need for broader participation in government as one of its causes. The rulers who had quashed it preferred carefully prescribed, well-mannered forums. Scripted ceremonies, formal processions, speeches by "some of the most eminent and eloquent men," and artillery salutes offered more appropriate commemorations than did pole-climbing and full-throated cheers. One more sober report of the event, which lauded "this grand and imposing assemblage," insisted that "the enthusiasm with which the whole mass was animated may readily be conceived," but offered only the text of the eleven adopted resolutions as evidence. Once "the public proceeding had terminated," six hundred invited dignitaries "sat down to dinner in a temporary pavilion erected on the spot where the hero fell." To applaud the man who had unfurled the Union Jack would encourage such overly passionate, unsanctioned displays of patriotism; a polite dinner featuring speeches and "great loyalty evinced" set the proper tone. What Americans saw as indifference, Canadians considered propriety. Americans of a Whiggish mind-set who preferred order and refinement over the political and social tension of Jacksonian America likely agreed. The 1840 gathering at Queenston Heights concluded "with great dignity and judgment, and no accident occurred to interrupt the pleasures of the day."[115] Order prevailed, eliding Lett's radicalism and divisions, whether internal or international, from memories of Queenston Heights. By the 1840s the War of 1812 had lost some of its salience, as even the American wartime rallying cry, "Free Trade and Sailors' Rights!" had been overused for so many purposes that it lost much of its original meaning.[116]

Canadians also seem to have allowed the war to fade into the background. Not until August 1852 did they make significant progress in replacing Brock's cracked monument. The committee charged with completing the task selected a design that included a gallery on the ground level, a ninety-five-foot-high column enclosing a staircase, and a viewing platform at the column's apex, all "topped with a Statue of the hero." As in the 1824 monument, in the first floor basement "will be deposited the remains of General Brock, and those of his aide-de-camp, Col McDonnell."[117] Construction began once the bodies were "temporarily removed from the ruined column to an adjoining burial ground." On the battle's 1853 anniversary, a "splendidly fine" day, another formal procession and ceremony reinterred Brock's and McDonnell's remains and laid the foundation stone. Reports no longer mentioned the pristine condition of Brock's corpse, now moldering in the ground for forty years.[118] A "laudable anxiety" to complete the renovation motivated the committee to move forward with what an American newspaper called "an enduring proof of the just regard for the memory of a brave officer."[119] After the new monument's completion in 1856, at least one guidebook continued to mention the first monument's destruction by an "infamous act, said to have been perpetrated by a person concerned in the insurrection of 1837–38." But even that book devoted most of its attention to the "beautiful structure" now standing atop Queenston Heights, detailing its measurements, stone components, and the fenced area around the monument, which "left space for a grass-plot and walk."[120] Tourists approached the column up a tree-lined carriage road that terminated in a broad circular drive in front of the monument. The 1853 landscape plan also emphasized the viewing platform just below Brock's statue, designed "for persons to stand in to view the magnificent scenery and interesting objects which the grandeur of the situation affords."[121]

More than military history or even the gallantry of Brock and McDonnell, guidebooks lauded "the present handsome shaft" and its "gorgeous" view. One British publication claimed, "The eye wanders with untiring delight over the richest imaginable scene of woodland and water" from the top of the newly built monument. "In the midst flows the now tranquil River Niagara, calm and majestic in its recovered serenity."[122] The battlefield itself, partly obscured immediately below the tower, vanished from the spectators' gaze. They gained this perspective after ascending "a spiral staircase of stone" to the monument's top. "It is a most fatiguing journey, but, once attained, fully repays," wrote an American tourist. He expended such effort not in order to dissect regimental maneuvers, but rather to admire the vista: "The view is extended over miles of country, and down Niagara River until it flows into Ontario."[123] Even Canadian accounts emphasized "the view from this monument." The combination of scenic beauty and historical association rendered it a place "perhaps unsurpassed for magnificence by any on the American continent."[124] The aesthetic of the 1850s emphasized scenery as much as, or perhaps more than, the history of a place. One handsomely illustrated British book contained eight tinted views of American scenes, including "Outlet of the Niagara River." The accompanying text declared, "Memory recalls the many deeds of daring and bloodshed that have been enacted among these beautiful scenes." The panorama, not the history, dominated this landscape. "There is a strange blending of the rich with the wild, the soft with the savage, in our noble river scenery, that encircles it as with a halo of romance." Picturesque tourists found the perfect combination of scenery and historic ruins along the Niagara River; anecdotes of battles and memorials to fallen generals supplemented the scenery.[125] North Americans of British decent shared a common love of scenery, even on the sites where men still living had once spilled each other's blood.[126]

## Patriotic Landscapes

Tourist visits to 1812 battlefields along the Niagara River increased dramatically after 1840, with a new consensus about how to remember the war. More united Americans and Canadians than had divided them decades before. The desire for social status and an allegiance to their professional status as soldiers in a national institution united officers on both sides of the border into a cadre of responsible gentlemen. They shared a common goal of peaceful relations on the Niagara border, even if belligerence elsewhere seemed acceptable.[127] American expansionism looked beyond Niagara for conflict by the late 1830s and 1840s. Growing American self-confidence and faith in a cooperative relationship with Great Britain combined with the emerging sense of Manifest Destiny to shift the expansionist focus onto "nonwhite" peoples, especially Native Americans and Spanish-speaking Mexicans, to the south and west. Peace reigned along the northern border for several decades as memories of the War of 1812 lost some of their nationalistic urgency.[128] "War," said a veteran officer in an 1845 retelling of Queenston Heights, "is not between men, but between Governments. British and American officers will be personally good friends the day after a hard fight, and will be ready to fight again the next day, if the Country requires it of them."[129] Citizens of both nations came to remember martial valor and personal honor, not territory gained, the result of a particular battle, prewar grievances or ideological quarrels, as the war's central meaning. The river that politically divided the United States and Canada created a partially false border between Anglo-Americans.[130] "The proximity of the two countries, the same language, and similarity of pursuits, have so assimilated the inhabitants, that a stranger, not knowing the political division, in passing from

one to the other, would still think himself among the same people."
A Niagara Falls promoter insisted that any senses of difference that
occurred when citizens of either nation crossed into the other "arise
from the same source—love of country—of home, and veneration for
long cherished institutions."[131]

Yet crumbling forts and overgrown battlefields complicated any
simple transformation of the war's memory into trite lessons about
shared cultural values. The War of 1812's fortifications and battlefields provided fresh reminders of the struggle's bloodshed and indeci-
sive conclusion, and thus required cultural meaning. Catharine Maria
Sedgwick attempted to define the war's Niagara region sites in her 1821
trip, declaring, "This beautiful country stimulates my patriotism." But
hers was a patriotism not of specific battles or struggles to defend national honor. In an area where "grass has grown over the graves, and
for the most part they are inclosed in fruitful fields," she and other early
nineteenth-century tourists constructed a generic, emotional response
to place and history at Niagara's battlefields, "the 'spectre of sit and
sigh' amid their ruins."[132] The proximity of cultivated landscapes and
sites of destruction, whether battlefields or the natural power of the
Niagara River, provided an ideal setting for contemplating the opposing forces of civilization and wilderness. James Fenimore Cooper
repeatedly raised these themes in his frontier novels, including *The Spy*
(1821), based in part on his 1809 trip to Fort Niagara and up the Niagara
River. The novel's main character, Henry Birch, now at least seventy
years old, dies in the battle of Lundy's Lane, "devoted to his country,
and a martyr to her liberties." Niagara's "properly classic ground" allowed Cooper to resolve the Revolution's domestic conflicts, but in a
sentimental manner; Birch died clutching a tin box containing a note
of praise from George Washington. The romantic landscape around
Niagara Falls lent itself to such interpretations.[133]

Like Cooper, tourists frequently realized "that the very spot we
are standing on, may have drank the crimson streams of some unfortunate husband or of some hapless son, dying upon a distant field, far
from home, unknown and perhaps unpitied."[134] Niagara's battlefields
provided the opportunity to express sentimental emotions regarding warfare and sacrifice. Tourists sought the "melancholy pleasure, to tread the grounds upon which important battles have been
fought."[135] Such responses alone sufficed, and required few historical

lessons. People visited Lundy's Lane or Queenston Heights because of the scenic views and proximity to Niagara Falls. As one 1845 author lamented, "little is now thought of the places where these scenes occurred." He hoped that "in future ages there will be the shrines where pilgrims will come to worship the memory of heroes."[136] But into the middle of the nineteenth century, besides Brock's Monument—which commemorated a British hero—few such shrines existed. Visitors to Lundy's Lane preferred to ascend the observatory and avert their gaze from the battlefield; after all, they could see the falls from atop the tower's stairs.

# CHAPTER SIX

# The Value of Union

## Antebellum Commemoration
## and the Coming of the Civil War

Americans proposed six monuments at Revolutionary War battlefields between 1854 and 1860, more than during any other time in nineteenth-century America except the Revolution's centennial. Add in a seventh monument completed from an earlier effort and these commemorations constitute almost half of the sixteen battlefield monuments proposed or completed before the Civil War (see table 1). In commemorating the Revolutionary War, antebellum Americans derived new meaning from the old conflict, tinting it with the rising sectional conflicts of their own time, seeking to remember the war as either a moment of common national purpose or as a vindication of states' rights. That they brought these arguments to the very places where the nation's founders won independence with their own blood indicates an increased interest in the uses of battlefield commemoration. More than during any other time period to date, antebellum Americans sought out battlefields, no matter how small or local in importance, as subjects of commemoration. Growing Southern nationalism and the secession movement coincided with an increasing Southern desire to visit regional attractions and historic sites. In 1850 William Gilmore Simms published an important essay, "Summer Travel in the South," that announced the discovery of new historic destinations in the American South. After a summer of cholera

outbreaks and "abolition mania" in the North, "patriotic" Southerners declined to spend "time and money among a people whose daily
labor seems to be addressed to the neighborly desire of defaming our
character and destroying our institutions."[1] By identifying, visiting, and
commemorating their battlefields, Southerners invoked the Revolution's
legacy, using place as an authentic endorsement of their current political
position. They sought to draw martial inspiration from Revolutionary
War battlefields, "earth soaked with the blood of martyr-kinsman."[2] The
fifteen-foot-tall marble obelisk erected at Waxhaws, South Carolina, in
1860 honored the American soldiers killed in that "bloody massacre."
More important, the monument "will never fail to kindle a feeling of
indignation in the bosom of the patriot."[3] Northerners rediscovered and
used their battlefields for similar purposes, although they tended to continue emphasizing national unity amid sectional crisis. The antebellum
increase in battlefield commemoration employed old rhetoric in new
ways by using place as a legitimizing factor in sectional political rhetoric.[4]

## Blood-Soaked Ground

Like many speakers before them, 1850s orators employed the imagery
of blood to sanctify their causes. During and immediately after the
Revolution, "descriptions of blood soaking the American soil to con-
secrate it as holy ground filled printed materials and commemorations
of all kinds." Bloodshed served to unite Americans in shared sacrifice.
This idealized nation preserved the memory of fallen heroes by envi-
sioning a national community of shared concepts of liberty and patriotism. During the early republic such expressions took place in print or
on battle anniversaries.[5] The thirtieth-anniversary commemoration of
Kings Mountain honored "the precious blood of many of the citizens
of this part of the country" that "flowed freely in defense of Liberty and
the rights of man." It took place hundreds of miles away from the battlefield, in Abingdon, Virginia, amid the mountain region from which
many of the Kings Mountain veterans had marched.[6] Only once, in
1815, did people gather on the actual battlefield of Kings Mountain to
commemorate the American victory.

When Southerners did congregate on battlefields, they employed
familiar rhetoric. Speaking on the fifty-fourth anniversary of the battle

of Cowpens, the historian Benjamin Franklin Perry emphasized, "We have met too on the very plain—now consecrated as the Field of Battle and of Victory—*enriched* with the *blood* of our Countrymen, and *bleached* with the *bones* of their Enemies." Perry declared the battlefield a "glorious and sacred spot" worthy of respect. "The earth, on which we now stand, was soon *crimsoned* with the *blood,* and *covered* with the *fallen bodies* of the contending armies!"[7] Likewise, the 1839 commemoration of Huck's Defeat in Brattonsville, South Carolina, contrasted "the waters of the spring below us, that now gush forth so clear and transparent," with past events. During the battle the waters were "completely crimsoned with the blood of tories and British soldiery."[8] The rhetoric of blood and sacrifice gained additional power when uttered on the field of battle.

Yet well into the 1830s and 1840s orators declined to use battlefield commemorations to promote sectional causes. At Cowpens in 1835, Perry denounced the "Demon of Nullification" and exhorted his fellow citizens "to look to this sacred Union—reared by the wisdom and cemented with the blood of your fathers—as the bulwark of your freedom"; and John Tyler, the future president of the United States, decried "the action of sectional and local feelings" at the 1837 commemoration of Yorktown. Tyler imagined a "constellation" of states united in a confederacy. "To obliterate a single star—nay, to dim a single ray that issues from it, would be to blot out the whole from the Heavens, and to bring on one long night of Despotism." Should such a Union ever dissolve, Tyler wished that he "might go down with it to my grave."[9] Having staked out a pro-Union position that simultaneously defended states rights, in 1840 Tyler became the Whig Party nominee for vice president. He articulated his position on the Yorktown battlefield in order to emphasize the symbolic patriotic meaning that that place held.

If commemorations avoided sectionalism, partisan causes were perfectly appropriate topics for battlefield speeches. Tyler's party adroitly employed the Revolution's legacy during the 1840 campaign. The "Grand Whig Convention" held on Bunker Hill during the fall campaign attracted "friends of Liberty and sound republican principles, from all parts of the Union."[10] Four years later "the Democracy of Saratoga assembled on the battle ground." Drawing inspiration "on that spot," the party faithful "retired better calculated to wage a battle of the most determined kind."[11] That same year a gathering of thirty thousand Democrats "densely covered more than ten acres of ground" on the Oriskany battlefield near Utica, New York. The attendees made clear their partisan intentions and "the iniquity of the present tariff." Flags and banners marked "the very spot where the contest had raged the fiercest, and adjacent to the knoll where Herkimer received his death wound." Lieutenant Governor Daniel S. Dickinson, a staunch Democrat, outlined "the recent history of the two parties, in a style of witty and touching eloquence." Held beneath "very tasty" banners which "bore inscribed upon them some article of the democratic creed," the meeting adjourned "in the midst of hearty cheers," with "the complete rout of federalism" nearly assured.[12] Indeed, the Democrats won statewide and national races that November. The sacred ground of Saratoga and Oriskany successfully motivated partisan politics in upstate New York.

The rival Whig party in North Carolina capitalized on the presence of Guilford Courthouse in that state. During the 1840 campaign they paraded the "Guilford Log Cabin" across North Carolina, topped with banners promoting the gubernatorial candidate and presidential ticket, "For Harrison and Tyler." Inside the cabin, "constructed with poles cut from the same ground" as the battle, lay "*relics* from the old Guilford battle ground, such as swords, balls, shot and bayonets." When the cabin approached the Guilford Courthouse battlefield, "a large Canoe" joined the procession, expressing the link between the Revolutionary War victory and the patriotism of "Tippecanoe," as Whigs called their presidential candidate, William Henry Harrison, the hero of the 1811 battle of Tippecanoe.[13]

Partisan interest in the war's military legacy did not transform into sectional rivalry until after an event often considered a moment of common memory and national unity, the 1843 dedication of the Bunker Hill Monument. Southerners complained that Massachusetts politician Daniel Webster's dedication oration implied "that the other colonies of the United States were only the abettors and assistants of Massachusetts in the vigorous prosecution of the war of American Independence, and not, as they really were, sharers and participants in the toil, blood and glory of that eventful epoch!" To characterize Bunker Hill as "the blow which determined the contest," as Webster did, denigrated the contributions of Southern patriots. But Webster paid little attention to their contributions, arguing by omission that the "blood of his noblest countrymen" shed on "the fields of Yorktown and Cowpens, were of no substantial benefit in prosperously terminating that long and arduous contest." While all Americans owed a debt of gratitude to the heroes of Bunker Hill, defenders of the South's Revolutionary legacy could "never consent to remain quiet and have it concluded that those services were in themselves productive of such important consequences as to supersede the necessity of the hardy and daring exploits of our ancestors subsequently performed" on Southern battlefields.[14] By the 1840s the commemorative imperative had changed, as place gained increasing power to legitimate politicians' claims to the Revolutionary mantle. Americans now conjoined place and memory, as well as politics, more than during any previous era. Two distinct views of American nationalism emerged, in part, from battlefield commemorations in the North and South, and the dialogue between events in both regions.[15]

## Revived Nationalism

Other than Washington's grave at Mount Vernon, no other Southern historic site rose to the status of a shrine that required a pilgrimage by patriotic Americans. William Gilmore Simms determined to set the record straight by listing the South's "several points of attraction." The South contained underdeveloped "memorials" that tourists "will love to tread, with a passionate veneration." Historically minded Southerners already knew the tales of Pocahontas, Opechancanough, and John Smith along the James River and revered Mount Vernon. Simms sought to emphasize less-prominent sites that played a large role in winning independence. He reminded scenic tourists that amid the visible peaks in upper South Carolina stood "Kings Mountain, famous for the defeat of Ferguson, in the Revolution." In the same region tourists might find that "the famous battle-field of the Cowpens affords a point of great attraction to him who loves to seek the memory of the Revolution."[16] As Simms said in an earlier effort to stimulate Southern nationalism, "The battle fields which have been distinguished by Carolina valor, and rendered sacred by her blood, are among the most holy memorials of the republic."[17]

Southern patriots answered Simms's call to better develop their historic battlefields. They proposed monuments at Kings Mountain in

1855, and at Guilford Courthouse and Moore's Creek in 1857, and completed monuments at Cowpens in 1856 and Waxhaws and York-town in 1860. This effort marked a new trend in monument building, as only two small markers stood on Southern battlefields before 1856: the grave marker of Baron DeKalb at Camden, erected in 1825, and the 1815 Major Chronicle stone at Kings Mountain. Speaking to the second annual meeting of the Virginia Historical Society in 1849, its president noted that other states "have set us a noble example by mark-ing those spots of their territory which have been the scenes of great historical events by simple but appropriate monuments.... Are not York and James Town, worthy to be thus commemorated with Bunker-Hill and Plymouth?"[18] William C. Rives only echoed the comments of a visitor to the ruins at Yorktown, who wondered aloud: "The patrio-tism of the North has erected a sublime monument on Bunker Hill, to commemorate the portentous dawn of the revolution; when shall the patriotism of the South raise such a one, on the field of Yorktown, to commemorate the parting glories of the sunset?"[19] During the de-cade before the Civil War, Southerners sought to correct the monu-ment deficit in their region, with an emphasis on advancing Southern nationalism.

Northerners sought to apply their own veneer of interpretation to commemorating Revolutionary War battlefields as well. Simply re-membering an important general like Baron von Steuben, whose rural grave "had not a flag to droop over his hearse, or a soldier to discharge his farewell shot above his grave," gained importance. Steuben "was left alone in the forest" of upstate New York, "with the tall stems of the trees standing like sentinels about him, and the wind sighing through their tops his only dirge." The forgotten patriot "sleeps well beneath the soil of the land he helped to free; and though the nation refuses to erect a monument to his worth, when we cease to remember his deeds, we shall be unworthy of the heritage he left us."[20] But in an era when old soldiers like Ralph Farnham served as antiquarian curiosities, commemorations carried additional weight. At 105 years old in 1860, Farnham earned fame as "the sole survivor of the battle of Bunker Hill" and traveled from his Maine home to Boston for a celebration of his feats.[21] With fewer and fewer aged veterans still living to remind North-erners of the Revolution's legacy, they turned to stone monuments for permanent remembrances.

During the 1850s, patriotic Northerners proposed monuments at battlefields such as Bennington, Hubbardton, Oriskany, Stony Point, Trenton, and others. An 1856 meeting on the Saratoga battlefield declared, "Bunker Hill has its monument, and so should Saratoga."[22] New statues to Ethan Allen and Joseph Warren gained supporters, and individual towns like Chelmsford, Massachusetts, erected monuments to their Revolutionary War veterans.[23] New Yorkers even considered a coordinated monument-building effort for the battles at Oriskany and Saratoga, and at key sites along the Hudson River. Despite the region's vital role in the Revolution, "to this day we have no monument consecrated to the memory of the noble deeds of the gallant patriots of the days that tried men's souls" in the Hudson River Valley.[24]

Such sacred ground carried increasing importance as the 1850s progressed. In 1852 over ten thousand people attended the seventy-fifth-anniversary commemoration "on the battle field" at Bennington, and returned for almost annual events later in the decade.[25] Speaking near the site of the battle of Lake George in 1855, Cortlandt Van Rensselaer declared, "Monuments are of great public use. They are pages of history to the people; they are the rallying-points of earnest patriotism; they are records of national gratitude." He concluded that the Seven Years' War, when Americans fought alongside Great Britain against a common French foe, demonstrated how "the colonies practically learned the value of union and the unconquerable energies of a free people."[26] At a similar dedication in 1859, Van Rensselaer asserted that "self denial and suffering" helped win independence, and that "the true defences of a country against an invading foe consist in the intelligence, the virtue, the hardihood, and the skill in arms, of the yeomanry of the land."[27] The virtues existed in the North, but not the slaveholding South. Like his Southern counterparts, Van Rensselaer advocated battlefield commemoration that reified regional nationalism. By the late 1850s such pronouncements carried an increasingly strident, sectional tone that invoked contemporary political quarrels, especially when issued on the battlefield.

## Southern Nationalism

After 1848 the South moved quickly to address its earlier neglect of Revolutionary War battlefields. With dozens of battlefields to choose from, Southern nationalists commemorated victories that reflected well on their cause. They identified victories where Southern troops had repelled a foreign invader. The slow but steady progress of the 1780–81 campaign in the backcountry, rather than the British capture of major ports early in the war, tended to garner attention. Places where sturdy yeomen defended their home soil resonated amid the sectional crisis.

## Kings Mountain

According to one memorial effort, "No event of the war was better timed, or had more influence on the [patriot] cause than the glorious victory" at Kings Mountain in October 1780. Residents of upcountry South Carolina began organizing a commemoration of Kings Mountain's seventy-fifth anniversary "on as grand a scale as possible," with a cornerstone-laying ceremony as its centerpiece. The organizers invited the governments of those Southern states whose involvement in the battle "entitles them to full and equal participation with ourselves. The glory of the achievement is as much their heritage as ours." A memorial from nearby Mecklenburg County, North Carolina, which had recently begun to claim that its May 20, 1775, Declaration of Independence marked the first formal break from Great Britain, endorsed the event as "creditable to the valor and patriotism of the people of Virginia, North Carolina and South Carolina." Kings Mountain deserved celebration as a distinctly *Southern* victory.[28]

The October 4, 1855, gathering attracted nearly fifteen thousand people for "a noble act of worship, at 'the grand old mountain.'" The night before the commemoration nearly one thousand tents dotted the mountain and surrounding glens, "all reflecting goldenly the last rays of a bright autumnal sunset." The emotional gathering honored the heroes "who for long years tenanted the abodes of silence and neglect." Their once "unmarked" remains "exhumed from forgotten graves; and with more than all the honors that glorious war can give...given back again to the honored earth marked by an everlasting monument," South Carolinians could rest assured that "a debt has been paid." It was, remarked a descendant of those who fought at Kings Mountain, "upon my soul...a heart-stopping scene."[29]

Encountering this "sacred spot and its sacred memory" lent Kings Mountain greater meaning. Besides the military drills, parades, music, and prayers, two speakers attempted to define the battle. John S. Preston, the event's organizer and keynote speaker, termed Kings Mountain a place "where liberty was born." He pleaded that "a monument rise upon its peak as a memorial of the heroism of our fathers—as an evidence of the piety of their sons." Because they stood "on the spot where the surrender took place, near the rock which pillowed the head of the dying Ferguson, and hard-by the spreading branches of the venerable tree from which the baker's dozen of traitor tories were hung," the thousands who gathered at Kings Mountain knew the price of liberty. Preston declared, "We came up to these places of worship, for they are sacred. There be those of us here today who are standing on earth soaked with the blood of martyr-kinsman. Through that gorge, along that ridge, rising that steep acclivity, our patriot sires trailed in their own sacred blood."[30]

The liberty purchased with that blood demanded constant vigilance, especially in 1855. The government "which our sires gave us—and in which we are still safe, strong and prospering—is but the temple in which we worship the living spirit." Preston privileged Revolutionary principles above the inherited government, insisting that "sacred as it is—might for great good as it is—this union, glorious and blessed as it has been, and is—is not the holy of holies." In the context of 1850s sectional discord, he dedicated a battlefield monument with more than honoring fallen heroes in mind. "This great confederation," Preston claimed, "this union of confederate empires, these states, their constitutions, may be shattered into a thousand fragments; their ashes may be scattered on the winds" if his fellow citizens betrayed the values and lessons of Kings Mountain. "Let us be true to ourselves, be true to our country, be true to the God who gave it to us, be faithful to the blood shed by our sires, and we will be the sires of freemen as long as the earth owns man for its master." Preston spoke these words not in a lecture hall, on the political stump, or even in a legislative body, but "as he kneels on this holy place." He tied the right to secede with the sacred ground of Kings Mountain. Among the traditional thirteen toasts for thirteen colonies they raised, the Carolinians praised "Virginia, North Carolina and South Carolina: Firmly united in the days of 1780, may they ever be found, side by side, battling in defence of their constitutional rights and liberties against a common foe."[31] With the 1855 ceremonies at Kings

Mountain, Southerners demonstrated that they possessed both the heritage and spirit necessary for self-defense.[32]

The nation's leading historian, Massachusetts-born George Bancroft, made brief comments after Preston's address. He echoed Preston's call for a monument to be erected and asked that "the Union stand like your own mountains, which the geologists tell us are the oldest and firmest in the world." Bancroft claimed that "the men of that day fought, not for Carolina, not for the south; they fought for America and for humanity." Commerce and transportation "bound together" the states, "but the recollections of the crowded hours of the glorious actions of our fathers speaks to the heart, and makes us feel, more than all the rest, that we are one people." Applause followed Bancroft's remarks, which deviated from the event's general theme. He had earned the crowd's approval by insisting that Northern gratitude for Kings Mountain flowed from "reciprocity." The South "cherishes the memory of every noble action in behalf of liberty, without regard to place."[33] Whether at Kings Mountain or Bunker Hill, Americans fought for the same ideals. One Southerner made the same connection as did Bancroft, characterizing the commemoration as "calculated at this particular time to have a fine effect upon the whole Southern and Northern country."[34] But this traditional use of battlefield commemoration to appeal to national unity fell flat in 1855 South Carolina.

A letter from D. R. Atchison of Platte City, Missouri, drew stark comparisons between 1855 and 1780. Unable to attend the ceremony, Atchison detected "a similar foe to encounter in Kansas" to the foe the patriot militia faced in Major Ferguson's loyalist forces. Atchison's "border ruffians," pro-slavery forces from Missouri who crossed into Kansas to counter anti-slavery partisans such as John Brown, metaphorically fought alongside the Kings Mountain's heroes, while "the Abolitionists—such men as fought with Ferguson," stood with the Tories. Pro-slavery forces "have the whole power of the northern states to contend with, single handed and alone, without assistance," just as Shelby, McDowell, and Sevier resisted the might of the British Empire. Few Southerners had openly supported the Kansas cause before the Kings Mountain committee extended Atchison an invitation to join the Kings Mountain celebration of Southern resistance to tyranny. Like those rugged Overmountain men of old, Kansas's defenders would have to go it alone. "The prosperity or the ruin of the whole south depends on the Kansas struggle," declared Atchison, just as the American Revolution had depended on Kings Mountain seventy-five years earlier. His partisans drew inspiration from the history of Kings Mountain, and delighted in the Committee of Invitation's last line: "three cheers for Atchison and Kansas!"[35] An excerpt from "the notorious" Atchison's letter ran in the Massachusetts newspapers under the headline: "To Be Remembered," motivating abolitionists as well as pro-slavery forces.[36] Kansas abolitionists, in stark contrast with the sentiments expressed at Kings Mountain, viewed the rejection of the pro-slavery Lecompton constitution as "Lexington," the Revolution's opening, and predicted that a vote on the compromise English bill would result in its defeat, "the grand finale of Yorktown."[37] No longer drawing on the common heritage of the Revolutionary War to define a unifying nationalism, at Kings Mountain Southerners constructed a regional nationalism based on their own memory of the Revolution.[38]

## Cowpens

Among the totems at Kings Mountain in 1855 was the flag of the Washington Light Infantry, a "company of gentlemen" based in Charleston. The militia unit held anniversary events for key battles, served as a South Carolina unit, and preserved the flag its namesake, Colonel William Washington, a distant cousin of the first president, had carried during the Revolution. On their way to "the battle-field of Cowpens...with a view to reconnoiter and make preparations for a grand demonstration on the ground next spring," their flag attracted attention at Kings Mountain as a "holy" relic of the Revolution. Reverence for place dominated memory in 1856 when the Washington Light Infantry sought to erect "a more enduring monument" to Colonel Washington at the Cowpens battlefield. "For over a half century they had cherished with honorable pride the associations of this important Revolutionary event, and the anniversaries of the battle have annually been celebrated by the corps" in Charleston. At the conclusion of their January 17, 1856, parade on the battle's seventy-fifth anniversary, they resolved to make a pilgrimage to Cowpens.[39]

What separated this event from other earlier commemorative events was that the Washington Light Infantry sought "not to deepen and renew inscriptions on moss covered monuments, but to erect for the first time a monument on a spot hallowed by duty and patriotic devotion."[40] More than a typical anniversary event, the Cowpens monument evoked new meanings from the old battle. The monument dedication would perpetuate "the germ of a living principle within you which proves that you are Old Carolina's true sons, and worthy to be the representative of the heroes of the Cowpens." Washington's "venerable flag" motivated "those among us, who, in times of peace are ready and willing to make the personal sacrifice to prepare themselves for war." The orator explicitly mentioned "the black and threatening cloud which darkens our northern horizon." In the context of heightened tensions over the status of Kansas as slave or free territory, "Among the strongest safeguards to the liberties of a people is a recollection of the deeds of valor and renown which wrung them from the tyrant's grasp, and disarmed him of his power." Monuments to such events, like Cowpens, "are the brightest jewels in the crown of a nation's glory" and reminded citizens of their usable Revolutionary past. "Should you in the course of human events be called from the quiet retreats of private life to drive back the enemies of our country, whether in defence of our national honor against a foreign foe, or of our own cherished institutions, our house-hold gods, and family altars, against the blind fury and folly of domestic fanaticism, may you like the immortal patriots of Eutaw and the Cowpens, armed with the panoply of a just cause, go forth" to battle, and presumably to victory. The foes, British tyranny or "domestic fanaticism," may have been different, but the outcome would be the same. The Washington Light Infantry's "absorbing veneration for this battle-field" provided an inspirational example of resisting external oppression.[41] The monument's base united South Carolinians in their opposition to invasion by including brick and water from the Eutaw Springs battlefield and "shell from the beach at Fort Moultrie, Sullivans Island."[42]

## Sullivan's Island

Charlestonians did not confine their battlefield commemoration to inland conflicts. Nearby Sullivan's Island provided an opportunity to redefine an important battle in the context of antebellum politics. On June 28, 1776, the southern tip of that sandy barrier island guarded Charleston harbor with a hastily constructed fort. The sand and palmetto logs

**Figure 18.** Washington Light Infantry Monument (1856), Cowpens National Battlefield. The Washington Light Infantry, a Charleston militia composed of some of the city's leading men, traced its lineage to the battle of Cowpens. In an attempt to unite their state amid growing sectional tensions, the group carried white shells from lowcountry Fort Moultrie to upcountry Cowpens, using the material to cement the monument's base. Note the shells inside the modern fence. Photograph by Andrew Kincannon for National Park Service.

absorbed cannon fire from British ships, several of which ran aground on the sandbar across the harbor entrance. Fort Sullivan's artillery pounded the ships into retreat, and the British burned the one vessel still stuck on the bar at day's end. Fort Moultrie, renamed in honor of its victorious commander, became "immortalized by its gallant reception of a British fleet" and earned a reputation as the beginning of South Carolina's resistance to British tyranny.[43]

Little remained to commemorate, however. Local preservationist Edmund Ravenel lamented the "destruction of the site of the Old Fort," as he called the original 1776 Fort Sullivan. During the Revolutionary War the "highwater mark was at least 150 yards farther from the present Fort" of the 1850s, and the protective sands and brickwork had disappeared. A few exposed palmetto log cribs indicated part of the original fort's rear wall, but even they "will in a very few years be completely destroyed and a small stone now confined in the cribs will disappear." Beachfront erosion could wash away even Fort Sullivan's bulwarks, which had so successfully repulsed the British attack. The antebellum breakwater "occupied the spot which was the center of the Palmetto Fort," as indicated by brick walls and a well "exposed by the encroachment of the tide a few years ago."[44]

Remains of the 1776 and 1780 fortifications, as well as earlier versions of the larger nineteenth-century Fort Moultrie, formed "the foundation of the Episcopal church" in the summer community of Moultrieville. An intrepid visitor might walk around the barrier island's beaches looking for traces of the fortifications, especially on the eastern tip, where there stood "a small battery of two guns, the brick foundation of which has lately been discovered, by the shifting of the sand."[45] By 1850 a two-story hotel capable of hosting two hundred guests supplemented wealthy families' beachfront cottages. The astutely named "Moultrie House" stood "within a short distance of *the spot,* where…on a rude rampart hastily thrown up, and constructed of Palmetto logs," Colonel Moultrie and his forces "triumphed on the memorable 28th June 1776, defended with Spartan virtue the passes to our City, against a proud squadron and a gallant army." By visiting the fort's "gateway, and its narrow postern, and its ramparts, well provided with wall pieces," guests could "call up the usual associations of the patriotic past."[46] Never mind that the extant fortification dated to 1811 and was the third Fort Moultrie located on Sullivan's Island. When Southerners visited the site, any ruins they saw probably related to something other than the valiant stand on June 28, 1776, but the ruins still carried historical association. So long as they were old, they could be used to call forth Revolutionary War successes.

The key events occurred "in the romantic days of…Sergeant Jasper's sad death in keeping upright and waving the banner presented him by the ladies of Charleston."[47] Sergeant William Jasper, only recently promoted from private in 1776, retrieved the fort's fallen standard, a white crescent on a blue field, amid heavy fire, "fixed it upon a sponge-staff, and planted it upon the ramparts again: Our flag once more waving in the air, revived the drooping spirits of our friends" watching from Charleston.[48] His defiant bravery symbolized the martial prowess of South Carolinians, and the "Palmetto Flag" became a patriotic emblem. When South Carolina contemplated secession in 1860, this flag, "under which the battle of Fort Moultrie was fought and won," flew from flagpoles across Charleston,

**Figure 19.** *The Dreamer at [Fort] Moultrie—1776 and 1861,* from *Harper's Weekly* (March 2, 1861): 136–37. The South Carolina soldier in the foreground equates his impending fight with the 1776 conflict on the same ground. Perhaps his forces, too, will repel the foreign force (in 1861 the United States, not Great Britain) and another hero will emerge, like William Jasper did in 1776. In this image Jasper holds the American, rather than the South Carolinian, flag (see figure 10). HarpWeek, LLC.

"suggested by the venerable Mr. Ruffin" as an evocative symbol of past glories. The fire-eating secessionist cited the Palmetto flag's "noble historical grounds for preference" as a banner "suitable to our cause" because Fort Moultrie "stood in the deadly breach and breasted the storm of tyranny." As Jasper had rallied patriots over eighty years ago, the *Charleston Mercury* hoped the flag, the crescent supplemented by a lone star and palmetto tree, "will grow and increase in strength" to become "the flag of the Southern Confederacy."[49] With only a few half-submerged brick walls to commemorate, Charlestonians adopted a physical symbol of the 1776 battle of Sullivan's Island to link secession to the Revolutionary War.

## National Unionism

Not all Americans, and not even all Southerners, employed Revolutionary War battlefields to promote sectional nationalism or justify secession

during the late 1850s. Instead, they echoed earlier invocations of sacred places to construct a national memory of the Revolutionary War
and to perpetuate the Union. An 1857 cornerstone-laying ceremony at
Stony Point, New York, sought to "contrast the scenes of the present
day with the disinterested services of our Revolutionary fathers...on
this national occasion." The virtuous and brave men who stormed the
British fort, armed only with bayonets, thought of more than their own
gain and political advantage. "On the spot where the deed, which they
would commemorate, had been performed," Americans should reflect
on their past "and profit largely" by the comparisons between "the triumph of peace and the destruction of war." Before nearly ten thousand
guests the keynote speaker declared, "If our great republic was yet to be
disseevered it would be from a neglect of those principles of Revolutionary times."[50] Similarly, an 1856 meeting designed to begin construction
of a Saratoga battlefield monument declared "our love of the union may
be strengthened by being reminded of the sacrifices made to achieve
our independence." Calling "abolitionists of the North, and Nullifi-
ers of the South—disunionists in principle and traitors at heart," the
meeting reminded Americans of the common ties "cemented by the
precious blood of a common ancestry." The gathering remained "concentrated and fixed immovably, on one idea—LIBERTY AND UNION,
NOW AND FOREVER."[51] The following year Massachusetts dedicated a
new, marble monument to General Joseph Warren near where he fell,
fighting as a common soldier, at Bunker Hill. An ode reminded the
ceremony's audience of the larger cause: "From sea to sea our UNION
swelling—/ Oh! forever may it stand."[52]

Pro-Union Southerners joined the national unionist chorus when the
long-neglected grounds at Guilford Courthouse gained their own preservation group, the Greene Monument Association. It formed in 1857
with an appeal "to the pride and patriotism of every North Carolinian."[53] Claiming that "the spirit of genuine, self-sustaining patriotism is
now at a low ebb in the hearts of our people," Greensboro's *Patriot and
Flag*, a Whig newspaper, called for more than "festivals and jubilees"
to commemorate the past.[54] The previous year an American Party rally
"at Old Guilford Battleground" had attempted to bolster support for
nativist principles and "old line Whig" candidates. Although thousands
of supporters heard numerous speeches over the course of two days, including "hundreds [who] remained on the ground all night," American

Party candidates lost the upcoming state elections. In November, Millard Fillmore lost North Carolina as well, marking the virtual end of the Whig Party as a viable force in North Carolina politics, most of its members having become Democrats.[55]

Seeing the limits of old battlefields as catalysts to electoral victory, Greensboro's Whig newspaper focused on engendering more generic patriotism among the citizenry. "Every battle field should have its monument; every hero, his obelisk." The nearby Guilford Courthouse battlefield led to Cornwallis's retreat and surrender at Yorktown, "yet nothing has been done. No stone, nor aught else has been reared in our county, to tell the day of that bloody fight, or to preserve and perpetuate the names and memories of the immortal GREENE and his brave compatriots in arms and dangers and death. Our ingratitude ought to crimson our cheeks with blushes of shame!" The newspaper proposed a "large and handsome monument of native granite" on "that consecrated battle-ground...the sacred place." Unlike the memorials at other Southern battlefields, that at Guilford Courthouse "will make us sacrifice our narrow, sectional prejudices and differences, which are worth nothing, for the preservation and continuance of that brotherly love, and national harmony, which alone can save and perpetuate our free and matchless institutions."[56] As early as 1848 local leaders had advocated "a Monument erected to the memory of Greene, and devoted to the perpetual Union of these States." Who could object to such a monument, "connected as it is with the South?" Patriotic citizens from North Carolina and across the South had contributed to Northern monuments.[57] "Objects equally *national* in their character, located in our native portion of the great national heritage," should garner even more generous donations.[58] Monument building could serve both sectional and national interests.

Instead, North Carolinians focused on "sectionalism, filibusterism, free-loveism, and all the isms, which ever cursed and disgraced a nation," and which were "rife in every quarter of the Union." The promoters of the Greene monument feared that "unless our differences are forgotten, unless party spirit is buried, unless devotion to our whole country is increased, unless our people are linked together by iron bands, and pointed by enduring monuments to Heaven," the Union will be "completely destroyed." Erecting a monument at Guilford Courthouse would constitute part of the urgent work needed "to avert

that worst of all national calamities, disunion and its inseparable con-
comitants, civil war and fraternal bloodshed."[59] It would remind "future generations of the cost and the worth of American liberty and the
American Union."[60] Seeing the symbol of the Revolution "should
smother trenchant thought in its conception, and wither the hand in its
traitorous act." Even with lifetime memberships of only one dollar, the
Greene Monument Association raised only $600 and never constructed
a monument before the Civil War rendered moot its attempt to preserve the Union by erecting obelisks.[61]

In 1857, the same year that heard renewed calls for a Guilford
Courthouse monument, no less an orator than Edward Everett invoked
General Warren's "lessons of fraternal affection which he taught us
in his death" at Bunker Hill. In his memory, "upon this sacred day,
and upon this immortal hill," Americans should "proclaim a truce to
sectional alienation and party strife." The hallowed ground of Bunker
Hill offered a physical reminder of "the kindly feelings that animated
our fathers," which should "revive in the bosoms of their sons." Should
any "malice, domestic or foreign levy invade us" and the nation's living
defenders fail, the statue's "marble sword would leap from its scabbard,
and the heaving sods of Bunker Hill give up their sheeted regiments
to the defense of the Union."[62] Three years later Everett, the eventual
vice presidential nominee of the Constitution Union Party, joined
the citizens of Lexington, Massachusetts, in proposing a monument
"on the spot where their fathers shed the first blood of the American
Revolution." They sought to honor and rekindle "the spirit which
animated our fathers on the momentous day, [which] was shared by
their fellow-citizens throughout the country." The proposed bronze
"Minute Man" figure invoked "comprehensive patriotism...in which
the whole country has an equal interest." Since each citizen of the
United States "has an equal share in the benefits of the great system of
Republican self-government," Everett expected donations from across
the nation.

> The present moment seems to be peculiarly adapted for an un-
> dertaking of this kind, which is so well calculated to carry back
> the mind to the times when the men of the South and the men of
> the North stood shoulder to shoulder in the field; when all hearts
> were united in one great national sentiment; and the names of

Lexington, Concord and Bunker Hill; of Bennington, Saratoga, and Princeton; of Kings Mountain and Yorktown, were uttered with equal pride and pleasure throughout the length and breadth of the Union.

Not just another monument, the Minute Man "shall be a national work on a spot of national renown." Lexington belonged not to Massachusetts or New England, but "to the people of the United States." April 19, 1775, was "equally important in its consequences, to every citizen of every state."[63]

Everett's Constitutional Union Party invoked the Revolution in arguing against secession, claiming at its 1860 nominating convention that "the Revolutionary blood in my veins rebels against every idea of disunion.... It comes to me from the battlefields of the Revolution, crying to me with the voice of my own father's blood to defend the Union as long as it lasts and as long as it breathes." The speaker, Tennessean Gustavus A. Henry, the grandson of founding father Patrick Henry, asked, "Are we to divide this heritage of graves? Am I to have no heritage in Bunker Hill—you none in Yorktown?"[64] The party's Georgia newspaper, the *Chronicle and Sentinel,* opined that "in the hearts of thousands, North and South, the story of the Revolution, the memory of Washington, the recollection of common struggles and common triumphs, the traditions of Bunker Hill and Guilford, or Trenton and the Cow Pens, of Lexington and of Yorktown, have kept alive a holy and reverential love of the Union." They sought to reclaim a spirit that had been gradually decreasing "for ten years past."[65] The governor of New Jersey wondered if Americans, having fought together during the Revolution "for the independence and liberty, not of a part, but of the whole American Union," could now avoid becoming "degenerate sons of patriotic sires."[66] Even Democrats, in hopes of making slavery a minor political issue throughout the 1850s, reminded voters that the shared sacrifices of countless battles meant that Americans from both sections "spilled" their blood for "that dear liberty for which they were contending." Northerners left slavery alone, and Washington, "a Southern man, a holder of slaves," led the nation to victory. "For seven long years" North and South "banded together, shoulder to shoulder" in the "battle for freedom."[67] As the Democratic nominee Stephen Douglas told a Vermont rally, "The glories of Bunker Hill, of

Bennington, of King's Bridge [*sic*], of Eutaw Springs, of Yorktown are our glories. We will have no dissolution!"[68]

## Sectional Memory

Others, like Republicans at an October 1856 meeting, ignored such calls for national unity and left no question as to on which side the Revolution's heroes stood. Holding a "grand gathering...on the ground where the Revolutionary Battle of Germantown was fought," Republicans hoped to invoke "a time hallowed in our country's history, [when] patriots poured out their blood in a struggle for freedom." Germantown would motivate men to fight for liberty once more: "the old battle ground will ring with the crys of freedom for Kansas!"[69] Patriots in Boston drew on black contributions during the Revolutionary War at a March 5, 1860, meeting at Faneuil Hall by linking the sacrifice of that day's hero ninety years previous, Crispus Attucks, to the liberty-depriving *Dred Scott* decision. That free blacks fought at "Bunker Hill...Lexington, Dorchester Heights, Brandywine, Princeton, Monmouth, Stony Point, Fort Moultrie, Green Bank, Croton Heights, Catskill, Bennington, and Yorktown" provided "satisfactory proof at least that they were citizens of the United States."[70] Political meetings across the North, including one held steps from the spot where patriot blood had first been spilled, remembered a Revolutionary War fought for freedom.

Northerners objected to Southern uses of the Revolutionary War for sectional ends, like the reported "desecration to the cenotaph and memory of" General Nathanael Greene. In November 1860 "at Savannah, the Colonial flag of Georgia was raised on Greene's monument, in the presence of an immense multitude." The Rhode Island officer who stood by Washington's side throughout the dark days of the Revolution, then headed south in 1780 to salvage victory from earlier defeats before becoming an adopted Georgian, provided a fitting symbol of national unity. Those who dishonored his memory "should have died of sun-stroke, as Greene did." Unionists expressed shock at the sight of "a rebel flag, flaunting defiance to the Union over the city where Pulaski fell fighting for that Union, and where Sergeant Jasper lives forever in memory for devotion to his country!"[71] Northerners reminded their countrymen that Southerners were "of the same blood as the South Carolinians who manned Fort Moultrie and defeated the British at Charleston in the Revolutionary War."[72] They should know better than to desecrate monuments to the nation's shared history.

Southern patriots ignored such scolding. They countered that on Bunker Hill "the banner of King George triumphed." Why should not "we of the sunnier South, not rear a like memorial on the ground where that banner drooped, and was down-trodden in defeat?" The monument at Moore's Creek Bridge deserved equal billing as "classic ground" where the nation actually defeated the British. Its 1857 erection created an "altar of freedom where we may ever rekindle the expiring fires of patriotism" and "swear...undying hostility to the enemies of our country." To the auditors of the dedication speech, the "tyrannies and trials which were practiced and endured" sounded familiar. "The minions of royalty made our own North Carolina alike their vassal and their victim, until, by reiterated aggression on her dearest rights, she was goaded to rebellion." Any dissolution of the union between Crown and colony lay squarely with the national power. Furthermore, "For ten long years we had remonstrated against the ungenerous and unconstitutional legislation of that power which claimed the right to rule us, and which sent its edicts over the water to degrade and destroy us." To prevent future assaults on liberty, "other men at other times" might have to "place their armed heel upon the...serpent of tyranny...and crush out its venom and its strength." Tyranny came in many forms, all of which North Carolinians stood ready to vanquish.[73]

Not willing to cede the Revolutionary War's memory, Virginians attempted to link the cause of states' rights to the war's culminating victory at Yorktown. An October 15–22, 1859, event included "some six or eight companies" of state militia ordered by Governor Floyd to attend and "a large number of visitors."[74] Plans to erect a monument to the Virginia men—not the Continental army, but Virginia state troops—who helped defeat the British in 1781 had to wait, as a fierce storm on October 19, the surrender's anniversary, prevented the Twenty-first Virginia militia from leaving its Gloucester County home and crossing the York River. They finally laid the cornerstone, dressed in their finest uniforms and marching in formation, on October 29. Dedicated on October 19, 1860, the fourteen-foot white marble obelisk sat atop a base of two large James River granite blocks placed on "the spot of the surrender of Cornwallis' sword." This was a Virginia monument resting on a base of Virginia stone, and the obelisk sought to claim Yorktown as a victory by and for the commonwealth.[75]

Just two years later Union troops approached Yorktown, which was defended by a Confederate army. Several Southern regiments encamped on a field outside the village, "within the remains of the old works, which the French had stormed nearly a century earlier." Many of the Confederate defenses merely consisted of "retouching to old British works," but the town itself had changed. Its "Revolutionary sleep" over, now the "quiet old Virginia county-seat, had waked up in all the bustle of a fortified camp." Old "worm-eaten" buildings transformed into warehouses, officers' quarters, and ammunition stores. The ancient wharf, "which had perhaps received Cornwallis' fleet, was now the landing place of hundreds of Southern troops," and its sheds would soon serve as hospitals. Even the one place that had actively remembered the earlier victory, the General Nelson house, from where "that eccentric shadow of the past...Capt. Robert Anderson, used to petition the Legislature every winter, to mount a cannon at that place for him to fire a patriotic salute on the nineteenth of each succeeding October," became a hospital, with the headquarters of Confederate General John B. Magruder located nearby. One observer estimated nearly "a thousand cannon and two hundred thousand muskets were assembled in and around Yorktown during this memorable siege." Most of its 1781 entrenchments "had been almost obliterated by these recent labors," and "the field where the Earl [Cornwallis] delivered up his sword was trodden bare, and dotted with ditches and ramparts." Occasionally troops found a few relics, like a "gold-hilted sword," on the old battlefield. In the optimistic early days of the conflict, before a fraction of the Civil War's blood had been shed, Americans wondered how "so paltry a settlement should have been twice made historic."[76]

The coincidence did not escape them. When Confederate troops marched from fortified Yorktown to meet Union troops at Bethel Church on June 10, 1861, "the place of rendezvous was in the road, opposite the monument, on the old battle-field below Yorktown."[77] That one of the Civil War's earliest battles occurred near the place where the United States won its independence, and that Confederate troops sallied forth from a monument to that victory, remained in the minds of troops from both sides. But if the South thought it could claim sole ownership

**Figure 20.** George N. Barnard, "Augustine Moore house, in which Lord Cornwallis signed the capitulation of 1781" (1862). This title is incorrect, however: Cornwallis was never in the house and the capitulation was signed elsewhere. When Union troops occupied Yorktown in May of 1862, these soldiers paused to have their photograph taken in front of one of the most potent symbols of the Revolutionary War. Its dilapidated condition indicates how far from the victorious unity of 1781 the United States had come. Presumably the Union soldiers hoped to force their current enemy, the Confederacy, to surrender as had Cornwallis. Courtesy of the Library of Congress.

of Yorktown's glory, Union troops held other ideas. When they marched into unoccupied Yorktown on May 4, 1862, the Union sought to re-claim the Revolution's legacy. But the small surrender monument had disappeared, "hacked to fragments by the Southerners, and carried away piecemeal." Confederate troops sought to prevent the Union's physical possession of both place and memory. In retaining pieces of the surren-der monument they kept their interpretation of the Revolutionary War intact.[78] If they could not control Yorktown, then they would carry its memory with them. Place and physical commemoration mattered in Civil-War era Americans' memories of the Revolution.

The commemorative power of battlefields, monuments, and military heroes merited contestation as the nation sought to define its past in the context of dissolution. The Revolutionary past possessed meaning that united the nation and provided political lessons for fractious antebellum politics. Not wanting to forget their past, antebellum Americans attempted to apply the Revolution to their current social and political struggles. During the 1850s the difference lay in where Americans made such appeals to the Revolution's legacy. Amid the increased interest in remembering the nation's past glories, sectional nationalism and national unionism both sought the old battlefields to lend credence to their respective ideologies. Speeches and ceremonies far from the scene of bloodshed no longer carried as much commemorative impact as they had in years past. In their varying battlefield celebrations and invocations of the Revolutionary past, Americans engaged in the "performative nature of regionalist discourse" that depended on competing visions of nationalism to define each section's identity and to mobilize its constituencies.[79] The unifying nationalism of the Revolution and the founding fathers so carefully constructed during the early republic could no longer submerge the perpetual tension between slavery and freedom.

## Conclusion

Decades before the harmonious Yorktown centennial, President James Monroe toured the Northern states, seeking to heal the sectional wounds inflicted by the War of 1812. The Revolutionary War veteran, severely wounded at the battle of Trenton in 1776, took notice of battlefields along his route, frequently embracing veterans he met there. Such places became "classic ground" because they had "been the scenes of blood, death and victory." Monroe's 1817 visits to American battlefields belong to a larger movement of touring and commemorating battlefields that gained popularity after his tour, although the motivations for visiting and responses to the sites varied over time. Battlefields had been "most celebrated by the ancient and modern epic poets," but in Monroe's era the task "still remains for the future poet to immortalize the plains" of America's great battles.[80]

As early as the late 1750s Anglo-Americans responded to history at places such as Braddock's Field and Ticonderoga. They lacked the framework to understand the scattered bones or crumbling earthworks they found at these Seven Years' War battlefields and frequently offered little more than musings on the folly of British military tactics, especially while visiting during the Revolutionary War. The errors of Braddock and Abercromby served to highlight the reasons for breaking from Great Britain or to advance the reputation of George Washington, but during the late eighteenth century too few visitors observed the bonefields to make these places central to American nationalism. It took the rise of picturesque tourism along the Northern Tour route, which included the Revolutionary War battlefields along the Hudson River and northern lakes, to bring battlefields to the forefront of American cultural consciousness. History provided ambience and opportunities to display sentiment when viewing old battlefields and ruins, especially if the site stood along a body of water or featured a scenic mountain backdrop. Tourism helped to commemorate battlefields, but emphasized personal interactions with place rather than historical knowledge. Such memories differed from the more nationalistic meanings public orators announced at monument dedications after 1826. Too few commemorative efforts resulted in completed monuments, though, for such official memories of the Revolutionary War to dominate the discourse of memory. Even the Marquis de Lafayette's famous 1824–25 tour of the United States, and his many stops at old battlefields, failed to spur a flurry of monument building. Americans were not yet ready to fully commemorate their past.

This was especially true at Revolutionary War battlefields in the South, where some of the war's harshest fighting had taken place. The region's battlefields, scattered across the rural inland or obliterated by urban expansion in Charleston and Savannah, left little physical evidence of the past to encounter. The lack of transportation infrastructure or nearby resorts meant that Southern battlefields never attracted the level of interest or visitation that northern battlefields experienced. Southern sites remained undisturbed or overgrown, if they still existed at all, and relied even more on the personal visits and responses of the few tourists who made their way to the battlefields. Tourists were more likely to encounter bones and bullets than monuments. In contrast, War of 1812 battlefields along the Niagara River gained fame, visitors, and monuments in the decades after that conflict. Scenery, efficient transportation, and the tourist magnet of Niagara Falls transformed 1812 battlefields like Lundy's Lane and Queenston Heights into popular destinations. Travelers could view both history and the region's splendid scenery on an afternoon carriage ride before returning to their hotels for dinner and a soft bed. Sentiment and generic patriotism—reverence for martial valor and fallen soldiers—prevailed at the Niagara River's battlefields, converting one of the War of 1812's bloodiest and most contest theaters into picturesque tourist attractions.

Such emotional and almost ahistorical responses to place began to fade as the sectional crisis intensified during the 1850s. South and North rediscovered Revolutionary War battlefields as places that held political meaning and could be used to advance sectional agendas. New efforts to construct monuments, or to complete ones proposed years earlier, invoked the Revolution's legacy as either evidence of sectional pride and self-sufficiency or lessons in national unity. Meaning became increasingly localized and political, as the broader memories of a gauzy Revolution of brave soldiers and tragic battles fought on scenic battlefields was relegated to secondary importance. During the antebellum period Americans did not necessarily interact with their battlefields more than they had in the past. Yet the meaning of place, and the memories constructed on historic ground, changed significantly as the motivation for visiting and commemorating battlefields evolved. Americans had performed nationalism all along, but the meaning of that nationalism and the nature of battlefield visits varied between the 1760s and 1850s.

Just a few years after the dedication of several monuments to a distinctly Southern or Northern memory of the Revolutionary War, President Abraham Lincoln invoked "the mystic chords of memory, stretching from every battlefield, and patriot grave" to unite the Union.[81] Where many antebellum politicians had used battlefield commemorations to tear the nation apart, Lincoln sought to bring it back together through the kind of national memory that had rarely dominated the discourse of battlefield tourism. Speechmakers may have favored it, but tourists preferred a picturesque scene and evocative story that varied from battlefield to battlefield. Not until almost a century after the Revolution, and a much bloodier war, would Lincoln's "mystic chords of memory" pervade American culture and result in the widespread preservation and commemoration of the nation's battlefields.

*Notes*

## Preface

1. Butch Street, *Statistical Abstract: 2010.* Natural Resource Data Series NPS/NRPC/SSD/NRDS—2011/147 (Fort Collins, CO: National Park Service, 2010), 3, 35.

2. John F. Sears, *Sacred Places: American Tourist Attractions in the Nineteenth Century* (New York: Oxford University Press, 1989).

3. "The British Are Coming…" *Ballston Journal,* September 24, 1980; "Battle Re-enacted during Heritage Weekend," *Ballston Journal,* October, 1, 1980; Edward F. Grose, *Centennial History of the Village of Ballston Spa, Including the Towns of Ballston and Milton* (Ballston Spa, NY: *Ballston Journal,* 1907), 17–19, 29–35.

## Introduction

1. "Yorktown," *New York Times,* October 23, 1879, p. 4, ProQuest Historical Newspapers: *New York Times* (1851–2007) (hereafter cited as NYT-PQ).

2. Ibid.

3. Phyllis A. Hall, "Yorktown Revisited: The Centennial and Sesquicentennial Celebrations," *Virginia Cavalcade* 31 (August 1981): 102–11; "Yorktown Victory Monument," National Park Service, www.nps.gov/york/historyculture/vicmon02.htm (accessed May 20, 2011).

4. "The Programme of the Yorktown Centennial Celebration," 1881, Yorktown Collection, Colonial National Historical Park; John Austin Stevens, *Yorktown Centennial Handbook: Historic and Topographical Guide to the Yorktown Peninsula* (New York: C. A. Coffin and Rogers, 1881), 48–51; "Yorktown," *Richmond Standard,* October 15, 1881, p. 2.

5. "Monument Bill in Congress," *New York Times,* May 30, 1880, p. 4, NYT-PQ; "The Yorktown Monument," *New York Times,* March 22, 1880, p. 1, NYT-PQ.

6. "Programme of the Yorktown Centennial Celebration," 48–51.

7. Stevens, *Yorktown Centennial Handbook,* 5; "Virginia's Welcome," *Richmond Daily Dispatch,* October 19, 1881, p. 2; "Laying the Cornerstone," *New York Times,* October 19, 1881, p. 1, NYT-PQ; "Memories of Yorktown," *New York Times,* October 20, 1881, p. 1, NYT-PQ.

8. Daniel Webster, *An Address Delivered at the Laying of the Corner Stone of the Bunker Hill Monument* (Boston: Cummings, Hillard, 1825); Daniel Webster, *An Address Delivered at the Completion of the Bunker Hill Monument, June 17, 1843* (Boston: Tappan and Dennet, 1843); Edward Everett, *An Oration Delivered at Concord, April the Nineteenth, 1825* (Boston: Cummings, Hillard, 1825); Edward Everett, *An Address, Delivered at Lexington, on the 19th (and 20th) April, 1835* (Charlestown, MA, William W. Wheildon, 1835).

9. David Waldstreicher, *In the Midst of Perpetual Fetes: The Making of American Nationalism, 1776–1820* (Chapel Hill: University of North Carolina Press, 1997), 2–14, 180–212; John F. Sears, *Sacred Places: American Tourist Attractions in the Nineteenth Century* (New York: Oxford University Press, 1989), 3–30. The extensive literature on memory in the early republic devotes the vast majority of its attention to ceremonies, anniversary events, individuals, and even structures, but spends little time discussing battlefields. The existing works minimize place to focus on such constructions and contestations along the dynamics of race, class, and gender, using sources of memory that are remarkably self-conscious—formal ceremonies and speeches commemorating the past. We know more about public celebrations or individual veterans than the places where they fought. See especially Mitchell Kachun, "From Forgotten Founder to Indispensable Icon: Crispus Attucks, Black Citizenship, and Collective Memory," *Journal of the Early Republic* 29 (Summer 2009): 249–86; Scott E. Casper, *Sarah Johnson's Mount Vernon: The Forgotten History of an American Shrine* (New York: Hill & Wang, 2008); Seth E. Bruggeman, *Here, George Washington Was Born: Memory, Material Culture, and the Public History of a National Monument* (Athens: University of Georgia Press, 2008); Mitchell Kachun, "Antebellum African Americans, Public Commemoration, and the Haitian Revolution," *Journal of the Early Republic* 26 (Summer 2006): 249–73; Francois Furstenberg, *In the Name of the Father: Washington's Legacy, Slavery, and the Making of a Nation* (New York: Penguin, 2006); Robert E. Cray Jr., "Remembering the USS *Chesapeake:* The Politics of Maritime Death and Impressment," *Journal of the Early Republic* 25 (Fall 2005): 445–74; Alfred F. Young, *Masquerade: The Life and Times of Deborah Sampson, Continental Soldier* (New York: Alfred A. Knopf, 2004); Mitchell Kachun, *Festivals of Freedom: Memory and Meaning in African American Emancipation Celebrations, 1808–1915* (Amherst: University of Massachusetts Press, 2003); Charlene Mires, *Independence Hall in American Memory* (Philadelphia: University of Pennsylvania Press, 2002); Andrew Burstein, *America's Jubilee, July 4, 1826: A Generation Remembers the Revolution after Fifty Years of Independence* (New York: Vintage Books, 2001); Robert E. Cray Jr., "Commemorating the Prison Ship Dead: Revolutionary Memory and the Politics of Sepulture in the Early Republic," *William and Mary Quarterly* 56 (July 1999): 565–90; Alfred F. Young, *The Shoemaker and the Tea Party: Memory and the American Revolution* (Boston: Beacon Press, 1999); John Resch, *Suffering Soldiers: Revolutionary War Veterans, Moral Sentiment, and Political Culture in the Early Republic* (Amherst: University of Massachusetts Press, 1999); Robert E. Cray Jr., "The Revolutionary Spy as Hero: Nathan Hale in the Public Memory," *Connecticut History* 38 (March 1999): 85–104; Len Travers, *Celebrating the Fourth: Independence Day and the Rites of Nationalism in the Early Republic* (Amherst: University of Massachusetts Press, 1997); Robert E. Cray Jr., "Major John André and the Three Captors: Class Dynamics and Revolutionary Memory Wars in the Early Republic, 1780–1831," *Journal of the Early Republic* 17 (Fall 1997): 371–97; Michael Kammen, *A Season of Youth: The American Revolution and the Historical Imagination* (Ithaca, NY: Cornell University Press, 1978).

10. "The Yorktown Centennial," *Richmond Dispatch,* September 29, 1881, p. 3; "Pleasant Routes to Yorktown during the Centennial," *Richmond Dispatch,* October 4, 1881, p. 1.

11. "Peninsula Branch of the Chesapeake and Ohio Railroad Now Nearly Completed to Yorktown and Newport News," *Richmond Dispatch,* September 30, 1881, p. 1; "Virginia's Great Fete: Scenes about the Camp in Historic Yorktown," *New York Times,* October 16, 1881, p. 1, NYT-PQ.

12. "The Yorktown Centennial," *Richmond Dispatch,* September 30, 1881, p. 4.

13. "Yorktown's Anniversary: Making Ready for the Great Celebration," *New York Times,* October 15, 1881, p. 1, NYT-PQ.

14. "The Celebration at Yorktown: Arrangements for the Monument—Accommodations for the Many Guests," *New York Times,* September 3, 1881, p. 2, NYT-PQ.

15. "Bad Management at Yorktown: No Quarters for the French Guests," *New York Times,* October 14, 1881, p. 1, NYT-PQ.

16. Stevens, *Yorktown Centennial Handbook,* 66–67.

17. "Yorktown Centennial," *Richmond Dispatch.*

18. Carl Bridenbaugh, ed., *Gentlemen's Progress: The Itinerarium of Dr. Alexander Hamilton, 1744* (Chapel Hill: University of North Carolina Press, 1948), xxvii.

19. Carl Bridenbaugh, "Baths and Watering Places of Colonial America," *William and Mary Quarterly,* 3rd Ser., vol. 3 (April 1946): 151–81; Cindy S. Aron, *Working at Play: A History of Vacations in the United States* (New York: Oxford University Press, 1999); Richard H. Gassan, *The Birth of American Tourism: New York, the Hudson Valley, and American Culture, 1790–1830* (Amherst: University of Massachusetts Press, 2008).

20. Barbara Carson, "Early American Tourists and the Commercialization of Leisure," in *Of Consuming Interests: The Style of Life in the Eighteenth Century,* ed. Cary Carson, Ronald Hoffman, and Peter J. Albert (Charlottesville: University of Virginia Press, 1994), 381–88; Dona Brown, *Inventing New England: Regional Tourism in the Nineteenth Century* (Washington, DC: Smithsonian Institution Press, 1995), 23–31; George Rogers Taylor, *The Transportation Revolution: 1815–1860* (New York: Harper & Row, 1968).

21. Aron, *Working at Play,* 15–18; Brown, *Inventing New England,* 31–35, 41–74; Sears, *Sacred Places;* John D. Cox, *Traveling South: Travel Narratives and the Construction of American Identity* (Athens: University of Georgia Press, 2005), 4; Thomas A. Chambers, *Drinking the Waters: Creating an American Leisure Class at Nineteenth-Century Mineral Springs* (Washington, DC: Smithsonian Institution Press, 2002); Charlene M. Boyer Lewis, *Ladies and Gentlemen on Display: Planter Society at the Virginia Springs* (Charlottesville: University of Virginia Press, 2001); Jon Sterngass, *First Resorts: Pursuing Pleasure at Saratoga Springs, Newport and Coney Island* (Baltimore: Johns Hopkins University Press, 2001); Theodore Corbett, *The Making of American Resorts: Saratoga Springs, Ballston Spa, Lake George* (New Brunswick, NJ: Rutgers University Press, 2001).

22. Peregrine Prolix [Philip Holbrook Nicklin], *Letters Descriptive of the Virginia Springs; the Roads Leading Thereto, and the Doings Thereat* (Philadelphia: H. S. Tanner, 1835), 29.

23. Washington Irving, "Style at Ballston," *Salmagundi No. 16,* Thursday, October 15, 1807, in *Salmagundi,* ed. Bruce I. Granger and Martha Hartzog (Boston: Twayne, 1977), 256–57.

24. Gideon Minor Davison, *The Fashionable Tour; or, a Trip to the Springs, Niagara, Quebeck, and Boston, in the Summer of 1821* (Saratoga Springs, NY: G. M. Davison, 1822); [James Kirke Paulding], *The New Mirror for Travellers; and Guide to the Springs* (New York: G. & C. Carvill, 1828), 5.

25. Edward Gibbon, *Memoirs of My Life,* ed. Georges A. Bonnard (New York: Funk & Wagnalls, 1966), 135; Lynne Withey, *Grand Tours and Cook's Tours: A History of Leisure Travel, 1750–1915* (New York: William Morrow, 1997), 3–31.

26. William Gilpin, "Essay on Picturesque Travel," in *Three Essays: On Picturesque Beauty; On Picturesque Travel; and On Sketching Landscape: To Which is Added a Poem, On Landscape Painting* (London: R. Blamire, 1792), 26, 48–50, 53; Edmund Burke, *A Philosophical Enquiry*

*into the Origin of Our Ideas of the Sublime and Beautiful* (London: J. Dodsley, 1757), 127–28, 213; Malcolm Andrews, *The Search for the Picturesque: Landscape Aesthetics and Tourism in Britain, 1760–1800* (Palo Alto, CA: Stanford University Press, 1989), pt. 1; Raymond Williams, *The Country and the City* (New York: Oxford University Press, 1973).

27. Daniel Kilbride, "Travel, Ritual, and National Identity: Planters on the European Tour, 1820–1860," *Journal of Southern History* 69, no. 3 (2003): 549–84.

28. John Conron, *American Picturesque* (University Park: Pennsylvania State University Press, 2000), 4–11; John Urry, *The Tourist Gaze* (London: Sage, 2002), 1–4; Brown, *Inventing New England*, 4–5, 34–38; Sears, *Sacred Places*, 3–10; Roger Haydon, ed., *Upstate Travels: British Views of Nineteenth-Century New York* (Syracuse, NY: Syracuse University Press, 1982), 8–9.

29. Thomas Cole, "American Scenery," *Northern Light* 1 (May 1841), as quoted in Bonnie Marranca, *Hudson Valley Lives* (New York: Overlook Press, 1991), 378–79, 383; Angela Miller, *Empire of the Eye: Landscape Representation and American Cultural Politics, 1825–1875* (Ithaca, NY: Cornell University Press, 1993), 11–17.

30. William H. Truettner and Alan Wallach, eds., *Thomas Cole: Landscape into History* (Washington, DC: National Museum of American Art, 1994); Kenneth Myers, "The Rise of Catskill Mountain Tourism, 1824–1838," in *The Catskills: Painters, Writers, and Tourists in the Mountains, 1820–1895* (Yonkers, NY: Hudson River Museum, 1987), 37–63; Bruce Robertson, "The Picturesque Traveller in America," in *Views and Visions: American Landscape before 1830*, ed. Edward J. Nygren (Washington, DC: Corcoran Gallery of Art, 1986), 187–211; Wayne Franklin, *James Fenimore Cooper: The Early Years* (New Haven, CT: Yale University Press, 2007).

31. Barbara Novak, *Nature and Culture: American Landscape, 1825–1875* (New York: Oxford University Press, 1980); Perry Miller, "The Romantic Dilemma in American Nationalism and the Concept of Nature," in *Nature's Nation* (Cambridge, MA: Harvard University Press, 1967), 197–207; Roderick Nash, *Wilderness and the American Mind*, rev. ed. (New Haven, CT: Yale University Press, 1973); Leo Marx, *The Machine in the Garden: Technology and the Pastoral Ideal in America* (New York: Oxford University Press, 1964); Stephen Daniels, *Fields of Vision: Landscape Imagery and National Identity in England and the United States* (Princeton, NJ: Princeton University Press, 1993).

32. Abigail May journal, July 20, 1800, p. 75, New York State Historical Association.

33. Theodore Dwight, *The Northern Traveller; Containing the Routes to the Springs, Niagara, and Quebec, and the Coal Mines; with the Tour of New England, and a Brief Guide to the Virginia Springs, and Southern and Western Routes* (New York: J. P: Haven, 1841), 102.

34. Benjamin Silliman, *Remarks Made on a Short Tour between Hartford and Quebec in the Autumn of 1819* (London: Sir Richard Philips and Co., 1822), 65.

35. Orville L. Holley, ed., *The Picturesque Tourist: Being a Guide through the Northern and Eastern States and Canada* (New York: Disturnell, 1844), 105.

36. Theodore Dwight, *The Northern Traveller; Containing the Routes to Niagara, Quebec, and the Springs; with Useful Descriptions of the Principal Scenes, and Useful Hints to Strangers* (New York: Wilder and Campbell, 1825); Dwight, *Northern Traveller* (1841).

37. "A Visit to Wyoming Monument," *National Magazine* 12 (January–June 1858): 249, 251.

38. Gassan, *Birth of American Tourism;* Brown, *Inventing New England*, 15–40. The standard works on the history of American tourism devote no specific, extended attention to battlefields, either as tourist destinations or as sites of memory.

39. John Bodnar, *Remaking America: Public Memory, Commemoration, and Patriotism in the Twentieth Century* (Princeton, NJ: Princeton University Press, 1992), 13–14, 19.

40. "Another Yorktown Siege: The Great Celebration of the Anniversary," *New York Times*, October 19, 1881, p. 1, NYT-PQ; "Yorktown on Sunday," *Richmond Dispatch*, October 18, 1881, p. 1; "Memories of Yorktown: Hosts and Guests Speaking of Days Gone By," *New*

*York Times,* October 20, 1881, p. 1, NYT-PQ; *Report of the Commission …for the Erection of a Monument at Yorktown, Va.* (Washington, DC: Government Printing Office, 1883), 36–52; "Yorktown's Anniversary," NYT-PQ.

41. Bodnar, *Remaking America; Report of the Commission,* 13. Such individualized responses to historic places on one hand, and formal commemorations on the other, seem different than the clash between the "official" memory of cultural elites, political leaders, and existing institutions that sought to minimize complexity and ambiguity in favor of an idealized reality, and the "vernacular" memory of ordinary citizens from small-scale and diverse communities that sought to express the felt reality of their everyday lives articulated by Bodnar. The tourists constructing such memory did not represent a marginalized minority intent on rejecting the consensus view imposed by those in power, and were seeking a kind of memory quite different from the official/vernacular dichotomy Bodnar applies to the late-nineteenth century.

42. Michael Kammen, *Mystic Chords of Memory: The Transformation of Tradition in American Culture* (New York: Vintage Books, 1993), 9–11; David Lowenthal, *The Past Is a Foreign Country* (Cambridge: Cambridge University Press, 1985), 194–95; John Bodnar, *The "Good War" in American Memory* (Baltimore: Johns Hopkins University Press, 2010), ix, 1–3.

43. "Memories of Yorktown," NYT-PQ; "Virginia's Welcome," *Richmond Daily Dispatch,* p. 1.

44. Yi-Fu Tuan, *Space and Place: The Perspective of Experience* (Minneapolis: University of Minnesota Press, 1977), 3–6, 130–37, 159; Yi-Fu Tuan, "Place: An Experiential Perspective," *Geographical Review* 65 (April 1975): 152.

45. Edward S. Casey, *Remembering: A Phenomenological Study* (Bloomington: Indiana University Press, 1987), 181–215.

46. Maurice Halbwachs, "The Social Framework of Memory," in *Maurice Halbwachs on Collective Memory,* ed. and trans. Lewis A. Coser (Chicago: University of Chicago Press, 1992), 37–191; Emile Durkheim, *The Elementary Forms of the Religious Life,* trans. Joseph Ward Swain (London: George Allen & Unwin, 1915); Casey, *Remembering,* 221–26.

47. Tuan, *Space and Place,* 174.

48. E. C. Relph, *Place and Placelessness* (London: Pion, 1976), 67–80; John Carman and Patricia Carman, *Bloody Meadows: Investigating Landscapes of Battle* (Stroud, UK: Sutton Publishing, 2006); Donald Keegan, *The Face of Battle: A Study of Agincourt, Waterloo, and the Somme* (New York: Penguin, 1983).

49. Christopher Tilley, *A Phenomenology of Landscape: Place, Paths and Monuments* (Oxford: Berg, 1994), 10–33; Setha M. Low and Irvin Altman, "Place Attachment: A Conceptual Inquiry," in *Place Attachment,* ed. Altman and Low (New York: Plenum, 1992), 4–10; Dolores Hayden, *The Power of Place: Urban Landscapes as Public History* (Cambridge, MA: MIT Press, 1997), 9–10.

50. Pierre Nora, *Realms of Memory: Rethinking the French Past,* vol. 1, *Conflicts and Divisions,* trans. Arthur Goldhammer, ed. Lawrence D. Kritzman (New York: Columbia University Press, 1996), 1–20; Pierre Nora, "Between Memory and History: Les Lieux de Memoire," *Representations* 26 (Spring 1989): 7–25; Eric Hobsbawn and Terence Ranger, eds., *The Invention of Tradition* (Cambridge: Cambridge University Press, 1983), 1–14. Relevant works on Revolutionary War battlefields include Edward Tabor Linenthal, "Lexington and Concord," in *Sacred Ground: Americans and Their Battlefields* (Urbana: University of Illinois Press, 1993), 3–5, 11–51; Sarah J. Purcell, *Sealed with Blood: War, Sacrifice, and Memory in Revolutionary America* (Philadelphia: University of Pennsylvania Press, 2002), 103–6, 164, 171–73; Lorett Treese, *Valley Forge: Making and Remaking a National Symbol* (University Park: Pennsylvania State University Press, 1995); Sarah J. Purcell, "Commemoration, Public Art, and the Changing Meaning of the Bunker Hill Monument," *Public Historian* 25 (Spring 2003): 55–71; Robert E. Cray Jr., "Bunker Hill Refought: Memory Wars and Partisan Conflicts, 1775–1825," *Historical Journal of Massachusetts* 29 (April 2001): 22–52. Among the many books on later American battlefields,

see especially Randy Roberts and James S. Olson, *A Line in the Sand: The Alamo in Blood and Memory* (New York: Free Press, 2003); Richard R. Flores, *Remembering the Alamo: Memory, Modernity, and the Master Symbol* (Austin: University of Texas Press, 2002); Timothy B. Smith, *This Great Battlefield of Shiloh: History, Memory, and the Establishment of a Civil War National Military Park* (Knoxville: University of Tennessee Press, 2004); Thomas A. Desjardin, *These Honored Dead: How the Story of Gettysburg Shaped American Memory* (Cambridge, MA: Da Capo Press, 2003).

51. Alon Confino, *Germany as a Culture of Remembrance: Promises and Limits of Writing History* (Chapel Hill: University of North Carolina Press, 2006), 241–43, 252–53; Jay Winter, *Sites of Memory, Sites of Mourning: The Great War in European Cultural History* (New York: Cambridge University Press, 1998); Marita Sturken, *Tourists of History: Memory, Kitsch, and Consumerism from Oklahoma City to Ground Zero* (Durham, NC: Duke University Press, 2008); James M. Mayo, *War Memorials as Political Landscape: The American Experience and Beyond* (New York: Praeger, 1988); Jennifer Iles, "Encounters in the Fields—Tourism to the Battle-fields of the Western Front," *Journal of Tourism and Cultural Change* 6, no. 2 (2008): 138–54; Chris Ryan, ed., *Battlefield Tourism: History, Place and Interpretation* (Amsterdam: Elsevier, 2007); Dean MacCannell, *The Ethics of Sightseeing* (Berkeley and Los Angeles: University of California Press, 2011), 167–81; Kendall R. Phillips, *Framing Public Memory* (Tuscaloosa: University of Alabama Press, 2004), 1–12. A broad overview of memory and American wars can be found in Wayne E. Lee, "Mind and Matter—Cultural Analysis in American Military History: A Look at the State of the Field," *Journal of American History* 93 (March 2007): 1135–38, and G. Kurt Piehler, *Remembering War the American Way* (Washington, DC: Smithsonian Books, 1995). Other works include Bodnar, *"Good War" in American Memory;* Jay Winter, *Remembering War: The Great War between Memory and History in the Twentieth Century* (New Haven, CT: Yale University Press, 2006); Susan Rubin Suleiman, *Crises of Memory and the Second World War* (Cambridge, MA: Harvard University Press, 2006); Philip West, Steven I. Levine, and Jackie Hiltz, eds., *America's Wars in Asia: A Cultural Approach to History and Memory* (Armonk, NY: M. E. Sharpe, 1998); Marita Sturken, *Tangled Memories: The Vietnam War, the AIDS Epidemic, and the Politics of Remembering* (Berkeley and Los Angeles: University of California Press, 1997).

52. David W. Blight, *Race and Reunion: The Civil War in American Memory* (Cambridge, MA: Belknap Press of Harvard University Press, 2001); Raphael Samuel argues British heritage tourism came to represent almost anything in an attempt to unite as many people as possible (*Theatres of Memory*, vol. 1, *Past and Present in Contemporary Culture* [London: Verso, 1994], 205–21). The scholarship on the Civil War / Reconstruction and memory is particularly rich and extensive. See John R. Neff, *Honoring the Civil War Dead: Commemoration and the Problem of Reconciliation* (Lawrence: University Press of Kansas, 2005); William Blair, *Cities of the Dead: Contesting the Memory of the Civil War in the South, 1865–1914* (Chapel Hill: University of North Carolina Press, 2003); Paul A. Shackel, *Memory in Black and White: Race, Commemoration, and the Post-bellum Landscape* (Walnut Creek, CA: Altamira Press, 2003); David W. Blight, *Beyond the Battlefield: Race, Memory, and the American Civil War* (Amherst: University of Massachusetts Press, 2002); Alice Fahs and Joan Waugh, eds., *The Memory of the Civil War in American Culture* (Chapel Hill: University of North Carolina Press, 2002); Martin H. Blatt, Thomas J. Brown, and Donald Yacovone, eds., *Hope and Glory: Essays on the Legacy of the Fifty-fourth Massachusetts Regiment* (Amherst: University of Massachusetts Press, 2001); Jennifer Ann Howell, *Sectional Healing: Reconciliation and the Image of Robert E. Lee, 1890–1910* (Cambridge, MA: Harvard University Press, 2000); Kirk Savage, *Standing Soldiers, Kneeling Slaves: Race, War, and Monument in Nineteenth-Century America* (Princeton, NJ: Princeton University Press, 1997); Thomas J. Brown, ed., *The Public Art of Civil War Commemoration: A Brief History with Documents* (Boston: Bedford / St. Martin's, 2004).

53. "Yorktown and the English," *New York Times,* October 20, 1881, p. 4, NYT-PQ.

54. "The Blue and the Gray," *Richmond Dispatch,* October 19, 1881, p. 1; "The Celebration," *Richmond Standard,* October 22, 1881, p. 1.

## 1. Accidental Tourists

1. Washington to Adam Stephen, July 20, 1776, in *The Papers of George Washington, Revolutionary War Series,* vol. 5, *June–August 1776,* ed. Philander D. Chase (Charlottesville: University of Virginia Press, 1993), 408–9.

2. Captain James Patterson journal, August 1, 1758, as quoted in Lewis Clark Walkinshaw, *Annals of Southwestern Pennsylvania* (New York: Lewis Historical Publishing, 1939), 1:137.

3. Walter Scott Dunn, *Choosing Sides on the Frontier in the American Revolution* (Westport, CT: Praeger, 2007), 155–67.

4. Charles I. Landis, "Jasper Yeates and His Times," *Pennsylvania Magazine of History and Biography* 46 (1922): 211–14.

5. Landis, "Jasper Yeates and His Times," 212–14; Douglas MacGregor, "Braddock's Field: How Brilliant the Morning, How Melancholy the Evening," *Western Pennsylvania History* 88 (Winter 2005): 22–29.

6. Fred Anderson, *Crucible of War: The Seven Years' War and the Fate of Empire in British North America, 1754–1766* (New York: Vintage, 2000), 94–107.

7. Fred Anderson, ed., "George Washington's 'Remarks,'" in *George Washington Remembers: Reflections on the French and Indian War,* ed. Fred Anderson (Lanham, MD: Rowman & Littlefield, 2004), 19–21. This document, written in response to a draft authorized biography by David Humphreys, is Washington's only autobiographical writing and covers his participation the 1750s Ohio campaigns.

8. George Washington to Francis Halket, April 12, 1758, *The Writings of George Washington from the Original Manuscript Sources, 1745–1799,* ed. John C. Fitzpatrick (Washington DC: Government Printing Office, 1931–44), 2:176.

9. Patterson journal, August 1, 1758, as quoted in Walkinshaw, *Annals of Southwestern Pennsylvania,* 1:137.

10. Anderson, *Crucible of War,* 267–85.

11. Forbes as quoted in Douglas R. Cubbison, *The British Defeat of the French in Pennsylvania, 1758: A Military History of the Forbes Campaign against Fort Duquesne* (Jefferson, NC: McFarland, 2010), 174.

12. Landis, "Jasper Yeates and His Times," 213.

13. John Galt, *The Life, Studies and Works of Benjamin West* (London: T. Cadell and W. Davies, 1820), 62–67; Anderson, *George Washington Remembers,* 49–52. West sketched the scene of Halket's reburial, but the patron who purchased *Death of General Wolfe* (1770) declined to commission a painting of the Halket story because he "thought it would not be interesting to the public" (Galt, 67–68). See Christie's, "Benjamin West, P.R.A. (1738–1820), *Discovering the Bones of Sir Peter Halket,*" http://www.christies.com/lotfinder/lot_details.aspx?intObjectID = 4998425 (accessed May 10, 2011).

14. Galt, *Life, Studies and Works of Benjamin West,* 62–67; Caroline Cox, *A Proper Sense of Honor: Service and Sacrifice in George Washington's Army* (Chapel Hill: University of North Carolina Press, 2004), 169–81, 193–96; Erik R. Seeman, *Death in the New World: Cross-Cultural Encounters, 1492–1800* (Philadelphia: University of Pennsylvania Press, 2010), 267–72.

15. David L. Preston, *The Texture of Contact: European and Indian Settler Communities on the Frontiers of Iroquoia, 1667–1783* (Lincoln: University of Nebraska Press, 2009), 216–64.

16. Jehu Eyre diary, September 1, 1760, as quoted in "Memorials of Colonel Jehu Eyre," ed. Peter D. Keyser, *Pennsylvania Magazine of History and Biography* 3 (1879): 303.

17. "Memoir of John Heckewelder," April 1, 1762, as quoted in Edward Rondthaler, *The Life of John Heckewelder,* ed. B. H. Coates (Philadelphia: Townshend Ward, 1847), 44.

18. "Extracts from the Journal of John Parrish, 1773," *Pennsylvania Magazine of History and Biography* 16 (1892): 446.

19. Franklin B. Dexter, ed., *The Diary of David McClure, 1748–1820* (New York: Knickerbocker Press, 1899), 48–49.

20. Nicholas Cresswell, *The Journal of Nicholas Cresswell, 1774–1777* (New York, L. MacVeagh, Dial Press, 1924), April 10, 1775, p. 63.

21. Wills DeHass, *History of the Early Settlement and Indian Wars of Western Virginia* (Wheeling, WV: H. Hoblitzell, 1851), 113.

22. Drew Gilpin Faust, *This Republic of Suffering: Death and the American Civil War* (New York: Alfred A. Knopf, 2008), 70–72, 202, 217, 226–27, 271.

23. Landis, "Jasper Yeates and His Times," 212–14.

24. *John Long's Journal, 1768–1782* (Cleveland: Arthur H. Clark, 1904 [1791]), 63.

25. Anderson, "George Washington's 'Remarks,'" 21. On Washington's care for his reputation, see Don Higginbotham, "Young Washington: Ambition, Accomplishment, and Acclaim," 67–87, and Anderson, "'Just as They Occurred to the Memory, They Were Committed': Speculations on George Washington's Autobiographical Remarks," 109–41, both in Anderson, *George Washington Remembers.*

26. Anderson, *A People's Army: Massachusetts Soldiers and Society in the Seven Years' War* (Chapel Hill: University of North Carolina Press, 1985); Charles Royster, *A Revolutionary People at War: The Continental Army and American Character, 1775–1783* (Chapel Hill: University of North Carolina Press, 1980).

27. Anderson, "'Just as They Occurred to the Memory,'" 126–34.

28. "Recollections of an Old Soldier: The Life of Captain David Perry" (1822), reprinted in *Magazine of History* 35, extra no. 137 (1928): 9–10.

29. Archelaus Fuller, "Journal of Col. Archelaus Fuller of Middletown, Mass., in the Expedition against Ticonderoga in 1758," *Essex Institute Historical Collections* 46 (1910): 214.

30. "Journal of an Officer Who Travelled in America and the West Indies in 1764 and 1765," in *Travels in the American Colonies,* ed. Newton Mereness (New York: Macmillan, 1916), 444.

31. Francis Grant, "Journal from New York to Canada, 1767," *Proceedings of the New York State Historical Association* 30 (1932): 319–20.

32. "Journal of an Officer," 444.

33. William De La Place to Thomas Gage, January 31, 1775, vol. 125, December 25–February 10, 1775, Thomas Gage Papers—American Series, William L. Clements Library, University of Michigan (hereafter cited as Clements).

34. Ethan Allen, *The Narrative of Colonel Ethan Allen* (Cambridge, MA: Applewood, 1989 [1779]), 6, 9, 11.

35. Mark Puls, *Henry Knox: Visionary General of the American Revolution* (New York: Palgrave Macmillan, 2008).

36. *Journals of the Continental Congress,* January 25, 1776, p. 38, as quoted in *A Century of Lawmaking for a New Nation: U.S. Congressional Documents and Debates, 1774–1875,* American Memory Project, Library of Congress, http://rs6.loc.gov/ammem/amlaw/lawhome.html (hereafter cited as *Journals*), accessed August 11, 2006.

37. George Washington to Philip J. Schuyler, October 22, 1776, Series 3b Varick Transcripts, *The George Washington Papers at the Library of Congress, 1741–1799.* American Memory Project, Library of Congress, http://memory.loc.gov/ammem/gwhtml/gwhome.html (hereafter cited as GW), accessed September 2, 2008.

38. "Journal of Charles Carroll of Carrollton, during His Visit to Canada, in 1776, as One of the Commissioners from Congress," appendix B of Kate Mason Rowland, *The Life of Charles Carroll of Carrollton, 1737–1832, with His Correspondence and Public Papers* (New York, 1898), 1:379–83; Ronald Hoffman, Sally D. Mason, and Eleanor S. Darcy, eds., *Dear Papa, Dear Charley: The Peregrinations of a Revolutionary Aristocrat, as Told by Charles Carroll of Carrollton and His Father, Charles Carroll of Annapolis, with Sundry Observations on Bastardy, Child-Rearing, Romance, Matrimony, Commerce, Tobacco, Slavery, and the Politics of Revolutionary America* (Chapel Hill: University of North Carolina Press, 2001), 1:299–300.

39. Charles Carroll of Annapolis to Charles Carroll of Carrollton, February 9, 1759, in Hoffman, Mason, and Darcy, *Dear Papa, Dear Charley,* 1:92–93.

40. "Journal of Charles Carroll of Carrollton," 1:379.

41. George Washington to Philip J. Schuyler, October 22, 1776: Series 3b Varick Transcripts, GW.

42. *Journals,* December 24, 1776, p. 1038.

43. George Washington to Massachusetts General Court, February 8, 1777 (also to New Hampshire Convention): Series 3c Varick Transcripts, GW.

44. Joseph Wood to Robert Morris, November 19, 1776, Nathanael Greene papers, vol. 1, 1762–77, Clements.

45. Anthony Wayne to George Clymer, December 15, 1776, as quoted in Charles J. Stille, *Major-General Anthony Wayne and the Pennsylvania Line in the Continental Army* (Philadelphia: J. B. Lippincott Co., 1893), 52.

46. Anthony Wayne to General Schuyler, January 2, 1777, as quoted in Stille, *Major-General Anthony Wayne,* 47.

47. Benjamin Beal journal, May 2, 1776, American Antiquarian Society, Worcester, MA.

48. Anthony Wayne to General Schuyler, January 2, 1777, as quoted in Stille, *Major-General Anthony Wayne,* 47.

49. Polly Wayne to Anthony Wayne, July 6, 1776, Wayne Family Papers, box 1756–June 1785, Clements.

50. Anthony Wayne to Colonel Joseph Penrose, August 23, 1776, as quoted in Stille, *Major-General Anthony Wayne,* 36–37.

51. George Washington to Philip J. Schuyler, July 10, 1777: Series 3b Varick Transcripts, GW.

52. Josiah Parker to John Page, August 5, 1777, box 2, James S. Schoff Revolutionary War Collection, Clements.

53. Don R. Gerlach, *Proud Patriot: Philip Schuyler and the War for Independence, 1775–1783* (Syracuse, NY: Syracuse University Press, 1987); Richard M. Ketchum, *Saratoga: Turning Point of America's Revolutionary War* (New York: Macmillan, 1999). The inquiry first appears in *Journals,* July 29, 1777, p. 585.

54. George Germain to John Burgoyne, March 26, 1777, Miscellaneous Manuscripts, box 14, December 1776–77, Clements.

55. George Germain to John Burgoyne, September 15 and October 1, 1777, Henry Clinton Papers, box 24, September 12–October 9, 1777, Clements.

56. *Journals,* March 27, 1778, p. 287. See also *Journals,* November 4, 1777, p. 863, and December 2, 1777, p. 987.

57. George Washington to President of Congress, July 16, 1783, as quoted in Fitzpatrick, *Writings of George Washington,* 27:69–70.

58. Elizabeth Cometti, ed., *Seeing America and Its Great Men: The Journal and Letters of Count Francesco dal Verme, 1783–1784* (Charlottesville, University of Virginia Press, 1969), 13–14.

59. David S. Robertson, ed., *An Englishman in America: Being the Diary of Joseph Hadfield* (Toronto: Hunter-Rose, 1933), 32.

60. Robertson, *Englishman in America,* 31–32, 168–69.

61. J. Robert Maguire, ed., *The Tour to the Northern Lakes of James Madison and Thomas Jefferson in 1791* (Ticonderoga, NY: Fort Ticonderoga Museum, 1995); Thomas Jefferson to Thomas Mann Randolph Jr., June 5, 1791, in *The Papers of Thomas Jefferson,* ed. Julian Boyd (Princeton, NJ: Princeton University Press, 1982), 20:464–65.

62. Mark Salber Phillips, "Distance and Historical Representation," *History Workshop Journal* 57, no. 1 (Spring 2004): 123–41; Joshua Goldstein, *War and Gender: How Gender Shapes the War System and Vice Versa* (New York: Cambridge University Press, 2001).

63. George Hamilton Journal, folders 2, August 1–7, 1783, pp. 1–9, American Travel Collection, Clements.

64. John Melish, *Travels through the United States of America, in the Years 1806 & 1807, and 1809, 1810, & 1811* (London, reprinted for G. Cowie and Co., 1818), 311.

65. Auguste Levasseur, *Lafayette in America in 1824 and 1825; or, Journal of a Voyage to the United States,* trans. John D. Goodman (Philadelphia: Carey and Lea, 1829), 2:180–81.

66. Anderson, *George Washington Remembers,* 54–55.

67. *François André Michaux's Travels West of Alleghany Mountains, 1802,* as quoted in *Early Western Travels, 1748–1846,* ed. Reuben Gold Thwaites (Cleveland: Arthur H. Clark Co., 1904), 3:328.

68. *Evans's Pedestrian Tour of Four Thousand Miles—1818* (Concord, NH: n.p., 1819), as quoted in Thwaites, *Early Western Travels,* 8:254.

69. William Amphlett, *The Emigrant's Directory to the Western States of North America* (London: Longman, Hurst, Rees, Orme, and Brown, 1819), 98.

70. William N. Blane, *An Excursion through the United States and Canada during the Years 1822–23* (London: Printed for Baldwin, Cradock, and Joy, 1824), 89.

71. Godfrey T. Vigne, *Six Months in America* (Philadelphia: T. T. Ash, 1833), 109.

72. Levasseur, *Lafayette in America,* 2:180–81.

73. Ebenezer Mack, *The Life of Gilbert Motier de Lafayette . . . from Numerous and Authentic Sources* (Ithaca, NY: Mack, Andrus & Woodruff, 1841), 325.

74. "Various Items," *Pittsfield (MA) Sun,* July 18, 1850, p. 3, America's Historical Newspapers, Early American Newspapers, Series 2, 1758–1900 (Chester, VT: Readex, 2004), http://www.newsbank.com/readex/product.cfm?product=11, accessed February 12, 2010.

75. Francis P. Lee to Sarah G. Lee, June 4, 1840, Francis P. Lee Papers, box 1, folder 63, Special Collections Research Center, Earl Greg Swem Library, College of William and Mary.

76. Nathaniel Hawthorne, "Old News," in *Tales, Sketches, and Other Papers,* ed. George Parsons Lathrop (Boston: Houghton, Mifflin, 1883), 251, 263, 269.

## 2. Forsaken Graves

1. Abigail May journal, July 20, 1800, p. 75, New York State Historical Association, Cooperstown (hereafter cited as NYSHA).

2. Benson J. Lossing, *The Pictorial Field-Book of the Revolution* (New York: Harper Bros., 1859 [1850]), 1:121, 127; Gregory M. Pfitzer, *Picturing the Past: Illustrated Histories and the American Imagination, 1840–1900* (Washington, DC: Smithsonian Institution Press, 2003), 40–63.

3. Theodore Dwight, *The Northern Traveller; Containing the Routes to Niagara, Quebec, and the Springs; with Useful Descriptions of the Principal Scenes, and Useful Hints to Strangers* (New York: Wilder and Campbell, 1825), 83–84, 113–14.

4. Elizabeth Ruffin, August 20, 1827, as quoted in *An Evening When Alone: Four Journals of Single Women in the South, 1827–1867,* ed. Michael O'Brien (Charlottesville: University Press of Virginia, 1993), 88.

5. John Urry, *The Tourist Gaze* (London: Sage, 2002), 1–4; Nick Yablon, *Untimely Ruins: An Archaeology of American Urban Modernity, 1819–1829* (Chicago: University of Chicago Press, 2009), 19–61; Nicholas William Yablon, "'Cities in Ruin': Urban Apocalypse in American Culture, 1790–1820" (Ph.D. diss., University of Chicago, 2002), 17–84.

6. Michael Kammen, *Mystic Chords of Memory: The Transformation of Tradition in American Culture* (New York: Vintage Books, 1993), 9–11, 59.

7. Harlow W. Sheidley, *Sectional Nationalism: Massachusetts Conservative Leaders and the Transformation of America, 1815–1836* (Boston: Northeastern University Press, 1998), 118–47. Raphael Samuel argues that British heritage tourism came to represent almost anything in an attempt to unite as many people as possible. Samuel, *Theatres of Memory* (London: Verso, 1994–98), 1:205–21. Robert A. Gross notes that attempts to unite Concord, Massachusetts, around a memorial commemorating the "shot heard 'round the world" reflected the broader tensions in the village and society. Gross, "The Celestial Village: Transcendentalism Tourism in Concord," in *Transient and Permanent: The Transcendentalist Movement and Its Contexts*, ed. Charles Capper and Conrad Edick (Boston: Massachusetts Historical Society, 1999), 251–71.

8. David Waldstreicher, *In the Midst of Perpetual Fetes: The Making of American Nationalism, 1776–1820* (Chapel Hill: University of North Carolina Press, 1997); Mitchell Kachun, *Festivals of Freedom: Memory and Meaning in African American Emancipation Celebrations, 1808–1915* (Amherst: University of Massachusetts Press, 2003); Len Travers, *Celebrating the Fourth: Independence Day and the Rites of Nationalism in the Early Republic* (Amherst: University of Massachusetts Press, 1997).

9. John Bodnar, *Remaking America: Public Memory, Commemoration, and Patriotism in the Twentieth Century* (Princeton, NJ: Princeton University Press, 1992), 13–14.

10. William Strickland diary, September 30, 1794, 5:118, and October 6, 1794, 7:163, New-York Historical Society, New York City (hereafter cited as N-YHS).

11. "Letters of an American Traveler…Written during an Excursion in the Year 1810," Letter 11th, 1:55, South Carolina Historical Society, Charleston (hereafter cited as SCHS).

12. John Maude, *Visit to the Falls of Niagara in 1800* (London: Longman, Rees, Orme, Brown and Green, 1826), 10–12.

13. "The Capture of Fort Montgomery," *Critic*, January 17, 1829, p. 189, American Antiquarian Society Historical Periodicals Collection, Series 2, 1821–37 (Ipswich, MA: EbscoHost, 2010), http://www.ebscohost.com/archives/featured-archives/american-antiquarian-society, accessed January 15, 2010 (hereafter cited as AAS2).

14. Charles West Thomson diary, July 24, 1824, N-YHS.

15. Ibid., July 29, 1824.

16. "Correspondence of the Constitution," *Constitution*, October 6, 1847, p. 2, AAS2.

17. "Palisades and Stony Point," *American Magazine of Useful and Entertaining Knowledge*, October 31, 1834, pp. 57–58, AAS2.

18. "View near Fort Montgomery," *New-York Mirror and Ladies' Literary Gazette*, December 20, 1823, pp. 162–63, AAS2.

19. Strickland diary, October 9, 1794, 9:194, N-YHS; J. B. Dunlop diary, 1810–11, N-YHS.

20. Washington Irving, "The Legend of Sleepy Hollow," in *The Sketch Book of Geoffrey Crayon, Gent.*, in *Washington Irving: History, Tales, Sketches* (New York: Library Classics, 1983), 1059, 1076, 1077–78, 1081–82, 1086–87.

21. Robert E. Cray Jr., "Major John André and the Three Captors: Class Dynamics and Revolutionary Memory Wars in the Early Republic, 1780–1831," *Journal of the Early Republic* 17 (Fall 1997): 371–97; Michael Marenze, "Major André's Exhumation," in *Mortal Remains: Death in Early America*, ed. Nancy Isenberg and Andrew Burstein (Philadelphia: University of Pennsylvania Press, 2002), 123–35; Robert E. Cray Jr., "The John André Memorial: The Politics of Memory in Gilded Age New York," *New York History* 77 (January 1996): 5–32.

22. "Diary of a Scot Touring the Eastern United States," 1821–1824, "Visit to West Point," N-YHS.

23. Wayne Franklin, *James Fenimore Cooper: The Early Years* (New Haven, CT: Yale University Press, 2007), 276–85.

24. Ibid., 343–51, 420–71; Michael Kammen, *A Season of Youth: The American Revolution and the Historical Imagination* (Ithaca, NY: Cornell University Press, 1978), 145–85.

25. Franklin, *James Fenimore Cooper,* 351, 376–78.

26. William H. Truettner and Alan Wallach, *Thomas Cole: Landscape into History* (New Haven, CT: Yale University Press, 1994), 23, 43–46, 64–65, 84.

27. Timothy Dwight, *Travels; in New-England and New-York* (New Haven, CT: S. Converse, 1822), 3:361.

28. "Interesting Revolutionary Reminiscences of Fort Washington," *New York Herald,* January 10, 1858, p. 1, America's Historical Newspapers, Early American Newspapers, Series 2, 1758–1900 (Chester, VT: Readex, 2004), http://www.newsbank.com/readex/product.cfm?product=11, accessed February 12, 2010, (hereafter cited as AHN2).

29. Richard M. Ketchum, *Saratoga: Turning Point of the Revolution* (New York: Henry Holt, 1997).

30. Netta, "First Impressions of Saratoga, No. 3," *National Era* 13, no. 660 (August 25, 1859): 1; Anonymous, "Diary of a Tour of New York and Canada," 1834, p. 192, N-YHS.

31. Benjamin Silliman, *Remarks Made on a Short Tour between Hartford and Quebec in the Autumn of 1819* (London: Sir Richard Philips and Co., 1822), 22.

32. "Letters of an American Traveler," Letter 11th, 1:60, SCHS.

33. Philip Stansbury, *A Pedestrian Tour of Two Thousand Three Hundred Miles, in North America* (New York: Myers & Smith, 1822), 36, 43–44.

34. "General Hoyt's Visit to the Battle Ground in 1825," in *Visits to the Saratoga Battle Grounds, 1780–1880,* ed. William L. Stone (Albany, NY: Munsell, 1895), 182, 197, 210; "Diary of a Scot," "The Battle of Saratoga," no. 25, New York, June 4, 1824, N-YHS.

35. Duke de la Rochefoucauld-Liancourt, *Travels through the United States of North America, of the Country of the Iroquois, and Upper Canada, in the Years 1795, 1796, and 1797* (London: R. Phillips, 1799), 1:373–74.

36. Marquis de Chastellux, *Travels in North America, in the Years 1780–81–82* (New York, 1828), 1:188–89.

37. Stansbury, *Pedestrian Tour,* 38–39, 42.

38. "General Hoyt's Visit to the Battle Ground in 1825," 185.

39. Ibid., 190, 196, 199; Stansbury, *Pedestrian Tour,* 37.

40. "Diary of a Scot," "Battle of Saratoga," N-YHS.

41. "Visit of Hon. William Wirt in August, 1821," in Stone, *Visits to the Saratoga Battle Grounds,* 153–54.

42. "General Hoyt's Visit to the Battle Ground in 1825," 188–89.

43. "Diary of a Scot," "Battle of Saratoga," N-YHS; "The Field of Saratoga," *Newport Mercury,* July 29, 1843, p. 2, AHN2.

44. Stansbury, *Pedestrian Tour,* 36.

45. Dwight, *Travels,* 3:219, 232.

46. Silliman, *Remarks Made on a Short Tour,* 25–26, 32.

47. "General Hoyt's Visit to the Battle Ground in 1825," 196–97.

48. Elkanah Watson, "Journal of Remarks from Albany to Lake Champlain," box 3, Journal E, August 23, 1805, p. 74, Elkanah Watson Papers, New York State Library and Archives, Albany (hereafter cited as NYSLA); Nicholas Westbrook, "Ticonderoga in Print: Prints from the Fort Ticonderoga Museum Collection," *Imprint* 26 (Spring 2001): 2–18.

49. "Echo Near Lake George," *Peabody's Parlor Journal,* December 27, 1834, p. 288, AAS2.

50. Anonymous Travel Journal, September 1849, SCHS; Theodore Corbett, *The Making of American Resorts: Saratoga Springs, Ballston Spa, Lake George* (New Brunswick, NJ: Rutgers University Press, 2001), 42–49; Franklin, *James Fenimore Cooper,* 438–40.

51. "Journey through NY State and Upper & Lower Canada, 1834," 219–22, N-YHS.

52. "View of Ticonderoga," *Analectic Magazine* 11 (April 1818): 325.

53. Lossing, *Pictorial Field-Book of the Revolution,* 1:128.

54. Watson, "Journal," August 23, 1805, p. 75, NYSLA; Priscilla Wakefield, *Excursions in North America: Described in Letters from a Gentleman and His Young Companion to Their Friends in England* (London: Darton, Harvey and Darton, 1810), 268.

55. May journal, July 20, 1800, pp. 76, 77, NYSHA.

56. Silliman, *Remarks Made on a Short Tour,* 184–85.

57. May journal, July 20, 1800, pp. 76–77, NYSHA.

58. Watson, "Journal," August 23, 1805, p. 75, NYSLA.

59. Lucinda A. Brockway, *A Favorite Place of Resort for Strangers: The King's Garden at Fort Ticonderoga* (Ticonderoga, NY: Fort Ticonderoga Museum, 2001), 29–38; Indenture, William F. Pell and Mary, his wife, and Morris Shipley (trustee), and Duncan C. Pell, September 26, 1840, Manuscripts Collection, N-YHS.

60. Theodore Dwight, *The Northern Traveller; Containing the Routes to Niagara, Quebec, and the Springs, with the Tour of New-England, and the Route to the Coal Mines of Pennsylvania* (New York: A. T. Goodrich, 1826), 173.

61. Ibid., 173.

62. "Lake George Steam Boat Association, Articles of Agreement with A. W. Hyde & Others," October 15, 1840, Clark/Field Family Papers, 1–12, Special Collections, Bailey-Howe Library, University of Vermont.

63. Alexander Bliss journal, July 19, 1825, American Antiquarian Society, Worcester, MA (hereafter cited as AAS).

64. Catharine Maria Sedgwick, "Journal of a Trip to New York and Canada," July 17, 1821, Massachusetts Historical Society, Boston (hereafter cited as MHS); Silliman, *Remarks Made on a Short Tour,* 64; Edward Thomas Cole, *A Subaltern's Furlough: Descriptive Scenes in Various Parts of the United States, Upper and Lower Canada, New Brunswick, and Nova Scotia during the Summer and Autumn of 1832* (London: Saunders and Otley, 1832), 158.

65. "Saturday Visitor," *New Hampshire Patriot,* October 9, 1845, p. 4, AHN2.

66. "Ticonderoga," *Monthly Repository and Library of Entertaining Knowledge* 3, no. 5 (October 1832): 148.

67. Dwight, *Northern Traveller* (1825), 127–28.

68. Sheidley, *Sectional Nationalism,* 119.

69. James Wilkinson, *Memoirs of My Own Times* (Philadelphia: Abraham Smalls, 1816).

70. Anonymous Travel Journal, September 1849, SCHS.

71. Anon., "Journey through NY State and Upper & Lower Canada, 1834," pp. 236–40, N-YHS.

72. "Ticonderoga," *Monthly Repository,* 147.

73. May journal, June 21, 1800, p. 45, NYSHA; William Heath, *Memoirs of Major-General Heath Containing Anecdotes, Details of Skirmishes, Battles, and Other Military Events, during the American War* (Boston: I. Thomas and E. T. Andrews, 1798).

74. "Ticonderoga," *Ariel: A Literary and Critical Gazette* 2, no. 7 (July 26, 1828): 1; "View of Ticonderoga," 325.

75. L. Q. C. Bolles, "From New York" diary, October 9, 1824, MHS.

76. Bliss journal, July 19, 1825, AAS.

77. Hawlam, "The Aged Visitant of Ticonderoga," *Guardian and Monitor* 7, no. 4 (April 1825): 130; "Historical Recollections," *Telescope* 3, no. 22 (October 28, 1826): 87.

78. Dwight, *Travels,* 3:383.

79. Watson, "Journal," August 23, 1805, pp. 72, 75, NYSLA.

80. Hawlam, "Aged Visitant," 127. Emotional responses are an essential component of modern "death tourism" to European battlefields. See Jennifer Iles, "Encounters in the Fields: Tourism to the Battlefields of the Western Front," *Journal of Tourism and Cultural Change* 6, no. 2 (2008): 138–54.

81. Kammen, *Mystic Chords of Memory,* 32–39, quote p. 35; Kammen, *Season of Youth,* 33–58.

82. James Kirke Paulding, *Letters from the South, Written during an Excursion in the Summer of 1816* (New York: James Eastburn, 1817), 1:184.

83. Giulian C. Verplanck, "Gelyna: A Tale of Albany and Ticonderoga Seventy Years Ago," in *The Talisman for 1830* (New York: Elam Bliss, 1829), reprinted in *Bulletin of the Fort Ticonderoga Museum* 8, no. 5 (Winter 1950): 179–89, quotes pp. 186–87, 189. Truettner and Wallach, *Thomas Cole,* 79.

84. Anon., "Journey through NY State and Upper & Lower Canada, 1834," pp. 175–76, 236–40, N-YHS.

85. Anonymous Travel Journal, September 1849, SCHS.

86. Amelia Murray, *Letters from the United States, Cuba and Canada* (New York: G. P. Putnam, 1856), 377.

87. Jane Caroline North, September 14, 1852, in O'Brien, *Evening When Alone,* 215–16.

88. Dwight, *Travels,* 3:341; May journal, July 20, 1800, p. 76, NYSHA.

89. Chastellux, *Travels in North America,* 1:193.

90. Silliman, *Remarks Made on a Short Tour,* 25–27.

91. "Visit of Hon. William Wirt in August, 1821," 150–51; "Diary of a Scot," "Battle of Saratoga," N-YHS.

92. Silliman, *Remarks Made on a Short Tour,* 32–34, 38, 40.

93. Chandos Michael Brown, *Benjamin Silliman: A Life in the Young Republic* (Princeton, NJ: Princeton University Press, 1989), 323; George B. Forgie, *Patricide in the House Divided: A Psychological Interpretation of Lincoln and His Age* (New York: W. W. Norton, 1979), 20–22.

94. Theodore Dwight, *Sketches of Scenery and Manners in the United States* (New York: A. T. Goodrich, 1829), 91–92, 105; John Resch, *Suffering Soldiers: Revolutionary War Veterans, Moral Sentiment, and Political Culture in the Early Republic* (Amherst: University of Massachusetts Press, 1999), 76, 93–118, 199; Lorett Treese, *Valley Forge: Making and Remaking a National Symbol* (University Park: Pennsylvania State University Press, 1995), 2; Gregory T. Knouff, *The Soldiers' Revolution: Pennsylvanians in Arms and the Forging of Early American Identity* (University Park: Pennsylvania State University Press, 2004), 236–71.

95. "Battle of Groton Heights," *Army and Navy Chronicle,* August 10, 1837, p. 92, AAS2.

96. E. Mattoon, "Battle of Saratoga," *Family Magazine* 1 (August 1836): 374, AAS2.

97. Stansbury, *Pedestrian Tour,* 37.

98. Nathaniel Hawthorne, "Old Ticonderoga: A Picture of the Past," *The Family Magazine* 1 (May 1836): 414–15, reprinted from *American Monthly Magazine* 1 (February 1836): 138–42; Judy R. Smith, "'Old Ticonderoga': An Early Example of Hawthorne's Narrative Strategy," *Nathaniel Hawthorne Society* 10 (Fall 1984): 10–11.

99. Mark Salber Phillips, "Distance and Historical Representation," *History Workshop Journal* 57 (Spring 2004): 123–41.

100. Forgie, *Patricide in the House Divided,* 47–49.

101. Knouff, *Soldiers' Revolution,* 236–71; Resch, *Suffering Soldiers;* Alfred F. Young, *The Shoemaker and the Tea Party: Memory and the American Revolution* (Boston: Beacon Press, 1999), 166–71.

102. Mrs. John S. Van Winkle diary, August 20, 1850, p. 35, Fort Ticonderoga Museum; Cyrus Morton, Middlebury, VT, to Peter Vaughan, Middleborough, MA, April 26, 1849, Fort Ticonderoga Museum, Ticonderoga, NY.

103. Lossing, *Pictorial Field-Book of the Revolution,* 1:121–22, 129–30.

104. Kammen argues that Lossing's *Field-Book* "may have done more than any other publication to foster popular pride in United States history during the second half of the nineteenth century" (*Season of Youth,* 52); Thomas A. Chambers, "A Soldier of the Revolution; Or, Will the Real Isaac Rice Please Stand Up," *Prologue* 42, no. 3 (Fall 2010): 34–41.

105. Paul E. Johnson, *Sam Patch: The Famous Jumper* (New York: Hill & Wang, 2003), 79–125.

106. Lossing, *Pictorial Field-Book of the Revolution,* 1:128–30 (emphasis in original).

## 3. Retrieved Relics and New Monuments

1. Samuel L. Knapp, ed., *Memoirs of General Lafayette. With an Account of His Visit to America, and the Reception by the People of the United States; from His Arrival, August 15th, to the Celebration at Yorktown, October 19th, 1824* (Boston: E. G. House, 1824), 244.

2. John Foster, *A Sketch of the Tour of General Lafayette, on His Late Visit to the United States, 1824* (Portland, ME: A. W. Thayer, 1824), 208.

3. Jerome A. Greene, *The Guns of Independence: The Siege of Yorktown, 1781* (New York: Savas Beatie, 2009), 309–10.

4. Edward M. Riley, ed., "St. George Tucker's Journal of the Siege of Yorktown, 1781," *William and Mary Quarterly,* 3rd Series, vol. 5 (July 1948): 391.

5. Evelyn M. Acomb, trans. and ed., *The Revolutionary Journal of Baron Ludwig von Closen, 1780–1783* (Chapel Hill: University of North Carolina Press, 1958), 155.

6. C. C. Robin, *New Travels through North America* (Philadelphia: Robert Bell, 1783), 65.

7. Greene, *Guns of Independence,* 311–12.

8. Donald O. Dewey, ed., "'To Level the Works at York': A Letter of David Jameson," *Virginia Magazine of History and Biography* 71 (1963): 150–52.

9. Isaac Weld, *Travels through the States of North America, and the Provinces of Upper and Lower Canada, during the Years 1795, 1796, and 1797* (London: John Stackpole, 1807), 1:165.

10. Ibid., 1:164.

11. Edward C. Carter II, ed., *The Virginia Journals of Benjamin Henry Latrobe, 1795–1798* (New Haven, CT: Yale University Press, 1977), April 5, 1796, 1:86.

12. Pleasants Murphy Diary, January 10, 1815, Special Collections Research Center, Earl Gregg Swem Library, College of William and Mary (hereafter cited as Swem).

13. William Cutter, *The Life of General Lafayette* (New York: G. F. Coolege & Brother, 1849), 360.

14. *The Siege of York, in 1781: and Its Celebration, in 1824, Written by a Revolutionary Officer, Who Partook of Both; and Inscribed to His Old and Beloved General, Lafayette* (Richmond, VA: P. DuVal, 1825), 1.

15. Auguste Levasseur, *Lafayette in America in 1824 and 1825; or, Journal of a Voyage to the United States,* trans. John D. Goodman (Philadelphia: Carey and Lea, 1829), 1:183.

16. *Siege of York,* 1.

17. Foster, *Sketch of the Tour of General Lafayette,* 197.

18. Levasseur, *Lafayette in America,* 1:185.

19. Knapp, *Memoirs of General Lafayette,* 55, 58.

20. Andrew Burstein, *America's Jubilee, July 4, 1826: A Generation Remembers the Revolution after Fifty Years of Independence* (New York: Vintage, 2001), 8, 16–18, 32.

21. Knapp, *Memoirs of General Lafayette,* 17–39; *A Complete History of the Marquis de La-fayette* (Hartford, CT: Andrus, 1850), 364.

22. Knapp, *Memoirs of General Lafayette,* 134.

23. Ibid., 153.

24. Levasseur, *Lafayette in America,* 1:29.

25. Cutter, *Life of General Lafayette,* 359.

26. Stanley Idzerda, Anne C. Loveland, and Marc H. Miller, *Lafayette, Hero of Two Worlds: The Art and Pageantry of His Farewell Tour of America, 1824–1825* (Hanover, NH: University Press of New England).

27. Caroline Olivia Bal Laurens Diary, March 1825, South Carolina Historical Society, Charleston.

28. Martha Fanny B. Rochelle Scrapbook, 1819–1864, Rochelle Family Papers, 1817–1967, Section 1, p. 41, Virginia Historical Society, Richmond (hereafter cited as VHS).

29. Foster, *Sketch of the Tour of General Lafayette,* 69–70.

30. Lafayette to John Steward Skinner, November 12, 1824, Greene Family Papers, 1795–1947, Section 7, a 36, VHS.

31. Lafayette to John Steward Skinner, August 27, 1825, copied from *National Intelligencer,* September 1, 1825, Greene Family Papers, 1795–1947, Section 7, a 37, VHS.

32. "At a Meeting of the General Committee appointed by the citizens of Petersburg to make arrangements for the reception of Gen'l. La Fayette," Lewis Mabry Papers, 1816–1833, b1, VHS.

33. Levasseur, *Lafayette in America,* 1:211–12.

34. "At a Meeting of the General Committee," VHS.

35. Levasseur, *Lafayette in America,* 1:212.

36. "At a Meeting of the General Committee," VHS.

37. John Peck to Isaac J. Peck, Isaac Gorham Peck Papers, 1822–38, Section 2, b 7, VHS.

38. Foster, *Sketch of the Tour of General Lafayette,* 54.

39. *Acts Passed at a General Assembly of the Commonwealth of Virginia, 1824–1825* (Richmond, VA: Thomas Ritchie, 1825), 6–7.

40. George Fayette Washington to George W[ashington] Bassett, October 27, 1824, VHS.

41. Robert Waln, *Life of the Marquis de La Fayette; Major General in the Service of the United States of America, in the War of the Revolution* (Philadelphia: J. P. Ayres, 1826), 386.

42. Levasseur, *Lafayette in America,* 1:22.

43. Knapp, *Memoirs of General Lafayette,* 163.

44. Levasseur, *Lafayette in America,* 1:165.

45. Ibid., 1:37–38; Knapp, *Memoirs of General Lafayette,* 209–10.

46. Knapp, *Memoirs of General Lafayette,* 200.

47. Waln, *Life of the Marquis de La Fayette,* 371.

48. Foster, *Sketch of the Tour of General Lafayette,* 175–76.

49. Ibid., 186; newspaper clippings, *Fredericksburg Virginia Herald,* October 16, 1824, VHS; George Dekker, *The American Historical Romance* (New York: Cambridge University Press, 1987), 29–35; Seth E. Bruggeman, *Here, George Washington Was Born: Memory, Material Culture, and the Public History of a National Monument* (Athens: University of Georgia Press, 2008), 33–49. The tent was also used in Washington and Richmond and was passed to "Charles Cotesworth Pinckney, of South Carolina, the immediate successor of Washington as President General of the Cincinnati of the United States." It currently resides at the Yorktown Battlefield Visitor Center, Colonial National Historical Park.

50. Levasseur, *Lafayette in America,* 1:165.

51. Leroy Anderson, *Half an Hour's Amusement at York and James-Town; Preparatory to a Narrative of La Fayette's Return, and Reception in Virginia* (Richmond, VA: n.p., 1824), 3.

52. *A Complete History of the Marquis de Lafayette* (Hartford, CT: Andrus, 1850), 366.

53. Foster, *Sketch of the Tour of General Lafayette*, 82.

54. Knapp, *Memoirs of General Lafayette*, 136.

55. Waln, *Life of the Marquis de La Fayette*, 433.

56. Knapp, *Memoirs of General Lafayette*, 142–43.

57. Ibid., 162.

58. Foster, *Sketch of the Tour of General Lafayette*, 106.

59. Knapp, *Memoirs of General Lafayette*, 143, 155.

60. *Norfolk and Portsmouth Herald,* October 29, 1824, VHS.

61. Waln, *Life of the Marquis de La Fayette*, 356.

62. "The Veteran of Ninety-Six," *Universalist Magazine* 6, no. 48 (May 21, 1825): 192, American Antiquarian Society Historical Periodicals Collection, Series 2, 1821–37 (EbscoHost).

63. S. Putnam Waldo, *Tour of James Monroe, President of the United States, through the Northern and Eastern States, in 1817; His Tour in 1818; Together with a Sketch of His Life* (Hartford, CT: Silas Andrus, 1820), 128–29, 230.

64. John Resch, *Suffering Soldiers: Revolutionary War Veterans, Moral Sentiment, and Political Culture in the Early Republic* (Amherst: University of Massachusetts Press, 1999); Marcus Cunliffe, *Soldiers and Civilians: The Martial Spirit in America, 1775–1865* (Boston: Little, Brown, 1968).

65. Levasseur, *Lafayette in America*, 1:34; Cutter, *Life of General Lafayette*, 371.

66. Levasseur, *Lafayette in America*, 2:231.

67. John E. Selby, *The Revolution in Virginia, 1775–1783* (Williamsburg, VA: Colonial Williamsburg Foundation, 1988), 265–309.

68. Knapp, *Memoirs of General Lafayette*, 244.

69. W. G. Saunders to Mrs. S. A. Saunders, October 19, 1824, VHS.

70. Judith H. Tomlin to Virginia Savage, September 23, 1824, Brown-Coalter-Tucker Papers, box 4, folder 4, Swem.

71. Levasseur, *Lafayette in America*, 1:180–83.

72. Virginia Adjutant General's Office, "General Orders" October 1, 1824, Small Special Collections, University of Virginia Library (hereafter cited as UVa).

73. *Siege of York*, 4–5.

74. Knapp, *Memoirs of General Lafayette*, 250; John Myers to Brigr. Genl. [John Hartwell] Cocke, October 17, 1824, UVa.

75. Levasseur, *Lafayette in America*, 1:183.

76. Knapp, *Memoirs of General Lafayette*, 250–51.

77. To Mrs. John Shepherd, Norfolk, VA, n.d., VHS.

78. Waln, *Life of the Marquis de La Fayette*, 388.

79. Levasseur, *Lafayette in America*, 1:184.

80. To Mrs. John Shepherd, VHS.

81. Levasseur, *Lafayette in America*, 1:184.

82. Knapp, *Memoirs of General Lafayette*, 254. Rock Redoubt was Redoubt No. 10.

83. Ibid., 254–55, 256–57.

84. Levasseur, *Lafayette in America*, 1:184–85.

85. Foster, *Sketch of the Tour of General Lafayette*, 198; *Siege of York*, 17.

86. Foster, *Sketch of the Tour of General Lafayette*, 209–10.

87. Levasseur, *Lafayette in America*, 1:185; *Siege of York*, 18.

88. *Siege of York*, 21.

89. Ibid., 5.

90. Knapp, *Memoirs of General Lafayette*, 259.

91. George Fayette Washington to George W[ashington] Bassett, October 27, 1824, VHS.

92. Letters for July–October, 1824, reel 21, Correspondence March 19, 1823–November 23, 1825, Tucker-Coleman Papers, Swem.

93. Judith H. Tomlin to Virginia Savage, September 23, 1824, Swem; To Mrs. John Shepherd, VHS.

94. Levasseur, *Lafayette in America*, 1:185.

95. Ibid., 1:183.

96. Foster, *Sketch of the Tour of General Lafayette*, 201–2.

97. Knapp, *Memoirs of General Lafayette*, 254.

98. Levasseur, *Lafayette in America*, 1:186. David Riggs, curator, Yorktown Collection, Colonial National Historical Park, Yorktown, VA (hereafter cited as CNHP), has been unable to document this monument.

99. *The Virginia State Capitol Visitor's Guide* (Richmond, VA: House of Delegates, 2008), 4–5.

100. "Notes &c of Historical Events—Political, Military and Social," William Palmer Price Commonplace Book, 1857–88, p. 5, Palmer Family Papers, 1782–1894, Section 6, VHS (emphasis in original).

101. Robert Gilmor, "Notes Taken in a Tour through the States of Viriginia, North Carolina, and South Carolina, in the Year 1806," South Caroliniana Library, Columbia (hereafter cited as SCL).

102. Gerald E. Kahler, *The Long Farewell: Americans Mourn the Death of George Washington* (Charlottesville: University of Virginia Press, 2008), 10–18, 105–15.

103. Kirk Savage, "The Self-Made Monument: George Washington and the Fight to Erect a National Memorial," *Winterthur Portfolio* 22 (1987): 228–31; Kirk Savage, *Monument Wars: Washington, D.C., the National Mall, and the Transformation of the Memorial Landscape* (Berkeley and Los Angeles: University of California Press, 2009), 13, 32–44.

104. Savage, "Self-Made Monument," 231–32; George H. Rogers, Travel Diary and Commonplace Book, June 20, 1835, p. 2, UVa; "Washington's Monument: To Be Erected in Baltimore," *Niles Weekly Register,* July 1, 1815, pp. 306–8, American Antiquarian Society Historical Periodicals Collection, Series 1, 1690–1820 (Ipswich, MA: EbscoHost, 2009), http://www.ebscohost.com/archives/featured-archives/american-antiquarian-society, accessed January 15, 2010 (hereafter cited as AAS1); "Washington Monument," Greater Baltimore History Alliance, http://www.baltimoremuseums.org/washington.html (accessed March 22, 2010).

105. Levasseur, *Lafayette in America*, 2:33; Antonio Canova's original was displayed in the capitol building from 1820 to 1831 ("Tour of the State Capitol," North Carolina Historic Sites, http://www.nchistoricsites.org/capitol/stat_cap/tour.htm (accessed March 22, 2010).

106. David Hunter Strother, "North Carolina Illustrated, III," *Harper's New Monthly Magazine,* vol. 15 (July 1857), 155; David Hunter Strother, "Notes of Travel in the District of Columbia and Lower Virginia, November 1849," as quoted in "'Porte Crayon' in the Tidewater," ed. Cecil D. Eby Jr., *Virginia Magazine of History and Biography* 67 (October 1959): 440–41. Strother later published a revised version of his travel diary as "A Visit to the Shrines of Old Virginia," *Lippincott's Magazine,* vol. 23 (April 1879): 393–404.

107. National Park Service, *Washington Monument and Associated Structures: Historic Structures Report,* vol. 1: *Washington Monument* (Washington, DC: Government Printing Office, 2004), 1–12, n19; [Robert] M[ills], "Essay on Architectural Monuments," *Analectic Magazine* 13 (1820): 279, 288; Savage, *Monument Wars,* 49–55, 63, 76–79, 107–11.

108. Benjamin Reiss, *The Showman and the Slave: Race, Death, and Memory in Barnum's America* (Cambridge, MA: Harvard University Press, 2001), 1–63; Scott E. Casper, *Sarah Johnson's Mount Vernon: The Forgotten History of an American Shrine* (New York: Hill & Wang, 2008), 6–7, 31–34, 63–67.

109. Levasseur, *Lafayette in America*, 1:181–82.

110. Broadside, "Explanation of a Medal Struck by the Americans in the Year 1782," Bland Family Papers, 1713–1825, Section 18, VHS; J. F. Loubat, *The Medallic History of the United States of America, 1776–1876* (New York: Author, 1878), 1: l–liv, 90–91.

111. Architect of the Capitol, "The Surrender of Lord Cornwallis," http://www.aoc.gov/cc/art/rotunda/surrender_cornwallis.cfm, accessed February 22, 2010; Strother, "Notes of Travel," 440.

112. *Statutes at Large,* 18th Congress, 2nd Sess., p. 320: Private Acts of the Eighteenth Congress, Statue II, Chapter 2: An Act Concerning General Lafayette, December 28, 1824, American Memory Project, Library of Congress, http://memory.loc.gov/cgi-bin/ampage?collId = llsl&fileName = 006/llsl006.db&recNum = 421, accessed February 18, 2010.

113. William F. Brainard, *An Address, in Commemoration of the Sixth of September, 1781. Spoken on Groton Heights, Sept. 6, 1825* (New London, CT: S. Green, 1825), 25.

114. Levasseur, *Lafayette in America,* 1:225.

115. Ibid., 2:236–37.

116. Ibid., 2:237.

117. Christopher Tilley, *A Phenomenology of Landscape: Places, Paths and Monuments* (Oxford: Berg, 1994), 10–33, 67.

118. Ebenezer Mack, *The Life of Gilbert Motier de Lafayette . . . from Numerous and Authentic Sources* (Ithaca, NY: Mack, Andrus & Woodruff, 1841), 317–18; Levasseur, *Lafayette in America,* 2:41–42; Idzerda, Loveland, and Miller, *Lafayette, Hero of Two Worlds,* 139; *Reception of General Lafayette in Camden, South Carolina, and Ceremony of Removing and Reinterring the Remains of Major General Baron DeKalb, and Laying the Corner Stone of His Monument by General Lafayette, March 1825,* SCL pamphlet, 7.

119. Levasseur, *Lafayette in America,* 1:69.

120. Idzerda, Loveland, and Miller, *Lafayette, Hero of Two Worlds,* 136.

121. Levasseur, *Lafayette in America,* 2:59–60, 62, 196; Mack, *Life of Gilbert Motier de Lafayette,* 317–18; Michael Kammen, *Digging Up the Dead: A History of Notable American Reburials* (Chicago: University of Chicago Press, 2010), 17.

122. Sarah J. Purcell, *Sealed with Blood: War, Sacrifice, and Memory in Revolutionary America* (Philadelphia: University of Pennsylvania Press, 2002), 24–29, 103–7; Kammen, *Digging Up the Dead,* 47–48, 50–53; G. Kurt Piehler, *Remembering War the American Way* (Washington, DC: Smithsonian Institution Press, 1995), 23; Joel Tyler Headley, *Washington and His Generals* (New York: Baker and Scribner, 1847), 338.

123. Charles West Thomson, "A Traveller's Diary: Being a Journal of a Tour to the Springs in the Summer of 1824," July 25, 1824, box 4, Charles West Thomson Papers, New-York Historical Society, New York City (hereafter cited as N-YHS).

124. Purcell, *Sealed with Blood,* 125–26; inscription, Lexington Battle Monument, Lexington, MA; *Complete History of the Marquis de Lafayette,* 397; Charles Royster, *A Revolutionary People at War: The Continental Army and American Character, 1775–1783* (Chapel Hill: University of North Carolina Press, 1980).

125. Robert E. Cray Jr., "Commemorating the Prison Ship Dead: Revolutionary Memory and the Politics of Sepulture in the Early Republic," *William and Mary Quarterly,* 3d. Ser., vol. 56 (July 1999): 565–90; Edwin G. Burrows, *Forgotten Patriots: The Untold Story of American Prisoners during the Revolutionary War* (New York: Basic Books, 2008), 205–40; Benjamin Romaine, *Wallabout Monument,* N-YHS pamphlet, 1826, p. 12; Matthew Dennis, "Patriotic Remains: Bones of Contention in the Early Republic," in *Mortal Remains: Death in Early America,* ed. Nancy Isenberg and Andrew Burstein (Philadelphia: University of Pennsylvania Press, 2003), 136–48; Purcell, *Sealed with Blood,* 144–49; Kammen, *Digging Up the Dead,* 46–47; Antoine Prost, "Monuments to the Dead," in *Realms of Memory: Rethinking the French Past,* series ed. Pierre Nora, vol. 1: *Traditions,* trans. Arthur Goldhammer, ed. Lawrence D. Kritzman

(New York: Columbia University Press, 1997), 307–30; John R. Gillis, ed., *Commemorations: The Politics of National Identity* (Princeton, NJ: Princeton University Press, 1994), 9–17.

126. Thomas J. McGuire, *Battle of Paoli* (Mechanicsburg, PA: Stackpole, 2006), 184–90.

127. Brainard, *Address, in Commemoration of the Sixth of September, 1781,* 24–25, 30; Scott Laderman, "'They Set About Revenging Themselves on the Population': The 'Hue Massacre' and the Shaping of Historical Consciousness," in *Tours of Vietnam: War, Travel Guides, and Memory* (Durham, NC: Duke University Press, 2009), 87–123.

128. G. Kurt Piehler, "The Memory of a Nation Forged in War," in Piehler, *Remembering War the American Way,* 10–46; Burstein, *America's Jubilee;* John C. Dann, ed., *The Revolution Remembered: Eyewitness Accounts of the War for Independence* (Chicago: University of Chicago Press, 1980), xvi; Fred Somkin, *Unquiet Eagle: Memory and Desire in the Idea of American Freedom, 1815–1860* (Ithaca, NY: Cornell University Press, 1967).

129. "Revolutionary Events" newspaper clipping [1825], Martha Fanny B. Rochelle Scrapbook, 1819–64, Section 1, Rochelle Family Papers, 1817–1967, VHS; Elizabeth B. Wingo, *The Battle of Great Bridge* (Chesapeake, VA: Norfolk County Historical Society, 1964), 21, 24.

130. Levasseur, *Lafayette in America,* 1:42–43.

131. Knapp, *Memoirs of General Lafayette,* 167–68.

132. Ibid., 169.

133. Levasseur, *Lafayette in America,* 1:43.

134. Ibid., 2:202–5; Waln, *Life of the Marquis de La Fayette,* 418–22.

135. Daniel Webster, *An Address Delivered at the Completion of the Bunker Hill Monument, June 17, 1843* (Boston: Tappan and Dennet, 1843); Purcell, *Sealed with Blood,* 194–209.

136. Duke de la Rochefoucauld-Liancourt, *Travels through the United States of North America, of the Country of the Iroquois, and Upper Canada, in the Years 1795, 1796, and 1797* (London: R. Phillips, 1799), 1:375.

137. "General Hoyt's Visit to the Battle Ground in 1825," in *Visits to the Saratoga Battle Grounds, 1780–1880,* ed. William L. Stone (Albany, NY: Munsell, 1895), 211.

138. "Valley Forge," *Freemason's Magazine and General Miscellany,* October 1, 1811, p. 48, col. 1, AAS1; Lorett Treese, *Valley Forge: Making and Remaking a National Symbol* (University Park: Pennsylvania State University Press, 1995), 2–13.

139. "Cultural Resource Studies and Research," March–June 1974, Series 1.4, H, folder 39, Kings Mountain National Military Park; Susan Hart Vincent, *Kings Mountain National Military Park: Cultural Landscape Report* (Washington, DC: National Park Service, 2003), 9–14.

140. "Random Recollections of Revolutionary Characters and Incidents: Number One," *Southern Literary Journal, and Magazine of Arts* 4, no. 1 (July 1838): 47.

141. *Proceedings of a Celebration of Huck's Defeat, at Brattonsville, York District, South Carolina, July 12, 1839,* SCL pamphlet, pp. 3, 5.

142. William Henry Foote, *Sketches of North Carolina, Historical and Biographical* (New York: Robert, Carter, 1846), 66.

143. "Valley Forge," *Freemason's Magazine and General Miscellany,* October 1, 1811, pp. 48, 51, 52, AAS1; Lorett Treese, *Valley Forge: Making and Remaking a National Symbol* (University Park: Pennsylvania State University Press, 1995), 2–13.

144. On the slow and haphazard efforts to preserve Independence Hall, see Charlene Mires, *Independence Hall in American Memory* (Philadelphia: University of Pennsylvania Press, 2002), 32–78.

145. Burstein, *America's Jubilee,* 35; Idzerda, Loveland, and Miller, *Lafayette, Hero of Two Worlds,* 134–36.

146. American Battlefield Protection Program, National Park Service, Department of the Interior, *Report to Congress on the Historic Preservation of Revolutionary War and War of 1812 Sites in the United States* (Washington, DC, 2007), 23–29. NPS classifications: "Class A. Site of a military or naval action with a vital objective or result that shaped the strategy,

direction, outcome, or perception of the war. Class B. Site of a military or naval action with a significant objective or result that shaped the strategy, direction, or outcome of a campaign or other operation" (25). The report excluded "Associated Historic Properties" that were near or connected to a battle but did not see action, such as an encampment or hospital (e.g., Valley Forge, Morristown, New Windsor Cantonment). Eight sites in Canada are also omitted.

147. Edward Tabor Linenthal, *Sacred Ground: Americans and Their Battlefields* (Urbana: University of Illinois Press, 1993) estimates that commemoration did not begin until the late nineteenth century (1–4); Michael Kammen, *Mystic Chords of Memory: The Transformation of Tradition in American Culture* (New York: Vintage Books, 1993), dates the rise of memorial architecture to after the Civil War (33–37, 53–55).

148. Michael Kammen, *A Season of Youth: The American Revolution and the Historical Imagination* (Ithaca, NY: Cornell University Press, 1978); John F. Sears, *Sacred Places: American Tourist Attractions in the Nineteenth Century* (New York: Oxford University Press, 1989), 99–115; Drew Gilpin Faust, *This Republic of Suffering: Death and the American Civil War* (New York: Alfred A. Knopf, 2008).

149. John Carman, "Legacies of War in Creating a Common European Identity," *International Journal of Heritage Studies* 9, no. 2 (2003): 135–50; Jay Winter, *Sites of Memory, Sites of Mourning: The Great War in European Cultural History* (New York: Cambridge University Press, 1998), 78–115.

150. Gaillard Hunt, ed., *Journals of the Continental Congress, 1774–1789*, vol. 21, *July 23–December 31, 1781* (Washington, DC: Government Printing Office, 1912), 1081.

151. *Register of Debates in Congress* (Washington: Gales & Seaton, 1834), vol. 10, pt. 3, p. 4040.

152. "Yorktown Victory Monument," National Park Service, http://www.nps.gov/york/historyculture/vicmon03.htm (accessed February 22, 2010). See also House Resolution 497, 23rd Congress (1834); *Journal of the House of Representatives, 1835–1836* (Washington, DC: Blair and Rives, 1835), 29:116, 133.

153. *American State Papers: Military Affairs; House of Representatives, 25th Congress, 2d Session* (Washington, DC: Gales and Seaton, 1861), 7:207–8; *The Congressional Globe; 30th Congress, 2d Session* (Washington, DC: Blair and Rives, 1848), 85, 105, 112.

154. *American State Papers: Military Affairs*, vol. 7, *House of Representatives, 25th Congress, 2d Session* (Washington, DC: Gales and Seaton, 1861), 207.

155. *American State Papers: Military Affairs,* 7:207–8; Surrender Monument #608, Yorktown Collection, CNHP.

156. Alexis de Tocqueville, *Democracy in America,* ed. J. P. Mayer, trans. George Lawrence (New York: Harper Perennial, 1988), 469.

157. John Tyler, "An Oration at York Town, October 19, 1837," *Southern Literary Messenger* 3, no. 12 (December 1837): 747–48.

158. Charles Campbell, "The Stone House," *Southern Literary Messenger* 10, no. 1 (January 1844): 41.

159. "Moore's House at York Town," *Family Magazine* 3 (1835): 321–24.

## 4. Memory without Tourism

1. Robert Gilmor, "Notes Taken in a Tour through the States of Virginia, North Carolina, and South Carolina, in the year 1806," South Caroliniana Library, Columbia (hereafter cited as SCL).

2. Rowland Gibson Hazard to Isaac P. Hazard, May 16, 1832, Isaac Peace Hazard Papers, SCL.

3. Joseph Johnson, *Traditions and Reminiscences Chiefly of the American Revolution in the South: Including Biographical Sketches, Incidents and Anecdotes, Few of Which Have Been Published, Particularly of Residents in the Upper Country* (Charleston, SC: Walker & James, 1851), 380.

4. George Washington Diary, Southern Tour (hereafter cited as GW Diary), June 2, 1791, *The Papers of George Washington Digital Edition* (hereafter cited as *PGWDE*), ed. Theodore J. Crackel (Charlottesville: University of Virginia Press, Rotunda, 2007), http://rotunda.upress. virginia.edu/founders/GEWN.html.

5. Lawrence E. Babits and Joshua B. Howard, *Long, Obstinate, and Bloody: The Battle of Guilford Courthouse* (Chapel Hill: University of North Carolina Press, 2009).

6. E. W. Caruthers, *Interesting Revolutionary War Incidents: And Sketches of Character; Chiefly in the "Old North State"* (Philadelphia: Hayes & Zell, 1856), 135–36; Charles E. Hatch Jr., *Guilford Courthouse and Its Environs* (Washington, DC: National Park Service, 1970), 78–80; Thomas E. Baker, *Redeemed from Oblivion: An Administrative History of Guilford Courthouse National Military Park* (Washington, DC: National Park Service, 1995, 2003), chap. 1; John Hiatt, *Guilford Courthouse National Military Park: Cultural Landscape Report* (Atlanta, GA: National Park Service, 2003), 22–24.

7. Albert Matthews, ed., "Journal of William Loughton Smith, 1790–1791," *Proceedings of the Massachusetts Historical Society* 51 (October 1917–June 1918): May 4–5, 1791, p. 72.

8. George H. Rogers, Travel Diary and Commonplace Book, 1835, 1881–82, February 14, 1835, p. 14, Small Special Collections, University of Virginia Library (hereafter cited as UVa).

9. William Henry Foote, *Sketches of North Carolina, Historical and Biographical* (New York: R. Carter, 1846; reprint, Raleigh, NC, 1965), 277.

10. Porte Crayon [David Hunter Strother], "North Carolina Illustrated. Ch. III—Guilford," *Harper's New Monthly Magazine* 15, no. 86 (July 1857): 158–59.

11. Ibid. 158–59, 163–64.

12. Ibid., 157, 162.

13. Foote, *Sketches of North Carolina,* 277.

14. Rogers diary, February 14, 1835, p. 14, UVa.

15. Marquis de Chastellux, *Travels in North America in the Years 1780, 1781 and 1782,* trans. Howard C. Rice Jr. (Chapel Hill: University of North Carolina Press, 1963), 2:402–3.

16. Steele family genealogy, bone fragment from the skull of David Steele [1781], UVa.

17. Crayon, "North Carolina Illustrated," 163–64.

18. Louis B. Wright and Marion Tinling, eds., *Quebec to Carolina in 1785–1786: Being the Travel Diary and Observations of Robert Hunter, Jr., a Young Merchant of London* (San Marino, CA: Huntington Library, 1943), 256–58.

19. George Washington (hereafter GW) to Alexander Hamilton, Thomas Jefferson, and Henry Knox, April 4, 1791, *PGWDE*.

20. GW Diary, March 21, 1791, *PGWDE*.

21. GW Diary, May 18 and 22, 1791, *PGWDE*.

22. Wright and Tinling, *Quebec to Carolina in 1785–1786,* 260–64.

23. William Tell Harris, *Remarks Made during a Tour through the United States of America, in the Years 1817, 1818, and 1819* (London: Sherwood, Neely, and Jones, 1821), 57–58, 60–61.

24. GW to Tobias Lear, May 14, 1791, *PGWDE*.

25. George H. Rogers, Travel Diary and Commonplace Book, February 4, p. 9, February 27, p. 15, March 17, p. 17, 1835, UVa.

26. Wright and Tinling, *Quebec to Carolina in 1785–1786,* 274.

27. GW Diary, April 16, 1791, *PGWDE*.

28. "Letters of an American Traveler, Containing a Brief Sketch of the Most Remarkable Places in Various Parts of the United States and the Canadas, with Some Account of the Character and Manners of the People, Written during an Excursion in the Year 1810," vol. 1, Letter 1st, p. 7, South Carolina Historical Society, Charleston (hereafter cited as SCHS).

29. "Life and Travel in the Southern States," *Great Republic Monthly* 1 (1859): 80–84, as quoted in *Travels in the Old South: Selected from the Periodicals of the Time,* ed. Eugene L. Schwaab (Lexington: University of Kentucky Press, 1973), 2:490.

30. Ann Maury diary, December 28, 1847, Maury Family Papers, Group H, box 5, folder 10, Special Collections Research Center, Earl Greg Swem Library, College of William and Mary (hereafter cited as Swem).

31. William Blandford Journal, June 24, 1828, Rare Book, Manuscript, and Special Collections Library, Duke University (hereafter cited as Duke).

32. Gilmor, "Notes Taken in a Tour," SCL.

33. GW Diary, June 4, 1791, *PGWDE.*

34. "Journal of a Tour in the Interior of South Carolina," *United States Literary Gazette* 3 (November 15, 1825): 104–8, 140–43, as quoted in Schwaab, *Travels in the Old South,* 1:188.

35. Blandford Journal, June 23, 1828, Duke.

36. "Life and Travel in the Southern States," 80–84.

37. Mary Harper Beall to Mrs. C. E. Harper, November 19, 1858, Southern Historical Collection, University of North Carolina–Chapel Hill (hereafter cited as SHC).

38. Captain Basil Hall, *Travels in North America, in the Years 1827 and 1828* (Edinburgh: Robert Cadell, 1830), 3:118.

39. William Gilmore Simms, "Summer Travel in the South," *Southern Quarterly Review* 2, no. 3 (September 1850): 24, 32–33.

40. Charlene Boyer Lewis, *Ladies and Gentlemen on Display: Planter Society at the Virginia Springs, 1790–1860* (Charlottesville: University Press of Virginia, 2001); Thomas A. Chambers, *Drinking the Waters: Creating an American Leisure Class at Nineteenth-Century Mineral Springs* (Washington, DC: Smithsonian Institution Press, 2002); Cindy Aron, *Working at Play: A History of Vacations in the United States* (New York: Oxford University Press, 1999), 15–44; Susan Clair Imbarrato, *Traveling Women: Narrative Visions of Early America* (Athens: Ohio University Press, 2006), 53–88; Daniel Kilbride, *An American Aristocracy: Southern Planters in Antebellum Philadelphia* (Columbia: University of South Carolina Press, 2006); Daniel Kilbride, "Travel, Ritual, and National Identity: Planters on the European Tour, 1820–1860," *Journal of Southern History* 69, no. 3 (2003): 549–84; Barbara Carson, "Early American Tourists and the Commercialization of Leisure" in *Of Consuming Interests: The Style of Life in the Eighteenth Century,* ed. Cary Carson, Ronald Hoffman, and Peter J. Albert (Charlottesville: University of Virginia Press, 1994), 373–405; John Hope Franklin, *A Southern Odyssey: Travelers in the Antebellum North* (Baton Rouge: Louisiana State University Press, 1976).

41. GW Diary, May 4, 1791, *PGWDE;* Terry W. Lipscomb, *South Carolina in 1791: George Washington's Southern Tour* (Columbia: South Carolina Department of Archives and History, 1993), 29–30.

42. GW Diary, May 5, 1791, *PGWDE.*

43. Duke de la Rochefoucauld-Liancourt, *Travels through the United States of North America, of the Country of the Iroquois, and Upper Canada, in the Years 1795, 1796, and 1797* (London: R. Phillips, 1799), 2:374–76.

44. "Life and Travel in the Southern States," 2:492.

45. Karl Bernhard, Duke of Saxe-Weimar Eisenach, *Travels through North America, during the Years 1825 and 1826* (Philadelphia: Carey, Lea & Carey, 1828), 2:6.

46. Edwin C. Bearrs, *The First Two Fort Moultries: A Structural History* (Washington, DC: National Park Service, 1968), vi; Lipscomb, *South Carolina in 1791,* 35.

47. M. I. Manigault to Ms. Izard, July 5, 1800, SCL; A. Izard to Mrs. Manigault, May 23, 1801, SCL; A. Izard to Mrs. Manigault, October 1, 1801, SCL; M. I. Manigault to Mrs. Izard, October 8, 1802, Manigault Family Papers, 1750–1900, SCL.

48. Emilla Bennett to Samuel Andrew [brother], October 12, 1824, SCL.

49. "Letters of an American Traveler," vol. 2, Letter 25th, p. 85, SCHS.

50. Len Travers, *Celebrating the Fourth: Independence Day and the Rites of Nationalism in the Early Republic* (Amherst: University of Massachusetts Press, 1997), 19–20, 26–27, 223–25; Sarah J. Purcell, *Sealed with Blood: War, Sacrifice, and Memory in Revolutionary America* (Philadelphia: University of Pennsylvania Press, 2002), 44–48.

51. "Fire Works," *Southern Patriot,* June 30, 1845, p. 2, America's Historical Newspapers, Series 2.

52. "Oration Deliv'd at Moultrieville June 27, 1829. Commemoration of the Battle of Fort Moultrie on the 28th June," Timothy Ford Speeches, Ford-Ravenel Papers, SCHS.

53. GW Diary, May 14, 1791, *PGWDE.*

54. Travel Book of John Thompson Brown, January 1821, folder 17, box 14, Brown-Coalter-Tucker Papers, Swem.

55. Ralph Waldo Emerson, "Memo St. Augustine, 1827," in *The Journals and Miscellaneous Notebooks of Ralph Waldo Emerson,* vol. 3: *1826–1832,* ed. William H. Gilman and Alfred R. Ferguson (Cambridge, MA: Belknap Press of Harvard University Press, 1963), 114.

56. Johnson, *Traditions and Reminiscences,* 101, 247, 248–49, 254, 274.

57. David K. Wilson, *The Southern Strategy: Britain's Conquest of South Carolina and Georgia, 1775–1780* (Columbia: University of South Carolina Press, 2005); Jim Piecuch, *Three Peoples, One King: Loyalists, Indians, and Slaves in the Revolutionary South, 1775–1782* (Columbia: University of South Carolina Press, 2008).

58. GW Diary, May 20, 1791, *PGWDE.*

59. Ibid., May 26, 1791.

60. Ibid.

61. Matthews, "Journal of William Loughton Smith," May 6, 1791, p. 75.

62. Winslow C. Watson, ed., *Men and Times of the Revolution; or, Memoirs of Elkanah Watson* (New York: Dana, 1856), 259.

63. *Maryland Journal,* June 17, 1791, as quoted in editor's note, GW Diary, May 26, 1791, *PGWDE.*

64. William Drayton, "Remarks in a Tour through the Back-Country of the State of South Carolina, 1784," 30–32, SCHS.

65. *Reception of General Lafayette in Camden, South Carolina, and Ceremony of Removing and Reinterring the Remains of Major General Baron DeKalb, and Laying the Corner Stone of His Monument by General Lafayette, March 1825,* SCL pamphlet, p. 1.

66. Johnson, *Traditions and Reminiscences,* 357.

67. Harris, *Remarks Made during a Tour through the United States of America,* 62.

68. Drayton, "Remarks in a Tour through the Back-Country," 20, SCHS; Jerome A. Greene, *Ninety-Six: A Historical Narrative; Historic Resource Study and Historic Structure Report* (Denver, CO: National Park Service, 1979), 179–80, 187–90.

69. Micajah Adolphus Clark, as quoted in Thomas D. Clark, ed., *South Carolina: The Grand Tour, 1780–1865* (Columbia: University of South Carolina Press, 1973), 290.

70. Edwin C. Bearss, *Historic Grounds and Resource Study: Cowpens National Battlefield, South Carolina* (Denver, CO: National Park Service, 1974), 153–54, 160, 162.

71. Benjamin Franklin Perry, "Revolutionary Incidents, Number 7: Cowpens," 1835, reel 1, B. F. Perry Papers, SHC.

72. "Celebration of the Battle of Cowpens," *Army and Navy Chronicle* 1, no. 7 (February 12, 1835): 51, American Antiquarian Society Historical Periodicals Collection, Series 2.

73. William Snodgrass to "General," August 15, 1842, box 19, Campbell Family Papers, Duke.

74. "The Several Celebrations of the Battle of Kings Mountain, October 7, 1780. The First Celebration," Collection 2, Desk Reference, box 1A, folder 7, Kings Mountain National Military Park, Blacksburg, SC (hereafter cited as KM); Historical Resource Study Proposal, "Archaeological Investigation of American and British Burials, Kings Mountain National Military Park, South Carolina," 1971, Collection 2, Desk Reference, box 1A, folder 2, KM; "Cultural Resource Studies and Research," March–June 1974, Series 1.4, H, folder 39, KM; William Mac-Lean, "Memorial Address Delivered July 4, 1814, at the King's Mountain Battle Ground," State of North Carolina Department of Archives and History, copy in Collection 2, Desk Reference, box 1A, folder 6, KM; Susan Hart Vincent, *Kings Mountain National Military Park: Cultural Landscape* Report (Atlanta, GA: National Park Service, 2003), 9–14; *Celebration of the Battle of King's Mountain, October 1855, and the Address of the Hon. John S. Preston. Together with the Proceedings of the Meeting and Accompanying Documents* (Yorkville, SC: *Enquirer*, 1855), 31, 75.

75. Wright and Tinling, *Quebec to Carolina in 1785–1786*, 231–32.

76. Susanna Nelson Page to Mrs. Ralph F. [Lucy Calthorpe Smith] Digges, April 10, 1835, folder 1, Smith-Digges Papers, John D. Rockefeller Jr. Library, Colonial Williamsburg Foundation, Williamsburg, VA (hereafter cited as CWF).

77. "My Table, and its History," folder 2, Smith-Digges Papers, CWF.

78. Isaac Weld, *Travels through the States of North America, and the Provinces of Upper and Lower Canada, during the Years 1795, 1796, and 1797* (London: John Stackpole, 1807), 1:163.

79. Edward C. Carter II, ed., *The Virginia Journals of Benjamin Henry Latrobe, 1795–1798* (New Haven, CT: Yale University Press, 1977), April 5, 1796, 1:86; Henry Latrobe, "An Essay on Landscape," in ibid., 2:489.

80. Weld, *Travels through the States of North America*, 1:165.

81. Carter, *Virginia Journals of Benjamin Henry Latrobe*, 1:86; Latrobe, "Essay on Landscape," 2:487, 489; Elizabeth Coleman and John Hemphill, "View at Little York in Virginia," *Virginia Cavalcade* 1, no. 2 (Autumn 1951): 44–47.

82. Pleasants Murphy Diary, January 10, 1815, Swem. Also published as "Pleasants Murphy's 'Journal and Day Book,'" *William and Mary Quarterly*, 2d. Ser., vol. 3 (October 1923): 231–38.

83. Railroad Commissioner meeting notes for June 18 and July 2, 1832, folder 294, box 66, Robert Anderson Papers, CWF.

84. John W. Williams, compiler, *Index to Enrolled Bills of the General Assembly of Virginia, 1776 to 1910* (Richmond, VA: Davis Bottom, 1911), 717–18, 939–40; December 1852 petition "To the Senate and House of Delegates," folder 294, box 66, Robert Anderson Papers, CWF.

85. David Hunter Strother, "Notes of Travel in the District of Columbia and Lower Virginia, November 1849," as quoted in "'Porte Crayon' in the Tidewater," ed. Cecil D. Eby Jr., *Virginia Magazine of History and Biography* 67 (October 1959): 441, 443. Strother later published a revised version of his travel diary as "A Visit to the Shrines of Old Virginia," *Lippincott's Magazine* 23 (April 1879): 393–404; Scott E. Casper, *Sarah Johnson's Mount Vernon: The Forgotten History of An American Shrine* (New York: Hill & Wang, 2008), 33, 63–67.

86. "Notes," *Southern Literary Messenger* 3, no. 4 (April 1837): 238.

87. Ibid.

88. Henry Howe, *Historical Collections of Virginia* (Charleston, SC: 1845), 519–21, 530.

89. Strother, "Notes of Travel in the District of Columbia and Lower Virginia," 443.

90. "Pleasants Murphy's 'Journal and Day Book,'" 238.

91. Strother, "Notes of Travel in the District of Columbia and Lower Virginia," 443; Howe, *Historical Collections of Virginia*, 520.

92. "Register and ledger for the Swan Tavern at Yorktown, February 6–July 20, 1852," box 76, Robert Anderson Papers, CWF; Matthew Willis ledger, Swan Tavern, 1813–23, Swem.

93. Weld, *Travels through North America,* 1:165; Edward M. Riley, ed., "St. George Tucker's Journal of the Siege of Yorktown, 1781," *William and Mary Quarterly* 3d. Ser., vol. 5 (July 1948): 387; Carter, *Virginia Journals of Benjamin Henry Latrobe,* 1:86, 2:488.

94. Charles E. Hatch Jr., *"York under the Hill": Yorktown's Waterfront. Historical Resource Study* (Washington, DC: National Park Service, 1973), 175–78.

95. "Pleasants Murphy's 'Journal and Day Book,'" 238.

96. "Notes," *Southern Literary Messenger,* 238.

97. Benson Lossing, *Pictorial Field-Book of the Revolution* (New York: Harper Bros., 1850), 2:302–3.

98. "Domestic Intelligences," *Harper's Weekly,* January 22, 1859, p. 62, HarpWeek: The Civil War Era and Reconstruction I, 1857–1877 (Greenwich, CT: Harpweek LLC, 1997), http//www.harpweek.com, accessed April 10, 2010.

99. Carter, *Virginia Journals of Benjamin Henry Latrobe,* 2:489.

100. "Notes &c of Historical Events—Political, Military and Social," William Palmer Price Commonplace Book, 1857–88, Palmer Family Papers, 1782–1894, Section 6, March 26, 1857, p. 1, Virginia Historical Society, Richmond.

101. "Notes," *Southern Literary Messenger,* 238; Howe, *Historical Collections of Virginia,* 520.

102. "Variety—on the Vicissitudes of Life," n.d., p. 4, Ambler Papers, CWF.

103. Lossing, *Pictorial Field-Book,* 2:302.

104. Ibid., 2:303, 313, 324; Charles E. Hatch Jr., "The Evolution of the Concept of Colonial National Historical Park: A Chapter in the Story of Historical Conservation," June 28, 1964, report, pp. 9–10, Yorktown Collection, Colonial National Historical Park.

105. Strother, "Notes of Travel in the District of Columbia and Lower Virginia," 443.

106. "Yorktown in 1854," *Putnam's Magazine* 4, no. 19 (July 1854): 37–38, 40–41.

107. Ibid., 41.

108. Strother, "Notes of Travel in the District of Columbia and Lower Virginia," 443.

## 5. American Antiquities Are So Rare

1. Catharine Maria Sedgwick, "Journal of a Trip to New York and Canada," July 6, 1821, Massachusetts Historical Society, Boston (hereafter cited as MHS).

2. Philip Stanbury, *A Pedestrian Tour of Two Thousand Three Hundred Miles, in North America* (New York: J. D. Myers, 1822), 121.

3. Sedgwick, "Journal," June 16, 1821, MHS.

4. Walter R. Borneman, *1812: The War That Forged a Nation* (New York: Harper Perennial, 2005), 70–75, 106–8, 170–72, 185–98; Alan Taylor, *The Civil War of 1812: American Citizens, British Subjects, Irish Rebels, and Indian Allies* (New York: Alfred A. Knopf, 2010), 182–95, 217–18, 247–58, 387–407, quote p. 404.

5. Robert E. Cray Jr., "Remembering the Chesapeake: The Politics of Maritime Death and Impressment," *Journal of the Early Republic* 25 (Fall 2005): 445–74; Robert E. Cray Jr., "The Death and Burials of Captain James Lawrence: Wartime Mourning in the Early Republic," *New York History* 83 (April 2002): 132–64.

6. Gideon Minor Davison, *The Fashionable Tour, in 1825. An Excursion to the Springs, Niagara, Quebec and Boston* (Saratoga Springs, NY: G. M. Davison, 1825), 122.

7. Horatio A. Parsons, *The Book of Niagara Falls* (Buffalo, NY: Oliver G. Steele, 1836), 76.

8. O. L. Holley, *The Picturesque Tourist; Being a Guide through the Northern and Eastern States and Canada* (New York: J. Disturnell, 1844), 175.

9. Sedgwick, "Journal," June 29, 1821, MHS.

10. Roger Jones, "Journal of a Military Inspection Tour of the Western Lakes," June 6, 1819, Buffalo and Erie County Historical Society, Buffalo, NY (hereafter cited as BECHS), photostat of original in Library of Congress.

11. Auguste Levasseur, *Lafayette in America in 1824 and 1825; or, Journal of a Voyage to the United States,* trans. John D. Goodman (Philadelphia: Carey and Lea, 1829), 2:186.

12. R. J. Vanderwater, *The Tourist, or Pocket Manual for Travellers on the Hudson River, the Western Canal, and Stage Road, to Niagara Falls* (New York: Ludwig & Tolefree, 1831), 58; Theodore Dwight, *The Northern Traveller, and Northern Tour: With the Routes to the Springs, Niagara, and Quebec, and the Coal Mines of Pennsylvania; also, The Tour of New England* (New York: J. and J. Harper, 1831), 102.

13. *Peck's Tourist Companion to Niagara Falls, Saratoga Springs, the Lakes, Canada, Etc.* (Buffalo, NY: William B. and Charles E. Peck, 1845), 31.

14. Jones, "Journal," June 11, 1819, BECHS.

15. *Peck's Tourist Companion,* 32.

16. Dwight, *Northern Traveller,* 102.

17. *Peck's Tourist Companion,* 32.

18. Sedgwick, "Journal," June 30, 1821, MHS.

19. Augustus E. Silliman, *A Gallop among American Scenery: Or, Sketches of American Scenes and Military Adventure* (New York: Appleton, 1843), 113–14, 119.

20. Sedgwick, "Journal," June 30, 1821, MHS.

21. Jones, "Journal," June 10, 1819, BECHS.

22. *Peck's Tourist Companion,* 27; Holley, *Picturesque Tourist,* 173.

23. Miss Leslie, "Niagara," *Godey's Lady's Book,* December 1845, Early Travel Accounts, Binder 1—to 1850, Local History Department, Niagara Falls (New York) Public Library (hereafter cited as NFPLA).

24. Sedgwick, "Journal," July 3, 1821, MHS.

25. Edward Thomas Coke, *A Subaltern's Furlough; Descriptive of Scenes in Various Parts of the United States, Upper and Lower Canada, New-Brunswick, and Nova Scotia, during the Summer and Autumn of 1832* (New York: J. & J. Harper, 1833), 2:45; *Peck's Tourist Companion,* 42–43.

26. Mrs. [Anna Brownell] Jameson, *Summer Rambles in Canada* (London: Saunders and Otley, 1838), 1:81.

27. Sedgwick, "Journal," July 3, 1821, MHS; P. Stanhope, *A Pedestrian Tour of Two Thousand Three Hundred Miles, in North America* (New York: J. D. Myers and W. Smith, 1822), 125; Jones, "Journal," June 3, 1819, BECHS.

28. *Peck's Tourist Companion,* 42; Sedgwick, "Journal," July 3, 1821, MHS.

29. Samuel DeVeaux, *The Falls of Niagara, or Visitor's Guide to this Wonder of Nature* (Buffalo, NY: William B. Hayden, 1839), 150–51.

30. Sedgwick, "Journal," July 3, 1821, MHS; Jones, "Journal," June 2, 1819, BECHS.

31. S. Putnam Waldo, ed., *The Tour of James Monroe, President of the United States, through the Northern and Eastern States, in 1817* (Hartford, CT: Silas Andrus, 1820), 245–51, 255–60, 263.

32. Levasseur, *Lafayette in America,* 2:190–91.

33. *Peck's Tourist Companion,* 43–46.

34. "Annual Report of Operations at Fort Niagara during the Year Ending 30 Sept. 1847," Record Group 77, M 1702; "Annual Report of Operations at Fort Niagara during the Year Ending 30 Sept. 1848," Record Group 77, M 1816; "Annual Report of Work Conducted at Fort Niagara," August 16, 1858, Record Group 77, B 7843; all photostats from National Archives, Old Fort Niagara Association Archives, Youngstown, NY.

35. DeVeaux, *Falls of Niagara,* 118–22.

36. *The American Guide Book; Being a Hand-Book for Tourists and Travellers through Every Part of the United States* (Philadelphia: George S. Appleton, 1846), 162; *Peck's Tourist Companion,* 44.

37. Charles Casey, *Two Years on the Farm of Uncle Sam* (London: R. Bentley, 1852), 89.

38. *The Falls of Niagara and the Vicinity* (London: T. Nelson and Sons, 1860), 47–48.

39. Diary of Stephen Allen, 1830–33, 1835–47, New-York Historical Society, New York City.

40. DeVeaux, *Falls of Niagara,* 145.

41. Sedgwick, "Journal," June 30, 1821, MHS; Dwight, *Northern Traveller,* 89.

42. Jonathan Pearson, "Journal of a Tour from Schenectady to Niagara Falls in August 1833," Early Travel Accounts, Binder 1—to 1850, NFPLA.

43. James Boardman, *America, and the Americans . . . by a Citizen of the World* (London: Longman, Rees, Orme, Brown, Green, & Longman, 1833), 149–50.

44. Moses C. Cleveland, "Journal of a Tour from Riverhead, Long Island, to the Falls of Niagara," June 15, 1831, Early Travel Accounts, Binder 1—to 1850, NFPLA.

45. DeVeaux, *Falls of Niagara,* 145.

46. Vanderwater, *Tourist,* 57.

47. *Peck's Tourist Companion,* 132–33.

48. Holley, *Picturesque Tourist,* 175.

49. Jones, "Journal," June 4, 1819, BECHS.

50. Winslow C. Watson, ed., *Men and Times of the Revolution; or, Memoirs of Elkanah Watson* (New York: Dana and Co., 1856), 418.

51. Sedgwick, "Journal," July 3, 1821, MHS.

52. Davison, *Fashionable Tour,* 123.

53. Dwight, *Northern Traveller,* 91.

54. Davison, *Fashionable Tour,* 123.

55. "My First Visit to Niagara Falls," *New York Mirror,* December 14, 1833, Early Travel Accounts, Binder 1—to 1850, NFPLA.

56. John F. Sears, *Sacred Places: American Tourist Attractions in the Nineteenth Century* (New York: Oxford University Press, 1989).

57. Colin Read, *The Rebellion of 1837 in Upper Canada* (Ottawa: Canadian Historical Association, 1988); J. I. Little, *Loyalties in Conflict: A Canadian Borderland in War and Rebellion, 1812–1840* (Toronto: University of Toronto Press, 2008); Allan Greer, *The Patriots and the People: The Rebellion of 1837 in Rural Lower Canada* (Toronto: University of Toronto Press, 1993).

58. Samuel Watson, "United States Army Officers Fight the 'Patriot War': Responses to Filibustering on the Canadian Border, 1837–1839," *Journal of the Early Republic* 18 (Fall 1998): 485–519; "Review of a Regiment of British Troop by Gen. P. B. Porter," *Northern Journal* (New York), July 25, 1839, War of 1812—General Binder, NFPLA.

59. W. E. Hulett, *Every Stranger His Own Guide to Niagara Falls* (Buffalo, NY: Steele's Press, 1845), 14, 26.

60. *Peck's Tourist Companion,* 131–32.

61. *American Guide Book,* 160.

62. J. H. Alexander, "A Sleigh Ride in Canada West," 1843, Early Travel Accounts, Binder 1—to 1850, NFPLA.

63. "Battle Ground Observatory Guest Book," August 25, 1853, Niagara Falls (Ontario) History Museum (hereafter cited as NFHM).

64. "Mr. Bennett's Letters," *New York Morning Herald,* August 12, 1840, Early Travel Accounts, Binder 1—to 1850, NFPLA.

65. Miss Leslie, "Niagara," *Godey's Lady's Book,* December 1845, pp. 233–34, Early Travel Accounts, Binder 1—to 1850, NFPLA.

66. "Mr. Bennett's Letters," NFPLA.

67. Hulett, *Every Stranger His Own Guide,* 26.

68. James C. Morden, *Historical Monuments and Observatories of Lundy's Lane and Queenston Heights* (Niagara Falls, Ontario: Lundy's Lane Historical Society, 1929), 19; "Battle Ground Observatory Guest Book," August 27, 1853, NFHM.

69. William Ferguson, *America by River and Rail; or, Notes by the Way on the New World and Its People* (London, J. Nisbet and Co., 1856), 449.

70. Alexander, "Sleigh Ride in Canada West," NFPLA.

71. Coke, *Subaltern's Furlough,* 2:29.

72. *Peck's Tourist Companion,* 131.

73. Silliman, *Gallop among American Scenery,* 128–30.

74. Alexander, "Sleigh Ride in Canada West," NFPLA.

75. The Journal of J. Warner Irwin, August 10, 1856, Doran Collection, 1797–1880, Historical Society of Pennsylvania, Philadelphia.

76. Ibid.

77. "Letter from Niagara," *Salem (MA) Register,* July 29, 1858, Early Travel Accounts, Binder 2—1859–80, NFPLA.

78. "Letter from Niagara," NFPLA.

79. *An Account of the Battle of Lundy's Lane Fought in 1814, between the British & American Armies, from the Best and Most Authentic Sources* (Drummondville, Ontario: *Welland Reporter,* 1853).

80. Morden, *Historical Monuments and Observatories of Lundy's Lane and Queenston Heights,* 12–24; "Battle Ground Observatory Guest Book," August 4–31, 1853, NFHM.

81. Watson, *Men and Times of the Revolution,* 417.

82. Carl Benn, *The Iroquois in the War of 1812* (Toronto: University of Toronto Press, 1998), 89–99; [P. L. Chambers,] "The War in Canada, 1812–1814," 17, MG 40, G4, file 2, Library and Archives of Canada, as quoted in Taylor, *Civil War of 1812,* 189.

83. Taylor, *Civil War of 1812,* 443–44.

84. John Symons, ed., *The Battle of Queenston Heights: Being a Narrative of the Opening of the War of 1812, with Notices of the Life of Major-General Sir Isaac Brock, K.B., and Description of the Monument Erected to His Memory* (Toronto: Thompson & Co., 1859), 17–18.

85. Sedgwick, "Journal," July 3, 1821, MHS; Stanhope, *Pedestrian Tour,* 128.

86. Jones, "Journal," June 3, 1819, BECHS.

87. George Sheppard, *Plunder, Profit, and Paroles: A Social History of the War of 1812 in Upper Canada* (Montreal: McGill–Queen's University Press, 1994), 208; Symons, *Battle of Queenston Heights,* 21–22.

88. DeVeaux, *Falls of Niagara,* 149.

89. Symons, *Battle of Queenston Heights,* 22–25.

90. "Piece of General Brock's Original Coffin" object label, accession number L988.D.010.438, gift of Jemima Van Wyck family, NFHM.

91. William Bullock, *Bullock's Journey from New Orleans to New York, in 1827,* reprinted in Reuben Gold Thwaites, *Early Western Travels,* vol. 19 (Cleveland, 1905; London, 1827), 148.

92. Dwight, *Northern Traveller,* 82.

93. "A Letter from the Falls of Niagara: from an Officer of the 43d Regiment," *New York Albion,* January 5, 1839, Early Travel Accounts, Binder 1—to 1850, NFPLA.

94. Boardman, *America, and the Americans,* 143.

95. Horatio A. Parsons, *The Book of Niagara Falls* (Buffalo, NY: Oliver G. Steele, 1836), 44–45.

96. DeVeaux, *Falls of Niagara,* 149.

97. Ibid., 149–50; *Peck's Tourist Companion,* 123.

98. Sedgwick, "Journal," July 3, 1821, MHS.

99. Frances Trollope, *Domestic Manners of the Americans* (London: Whittaker, Teacher and Co., 1832), 301.

100. *Steele's Book of Niagara Falls* (Buffalo, NY: Oliver G. Steele, 1840), 110.

101. Hulett, *Every Strangers His Own Guide*, 26.

102. *Peck's Tourist Companion*, 125.

103. *Steele's Book of Niagara Falls*, 110.

104. Holley, *Picturesque Tourist*, 175.

105. *Steele's Book of Niagara Falls*, 110.

106. Sheppard, *Plunder, Profits, and Paroles*, 243; *Peck's Tourist Companion*, 125–26.

107. Chris Raible, "Benjamin Rebel Lett Terrorist," *Beaver* 82, no. 5 (October/November 2002): 10–15; Watson, "United States Army Officers Fight the 'Patriot War.'"

108. Symons, *Battle of Queenston Heights*, 25; Sheppard, *Plunder, Profits, and Paroles*, 243–51.

109. Michael Kammen, *Digging Up the Dead: A History of Notable American Reburials* (Chicago: University of Chicago Press, 2009), 50–53.

110. *Peck's Tourist Companion*, 124–25.

111. "Niagara from the Canadian Shore," *Ladies Repository*, August 1852, 301, Early Travel Accounts, Binder 2—1850–1880, NFPLA.

112. William Brown, *America: A Four Years' Residence in the United States and Canada* (Leeds, UK: Kemplay and Bolland, 1849), 72.

113. Holley, *Picturesque Tourist*, 175.

114. "Mr. Bennett's Letters," *New York Morning Herald*, August 7, 1840, Early Travel Accounts, Binder 1—to 1850, NFPLA.

115. Symons, *Battle of Queenston Heights*, 25–30.

116. Paul A. Gilje, "'Free Trade and Sailors' Rights': The Rhetoric of the War of 1812," *Journal of the Early Republic* 30 (Spring 2010): 21.

117. "The Brock Monument" broadside (Toronto: Hugh Scobie, 1853), Brock Monument Committee fonds, F1151, box MU 296, Archives of Ontario, Toronto.

118. Symons, *Battle of Queenston Heights*, 31.

119. "The Battle Fields of Canada," *Niagara Falls Gazette*, December 6, 1854, War of 1812—General Binder, NFPLA.

120. *Tourist's Guide to Niagara Falls, Lake Ontario, and St. Lawrence River* (New York: J. Disturnell, 1857), 13.

121. "Brock Monument," Archives of Ontario; Symons, *Battle of Queenston Heights*, 32.

122. *Falls of Niagara and the Vicinity*, 46.

123. "Letter from Niagara," NFPLA.

124. Symons, *Battle of Queenston Heights*, 35.

125. *American Views* (London: Thomas Nelson and Sons, ca. 1860); Kamille T. H. Parkinson, "The War of 1812 and the Tourist Encounter in Upper Canada: Eight Watercolour Views by Philip John Bainbrigge," *War of 1812 Magazine* 12 (November 2009), http://www.napoleon-series.org/military/Warof1812/2009/Issue12/c_Tourism.html (accessed April 10, 2011).

126. Patricia Jasen, *Wild Things: Nature, Culture, and Tourism in Ontario, 1790–1814* (Toronto: University of Toronto Press, 195), 38.

127. Watson, "United States Army Officers Fight the 'Patriotic War,'" 485–519.

128. Thomas Hietala, *Manifest Design: Anxious Aggrandizement in Late Jacksonian America* (Ithaca, NY: Cornell University Press, 1985); Reginald Horsman, *Race and Manifest Destiny: The Origins of American Racial Anglo-Saxonism* (Cambridge, MA: Harvard University Press, 1981).

129. *Tales of the Niagara Frontier* (Buffalo, NY: Steele's Press, 1851), 74.

130. Taylor, *Civil War of 1812*, 404–7.

131. DeVeaux, *Falls of Niagara,* 128.

132. Sedgwick, "Journal," June 29, 1821, MHS.

133. James Fenimore Cooper, *The Spy: A Tale of the Neutral Ground* (New York: Tauchnitz, 1842), 399–400; Wayne Franklin, *James Fenimore Cooper: The Early Years* (New Haven, CT: Yale University Press, 2007), 120–21.

134. Stanhope, *Pedestrian Tour,* 128.

135. Ibid., 127.

136. *Tales of the Niagara Frontier,* vii.

## 6. The Value of Union

1. William Gilmore Simms, "Summer Travels in the South," *Southern Quarterly Review* 2, no. 3 (September 1850): 24.

2. John S. Preston, *Address Delivered at the Celebration of the Battle of King's Mountain, October, 1855* (Yorkville, SC: *Enquirer,* 1855), 41.

3. *Lancaster Ledger,* May 16, 1860, as quoted in Buford's Massacre Site application, National Register of Historic Places registration form, December 11, 1989, Section 8, p. 4, South Carolina Department of Archives and History, Columbia.

4. Michael Kammen, *Mystic Chords of Memory: The Transformation of Tradition in American Culture* (New York: Vintage Books, 1993), 62–90; John Bodnar, *Remaking America: Public Memory, Commemoration, and Patriotism in the Twentieth Century* (Princeton, NJ: Princeton University Press, 1992), 26–28; Wilbur Zelinsky, *Nation into State: The Shifting Symbolic Foundations of American Nationalism* (Chapel Hill, University of North Carolina Press, 1988).

5. Sarah J. Purcell, *Sealed with Blood: War, Sacrifice, and Memory in Revolutionary America* (Philadelphia: University of Pennsylvania Press, 2002), 19–21, 39, 205.

6. "Oration Delivered by Gen'l Francis Preston, on Oct. 17, 1810, at Abingdon, Va.," in *Battle of Kings Mountain, South Carolina, Oct. 7, 1780: Memorial Addresses* (Abingdon, VA: Washington County Historical Society, 1939), 1–4.

7. B. F. Perry, *An Address Delivered at the Celebration of the 54th Anniversary of the Battle of Cowpens, on the Battle Ground, in Spartanburgh District, S.C. January 17, 1835* (Greenville, SC: *Mountaineer* office, 1835), 1–2.

8. *Proceedings of a Celebration of Huck's Defeat, at Brattonsville, York District, South Carolina, July 12, 1839,* pamphlet, 1839, p. 4, South Caroliniana Library, Columbia.

9. Perry, *Address Delivered at the Celebration of the 54th Anniversary of the Battle of Cowpens,* 11, 13; John Tyler, "An Oration at York Town, October 19, 1837," *Southern Literary Messenger* 3, no. 12 (December 1837): 750–52.

10. Whig Party (Massachusetts), "Bunker Hill Convention" (Boston: n.p., 1840), American Broadsides and Ephemera, Series 1, 1790–1860 (Chester, VT: Readex, 2005), http://www.newsbank.com/readex/product.cfm?product=2, accessed April 22, 2010 (hereafter cited as ABE1).

11. "Public Opinion," *New Hampshire Patriot,* July 25, 1844, America's Historical Newspapers, Early American Newspapers, Series 2, 1758–1900 (Chester, VT: Readex, 2004), http://www.newsbank.com/readex/product.cfm?product=11, accessed February 12, 2010, (hereafter cited as AHN2).

12. "The Oriskany Meeting," *New-Hampshire Patriot,* September 12, 1844, AHN2; "The Empire Meeting. From 30,000 to 50,000 Democrats in Grand Council on the Oriskany Battle Ground," *New-Hampshire Patriot,* August 15, 1844, AHN2; "New York," *New-Hampshire Patriot,* July 24, 1855, AHN2.

13. *Carolina Watchman,* July 10, 1840, and *Greensborough Patriot,* July 7, 1840, as quoted in Adrienne B. Monroy, "Remembrances of Revolution: Public Commemorations of the Battle of Guilford Courthouse" (unpublished paper, University of North Carolina–Greensboro, December 1998), 14–18, Guilford Courthouse National Military Park Archives, North Carolina (hereafter cited as GCHA).

14. "Mr. Webster's Bunker Hill Oration," *Southern Literary Messenger* 9, no. 12 (December 1843): 750–53; Daniel Webster, *An Address Delivered at the Completion of the Bunker Hill Monument, June 17, 1843* (Boston: Tappan and Dennet, 1843), 9.

15. Frank Wesley Craven, "Pride of Ancestry," in *The Legend of the Founding Fathers* (Ithaca, NY: Cornell University Press, 1965), 102–38; Mary Susan Grant, *North over South: Northern Nationalism and American Identity in the Antebellum Era* (Lawrence: University Press of Kansas, 2009); Harlow W. Sheidley, *Sectional Nationalism: Massachusetts Conservative Leaders and the Transformation of America, 1815–1836* (Boston: Northeastern University Press, 1998); Drew Gilpin Faust, *The Creation of Confederate Nationalism: Ideology and Identity in the Civil War South* (Baton Rouge: Louisiana State University Press, 1988); John M. McCardell, *The Idea of a Southern Nation: Southern Nationalists and Southern Nationalism, 1830–1860* (New York: W. W. Norton, 1979); Avery Craven, "The Coming of the War between the States: An Interpretation," *Journal of Southern History* 2 (August 1936): 303–22.

16. Simms, "Summer Travels in the South," 38–39, 52, 55, 65.

17. William Gilmore Simms, "An Oration on the Sixty-Ninth Anniversary of American Independence," *Southern Patriot,* August 14, 1844, AHN2.

18. "Address of William C. Rives, President of the Virginia Historical Society, Second Annual Meeting, Thursday 14 [December] 1848," *Virginia Historical Register* 2 (January 1849): 10.

19. Charles Campbell, "The Stone House," *Southern Literary Messenger* 10, no. 1 (January 1844): 41.

20. Joel Tyler Headley, *Washington and His Generals* (New York: Baker and Scribner, 1847), 309, 313.

21. "Ralph Farnham," *Harper's Weekly,* October 6, 1860, p. 629, HarpWeek: The Civil War Era and Reconstruction I, 1857–1877 (Greenwich, CT: Harpweek LLC, 1997), http//www.harpweek.com, accessed April 10, 2010.

22. *Proceedings of the Convention of the Soldiers of the War of 1812, in the State of New York, Held at Schuylerville, Saratoga County, October 17, 1856* (Albany, NY: Joel Munsell, 1857), 13, 19.

23. "Monument to the Revolution Heroes in Chelmsford, Mass.," *New York Herald,* September 25, 1859, AHN2.

24. "Affairs at the State Capitol," *New York Herald,* January 21, 1858, AHN2.

25. "Vermont News Items," *Brattleboro Weekly Eagle,* August 23, 1852, AHN2; "Anniversary of the Battle of Bennington," *New York Herald,* August 17, 1858, AHN2; "Celebration of the Battle of Bennington," *Boston Daily Atlas,* August 20, 1852, AHN2; *Barre (VT) Patriot,* August 11, 1854, AHN2; "Eastern News," *Deseret News* (Salt Lake City, UT), September 19, 1860, AHN2.

26. "An Historical Discourse, on the Occasion of the Centennial Celebration of the Battle of Lake George, 1755, Delivered at the Court House, Caldwell, N.Y., September 8th, 1855," in Cortlandt Van Rensselaer, *Miscellaneous Sermons, Essays, and Addresses* (Philadelphia, J. B. Lippincott & Co., 1861), 161, 168.

27. "An Historical Discourse, in Centennial Commemoration of the Capture of Ticonderoga, 1759, delivered at Ticonderoga, N.Y., October 11th, 1859," in Van Rensselaer, *Miscellaneous Sermons, Essays, and Addresses,* 564.

28. *Celebration of the Battle of King's Mountain, October 1855, and the Address of the Hon. John S. Preston. Together with the Proceedings of the Meeting and Accompanying Documents* (Yorkville, SC: *Enquirer,* 1855), 1, 4, 14, 18, 62.

29. *Celebration of the Battle of King's Mountain,* 4, 28–29; John Campbell to David Campbell, December 20, 1885, box 29, Campbell Family Papers, Rare Book, Manuscript, and Special Collections Library, Duke University (hereafter cited as Duke).

30. *Celebration of the Battle of King's Mountain,* 28, 34, 41.

31. Ibid., 34, 72–73.

32. William Gilmore Simms, "King's Mountain—a Ballad of the Carolinas," *Harper's New Monthly Magazine* 21 (October 1860): 670.

33. *Celebration of the Battle of King's Mountain,* 28, 34–35, 41, 61, 76–77, 79.

34. John Campbell to David Campbell, December 20, 1885, box 29, Campbell Family Papers, Duke.

35. *Celebration of the Battle of King's Mountain,* 88.

36. "To Be Remembered," *Boston Daily Atlas,* November 5, 1855, AHN2; *Barre (VT) Patriot,* November 9, 1855, AHN2.

37. "Editorial Department," *Baltimore (MD) Weekly Champion and Press,* June 5, 1858, AHN2.

38. Michael A. Morrison, *Slavery and the American West: The Eclipse of Manifest Destiny* (Chapel Hill: University of North Carolina Press, 1997).

39. *Proceedings at the Unveiling of the Battle Monument in Spartanburg, S.C., in Commemoration of the Centennial of the Battle of Cowpens* (Charleston, SC: Cowpens Centennial Committee, 1896), 3–4, 6; *Celebration of the Battle of King's Mountain,* 28, 62; R. L. Shreadley, *Valor and Virtue: The Washington Light Infantry in Peace and War* (Charleston, SC: Washington Light Infantry, 1997), 16–18, 30–38.

40. "The Battle of Cowpens," *Charleston Daily Courier,* April 17, 1856, Cowpens National Battlefield Archives, Chesnee, SC (hereafter cited as CNBA).

41. "The Washington Light Infantry," *Spartanburg (SC) Spartan,* April 25, 1856, CNBA.

42. Shreadley, *Valor and Virtue,* 93; Washington Light Infantry Monument, National Park Service List of Classified Structures form, February 11, 1976, folder 30, LCS, box H, cabinet C, CNBA; Susan Hart Vincent, *Cultural Landscape Report: Cowpens National Battlefield, South Carolina* (Atlanta, GA: National Park Service, 2000), 30–31.

43. Anonymous Travel Journal, November 1850, South Carolina Historical Society, Charleston (hereafter cited as SCHS).

44. "For the *Courier,*" n.d., Edmund Ravenel Writings, 1846–59, Ford-Ravenel Papers, SCHS; "Dr. Ravenel's Views of the Preservation of Fort Moultrie," transcript, n.d., Edmund Ravenel Writings, 1846–1859, Ford-Ravenel Papers, SCHS; Stanley South, "Palmetto Parapets: Exploratory Archaeology at Fort Moultrie, South Carolina, 38CH50," National Park Service Contract #CX50003584: "The First Fort Moultrie Exploratory Excavation, 1974," SCHS.

45. Joseph Johnson, *Traditions and Reminiscences Chiefly of the American Revolution in the South: Including Biographical Sketches, Incidents and Anecdotes, Few of Which Have Been Published, Particularly of Residents in the Upper Country* (Charleston, SC: Walker & James, 1851), 91, 95.

46. *Local Events and Incidents at Home* (Charleston, 1850), 3–4, 19, SCHS.

47. Anonymous Travel Journal, November 1850, SCHS.

48. William Moultrie, *Memoirs of the American Revolution, So Far as It Related to the States of North and South Carolina and Georgia* (New York: David Longworth, 1802), 1:179.

49. "The Palmetto Flag from the Charleston *Mercury,*" *Philadelphia Inquirer,* November 15, 1860, AHN2; William K. Scarborough, ed., *The Diary of Edmund Ruffin,* vol. 1: *Toward Independence, October, 1856–April, 1861* (Baton Rouge: Louisiana University Press, 1972),

November 10, 1860, p. 488; Len Travers, *Celebrating the Fourth: Independence Day and the Rites of Nationalism in the Early Republic* (Amherst: University of Massachusetts Press, 1997), 19–20, 26–27, 223–25.

50. "Anniversary of the Storming of Stony Point. Laying the Corner Stone of a Monument in Honor of the Event," *New York Herald*, July 17, 1857, AHN2.

51. *Proceedings of the Convention of the Soldiers of the War of 1812,* 31, 33.

52. J. H. Sheppard, *Ode on the Inauguration of the Statue of Gen. Warren, on Bunker Hill, June 17, 1857* (Boston: n.p., 1857), ABE1, no. 1380.

53. *Greensborough Patriot and Flag,* October 30, 1857, GCHA; John Hiatt, *Guilford Courthouse National Military Park: Cultural Landscape Report* (Washington, DC: National Park Service, 2003), 32.

54. "Address Delivered before the Greensborough Guards, on the 22nd of February, 1848, by L. Swaim, Esq.," as quoted in *Greensborough Patriot and Flag,* August 7, 1857, GCHA.

55. "Grand Rally of Americans: Five Thousand Freemen Assembled Together in Council at Old Guilford Battleground," *Greensborough Patriot and Flag,* August 8, 1856, GCHA; Michael F. Holt, *The Rise and Fall of the American Whig Party: Jacksonian Politics and the Onset of the Civil War* (New York: Oxford University Press, 1999), 969–70, 978–79.

56. *Greensborough Patriot and Flag,* October 30, 1857, GCHA.

57. "Address Delivered before the Greensborough Guards," GCHA.

58. *Greensborough Patriot and Flag,* March 5, 1858, GCHA.

59. Ibid., July 10, 1857.

60. Ibid., March 5, 1858.

61. "Address Delivered before the Greensborough Guards," GCHA; "The General Nathanael Greene Monument" fact sheet (2005), GCHA.

62. "The Bunker Hill Celebration," *Pittsfield (MA) Sun,* June 25, 1857, AHN2; Purcell, "Commemoration, Public Art, and the Changing Meaning of the Bunker Hill Monument," *Public Historian* 25 (Spring 2003): 55–71.

63. Edward Everett, "The Lexington Monument," *Farmer's Cabinet,* February 15, 1860, p. 1, AHN2.

64. "The Presidential Campaign," *New York Herald,* June 9, 1860, AHN2.

65. "Significant Words," *Washington Constitution,* October 11, 1860, AHN2.

66. "The Presidential Canvas," *New York Herald,* August 18, 1860, AHN2.

67. "The Presidential Campaign," *New York Herald,* February 22, 1860, AHN2.

68. "Douglas in New England," *Weekly Wisconsin Patriot,* August 25, 1860, AHN2.

69. *Boston Daily Atlas,* October 7, 1852, AHN2; "The Contest in Pennsylvania," *New York Herald,* November 13, 1856, AHN2.

70. William C. Cooper, "Ninetieth Anniversary of the Boston Massacre" (Boston, 1860), ABE1, no. 10755.

71. "Opinions of the Press," *Philadelphia Inquirer,* November 16, 1860, AHN2. Jasper died in Savannah on October 9, 1779, while unsuccessfully trying to plant his regiment's colors on the British lines.

72. "The Republican Party of Coercion," *New York Herald,* December 17, 1860, AHN2.

73. Josiah G. Wright, *Address Delivered at the Celebration of the Battle of Moore's Creek Bridge, February 27, 1857* (Wilmington, NC: Fulton & Price, 1857), 19, 23, 24.

74. "Steam Communication—Battle of York Town," *Washington Constitution,* October 1, 1859, AHN2; *Dallas Weekly Herald,* August 3, 1859, AHN2.

75. *Richmond Times-Dispatch,* April 11, 1854, in Surrender Monument file, #608, Yorktown Collection, Colonial National Historical Park (hereafter cited as CNHP); Charles E. Hatch Jr., "The Evolution of the Concept of Colonial National Historical Park: A Chapter in the Story of Historical Conservation," June 28, 1964, report, p. 9, CNHP; Clyde F. Trudell,

*Colonial Yorktown: Being a Brief Historie of the Place; Together with Something of Its Houses and Publick Buildings* (Richmond, VA: Dietz Press, 1938), 199–200.

76. "Peninsular Sketches," *Southern Literary Messenger* 37 (July 1863): 399–400, 402; Linda Mayo, ed., *Rustics in Rebellion: A Yankee Reporter on the Road to Richmond, 1861–1865* (Chapel Hill: University of North Carolina Press, 1950; reprint of George Alfred Townshend, "Campaigns of a Non-Combatant," 1866), 51–52.

77. "Peninsular Sketches," 403.

78. Mayo, *Rustics in Rebellion,* 51; Trudell, *Colonial Yorktown,* 199. During and after the Civil War, Republicans claimed the mantle of a "Second American Revolution" as they sought to remake Southern society in a more egalitarian, post-slavery image. See James M. McPherson, *Abraham Lincoln and the Second American Revolution* (New York: Oxford University Press, 1990), 3–7.

79. David Waldstreicher, *In the Midst of Perpetual Fetes: The Making of American Nationalism, 1776–1820* (Chapel Hill: University of North Carolina Press, 1997), 249–50.

80. S. Putnam Waldo, *Tour of James Monroe, President of the United States, through the Northern and Eastern States, in 1817; His Tour in 1818; Together with a Sketch of His Life* (Hartford, CT: Silas Andrus, 1820), 16–17, 251.

81. Abraham Lincoln, Second Inaugural Address, March 4, 1861, as quoted in *Abraham Lincoln: A Documentary Portrait through His Speeches and Writings,* ed. Don E. Fehrenbacher (Stanford, CA: Stanford University Press, 1964), 160.

# Index

Page numbers in italics refer to illustrations and maps.